W9-BWQ-368

# Front of the CLASS GRADE 2

The dog | chased the ball.

$$\begin{array}{r} 32 \\ +12 \\ \hline 44 \end{array}$$

ones   tens   hundreds

Thinking Kids®
An imprint of Carson-Dellosa Publishing LLC
P.O. Box 35665
Greensboro, NC 27425 USA

Thinking Kids®
An imprint of Carson-Dellosa Publishing LLC
P.O. Box 35665
Greensboro, NC 27425  USA

Printed in the USA • All rights reserved.                    ISBN  978-1-4838-2713-1
02-086171151

# Table of Contents

## Spelling

## Math

## Answer Key

# READING

Name ____________________________

# All About Me!

**Directions:** Fill in the blanks to tell all about you!

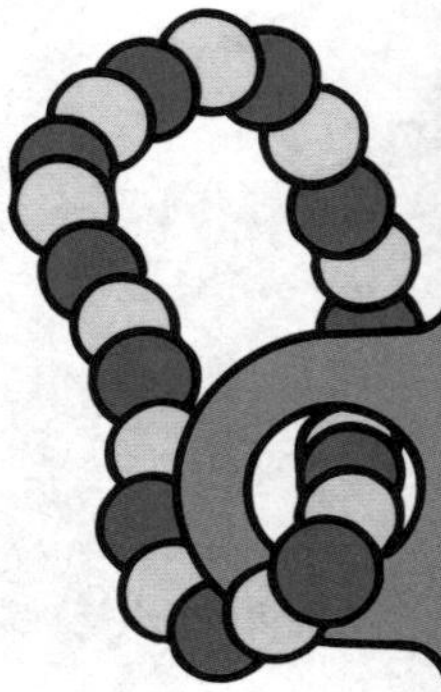

Name ____________________________
(First) (Last)

Address ____________________________

City ____________________ State __________

Phone number ____________________________

Age ____________________________

Places I have visited: ____________________________

____________________________

____________________________

____________________________

My favorite vacation: ____________________________

____________________________

____________________________

____________________________

# Beginning Consonants: b, c, d, f, g, h, j

**Directions:** Fill in the beginning consonant for each word.

**Example:** __c__ at

_____ ox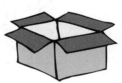

_____ acket

_____ oat

_____ ouse

_____ og

_____ ire

# Beginning Consonants: k, l, m, n, p, q, r

**Directions:** Write the letter that makes the beginning sound for each picture.

_____     _____     _____     _____

_____     _____     _____     _____

_____     _____     _____     _____

_____     _____     _____     _____

# Beginning Consonants: s, t, v, w, x, y, z

**Directions:** Write the letter under each picture that makes the beginning sound.

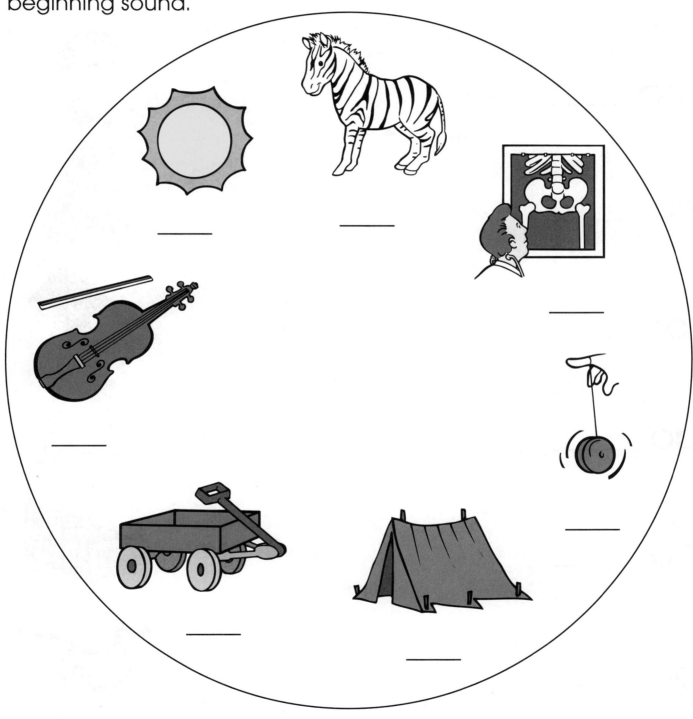

# Ending Consonants: b, d, f, g

**Directions:** Fill in the ending consonant for each word.

ma _____

cu _____

roo _____

do _____

be _____

bi _____

# Ending Consonants: k, l, m, n, p, r

**Directions:** Fill in the ending consonant for each word.

nai _____

ca _____

gu _____

ca _____

truc _____

ca _____

pai _____

# Ending Consonants: s, t, x

**Directions:** Fill in the ending consonant for each word.

ca _____

bo _____

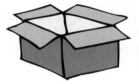

bu _____

fo _____

boa _____

ma _____

**Name** _____

# Consonant Blends

**Consonant blends** are two or three consonant letters in a word whose sounds combine, or blend. **Examples: br, fr, gr, pr, tr**

**Directions:** Look at each picture. Say its name. Write the blend you hear at the beginning of each word.

_____          _____          _____

_____          _____          _____

_____          _____          _____

_____          _____          _____

# Blends: fl, br, pl, sk, sn

**Blends** are two consonants put together to form a single sound.

**Directions:** Look at the pictures and say their names. Write the letters for the beginning sound in each word.

# Blends: bl, sl, cr, cl

**Directions:** Look at the pictures and say their names. Write the letters for the beginning sound in each word.

 _____ own

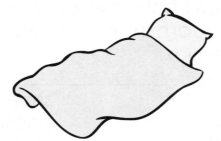 _____ anket

 _____ ayon

 _____ ock

 _____ ide

 _____ oud

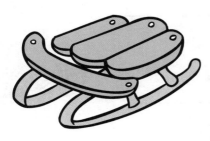 _____ ed

 _____ ab

 _____ ocodile

# Consonant Teams

**Consonant teams** are two or three consonant letters that have a single sound. **Examples: sh** and **tch**

**Directions:** Write each word from the word box next to its picture. Underline the consonant team in each word. Circle the consonant team in each word in the box.

| bench | match | shoe | thimble |
|-------|-------|------|---------|
| shell | brush | peach | watch |
| whale | teeth | chair | wheel |

Reading

# Consonant Teams

**Directions:** Read the words in the box. Write a word from the word box to finish each sentence. Circle the consonant team in each word. **Hint:** There are three letters in each team!

| splash | screen | spray | street | scream |
| screw | shrub | split | strong | string |

1. Another word for a bush is a _____ .

2. I tied a _____ to my tooth to help pull it out.

3. I have many friends who live on my_____ .

4. We always _____ when we ride the roller coaster.

5. A _____ helps keep bugs out of the house.

6. It is fun to _____ in the water.

7. My father uses an ax to _____ the firewood.

8. We will need a _____ to fix the chair.

9. You must be very _____ to lift this heavy box.

10. The firemen _____ the fire with water.

# Letter Teams: sh, ch, wh, th

**Directions:** Look at the first picture in each row. Circle the pictures that have the same sound.

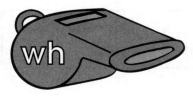
**whistle**

**shoe**

**chin**

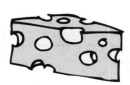

**thumb**

# Silent Letters

Some words have letters you can't hear at all, such as the **gh** in **night**, the **w** in **wrong**, the **l** in **walk**, the **k** in **knee**, the **b** in **climb** and the **t** in **listen**.

**Directions:** Look at the words in the word box. Write the word under its picture. Underline the silent letters.

| knife | light | calf | wrench | lamb | eight |
| wrist | whistle | comb | thumb | knob | knee |

_____    _____    _____    _____

_____    _____    _____    _____

_____    _____    _____    _____

# Hard and Soft c

When **c** is followed by **e, i** or **y**, it usually has a **soft** sound. The **soft c** sounds like **s**. For example, circle and fence. When **c** is followed by **a** or **u**, it usually has a **hard** sound. The **hard c** sounds like **k**.

**Example:** cup and cart

**Directions:** Read the words in the word box. Write the words in the correct lists. One word will be in both. Write a word from the word box to finish each sentence.

**Words with soft c**          **Words with hard c**

| pencil | cookie |
|--------|--------|
| dance | cent |
| popcorn | circus |
| lucky | mice |
| tractor | card |

<u>__pencil__</u>    _____

_____    _____

_____    _____

_____    _____

_____    _____

1.  Another word for a penny is a _____.

2.  A cat likes to chase _____.

3.  You will see animals and clowns at the _____.

4.  Will you please sharpen my _____?

# Hard and Soft g

When **g** is followed by **e**, **i** or **y**, it usually has a **soft** sound. The **soft g** sounds like **j**. **Example:** change and gentle. The **hard g** sounds like the **g** in girl or gate.

**Directions:** Read the words in the word box. Write the words in the correct lists. Write a word from the box to finish each sentence.

| engine | glove | cage | magic | frog |
|--------|-------|------|-------|------|
| giant | flag | large | glass | goose |

**Words with soft g**          **Words with hard g**

___engine___          _____

_____          _____

_____          _____

_____          _____

1. Our bird lives in a _____.

2. Pulling a rabbit from a hat is a good _____ trick.

3. A car needs an _____ to run.

4. A _____ is a huge person.

5. An elephant is a very _____ animal.

# Short Vowels

**Vowels** can make **short** or **long** sounds. The short **a** sounds like the **a** in **cat**. The short **e** is like the **e** in **leg**. The short **i** sounds like the **i** in **pig**. The short **o** sounds like the **o** in **box**. The short **u** sounds like the **u** in **cup**.

**Directions:** Look at each picture. Write the missing short vowel letter.

p___p          n___t          s ___ ck

___x          l___ps          h___t

f___x          t___nt          p___n

# Short Vowels

Vowels can make **short** or **long** sounds. The short **a** sounds like the **a** in **cat**. The short **e** is like the **e** in **leg**. The short **i** sounds like the **i** in **pig**. The short **o** sounds like the **o** in **box**. The short **u** is like the **u** in **cup**.

**Directions:** Look at the pictures. Their names all have short vowel sounds. But the vowels are missing! Fill in the missing vowels in each word.

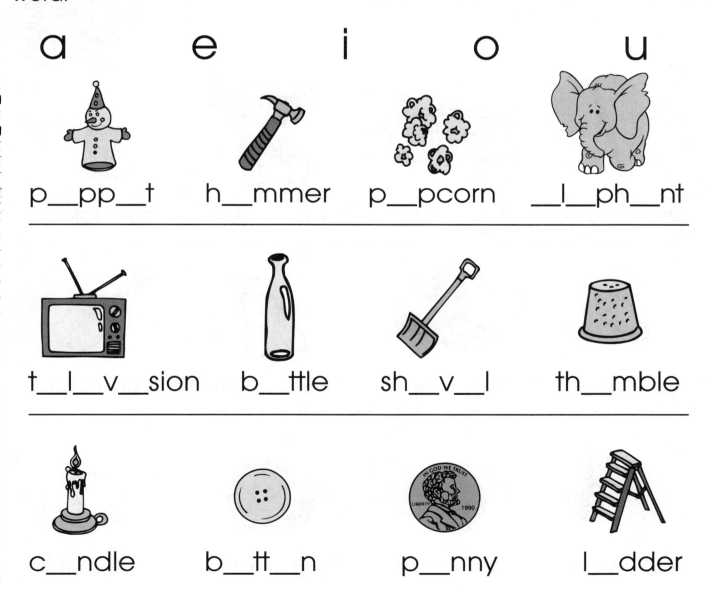

a      e      i      o      u

p__pp__t    h__mmer    p__pcorn    __l__ph__nt

t__l__v__sion    b__ttle    sh__v__l    th__mble

c__ndle    b__tt__n    p__nny    l__dder

# Super Silent e

Long vowel sounds have the same sound as their names. When a **Super Silent e** appears at the end of a word, you can't hear it, but it makes the other vowel have a long sound. For example: **tub** has a **short** vowel sound, and **tube** has a **long** vowel sound.

**Directions:** Look at the following pictures. Decide if the word has a short or long vowel sound. Circle the correct word. Watch for the **Super Silent e**!

| can  cane | tub  tube | rob  robe | rat  rate |

| pin  pine | cap  cape | not  note | pan  pane |

| slid  slide | dim  dime | tap  tape | cub  cube |

# Long Vowels

Long vowel sounds have the same sound as their names. When a **Super Silent e** comes at the end of a word, you can't hear it, but it changes the short vowel sound to a long vowel sound.

**Example:** rope, skate, bee, pie, cute

**Directions:** Say the name of the pictures. Listen for the long vowel sounds. Write the missing long vowel sound under each picture.

c ___ ke

h ___ ke

n ___ se

___ pe

c ___ be

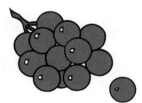

gr ___ pe

r ___ ke

b ___ ne

k ___ te

# R-Controlled Vowels

When a vowel is followed by the letter **r**, it has a different sound.

**Example: he** and **her**

**Directions:** Write a word from the word box to finish each sentence. Notice the sound of the vowel followed by an **r**.

| park | chair | horse | bark | bird |
|------|-------|-------|------|------|
| hurt | girl | hair | store | ears |

1. A dog likes to _____.

2. You buy food at a _____.

3. Children like to play at the _____.

4. An animal you can ride is a _____.

5. You hear with your _____.

6. A robin is a kind of _____.

7. If you fall down, you might get _____.

8. The opposite of a boy is a _____.

9. You comb and brush your _____.

10. You sit down on a _____.

# R-Controlled Words

**R-controlled vowel words** are words in which the **r** that comes after the vowel changes the sound of the vowel. **Examples:** bird, star, burn

**Directions:** Write the correct word in the sentences below.

| | |
|---|---|
| horse | purple |
| jar | bird |
| dirt | turtle |

1. Jelly comes in one of these. _____

2. This creature has feathers and can fly._____

3. This animal lives in a shell. _____

4. This animal can pull wagons. _____

5. If you mix water and this,
   you will have mud. _____

6. This color starts with the letter **p**. _____

# Double Vowel Words

Usually when two vowels appear together, the first one says its name and the second one is silent.
**Example: b<u>e</u>an**

**Directions:** Unscramble the double vowel words below. Write the correct word on the line.

 **ocat** _____

 **etar** _____

 **mtea** _____

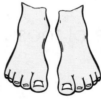 **eetf** _____

 **teas** _____

 **otab** _____

 **ogat** _____

 **spea** _____

 **atli** _____

 **apil** _____

# Vowel Teams

The vowel teams **ou** and **ow** can have the same sound. You can hear it in the words **clown** and **cloud**. The vowel teams **au** and **aw** have the same sound. You hear it in the words **because** and **law**.

**Directions:** Look at the pictures. Write the correct vowel team to complete the words. The first one is done for you. You may need to use a dictionary to help you with the correct spelling.

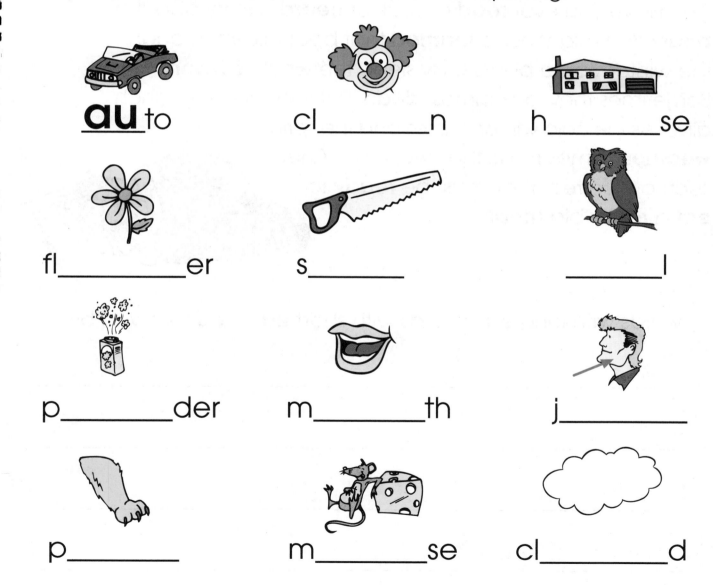

**au**to

cl_____n

h_____se

fl_____er

s_____

_____l

p_____der

m_____th

j_____

p_____

m_____se

cl_____d

# Vowel Teams

The vowel team **ea** can have a short **e** sound like in **head**, or a long **e** sound like in **bead**. An **ea** followed by an **r** makes a sound like the one in **ear** or like the one in **heard**.

**Directions:** Read the story. Listen for the sound **ea** makes in the bold words.

Have you ever **read** a book or **heard** a story about a **bear**? You might have **learned** that bears sleep through the winter. Some bears may sleep the whole **season**. Sometimes they look almost **dead**! But they are very much alive. As the cold winter passes and the spring **weather** comes **near**, they wake up. After such a nice rest, they must be **ready** to **eat** a **really** big **meal**!

| words with long **ea** | words with short **ea** | **ea** followed by **r** |
|---|---|---|
| _____ | _____ | _____ |
| _____ | _____ | _____ |
| _____ | _____ | _____ |
| _____ | _____ | _____ |

# Vowel Teams

The vowel team **ie** makes the long **e** sound like in **believe**. The team **ei** also makes the long **e** sound like in **either**. But **ei** can also make a long **a** sound like in **eight**.

**Directions:** Circle the **ei** words with the long **a** sound.

neighbor                    veil

receive                     reindeer

reign                       ceiling

---

The teams **eigh** and **ey** also make the long **a** sound.

**Directions:** Finish the sentences with words from the word box.

| chief | sleigh | obey | weigh | thief | field | ceiling |

1. Eight reindeer pull Santa's _____ .

2. Rules are for us to _____ .

3. The bird got out of its cage and flew up to the _____ .

4. The leader of an Indian tribe is the _____ .

5. How much do you _____ ?

6. They caught the _____ who took my bike.

7. Corn grows in a _____ .

# Vowel Teams: oi, oy, ou, ow

**Directions:** Look at the first picture in each row. Circle the pictures that have the same sound.

**oil**

**toy**

**couch**

**howl**

# Vowel Teams: ai, ee

**Directions:** Write in the vowel team **ai** or **ee** to complete each word.

r ___ ___ n

f ___ ___ d

s ___ ___ d

p ___ ___ l

s ___ ___ l

cr ___ ___ k

# Y as a Vowel

When **y** comes at the end of a word, it is a vowel. When **y** is the only vowel at the end of a one-syllable word, it has the sound of a long **i** (like in **my**). When **y** is the only vowel at the end of a word with more than one syllable, it has the sound of a long **e** (like in **baby**).

**Directions:** Look at the words in the word box. If the word has the sound of a long **i**, write it under the word **my**. If the word has the sound of a long **e**, write it under the word **baby**. Write the word from the word box that answers each riddle.

| happy | penny | fry | try | sleepy | dry |
| bunny | why | windy | sky | party | fly |

**my**                                            **baby**

_____          _____

_____          _____

_____          _____

_____          _____

_____          _____

_____          _____

1. It takes five of these to make a nickel.          _____

2. This is what you call a baby rabbit.          _____

3. It is often blue and you can see it if you look up. _____

4. You might have one of these on your birthday.          _____

5. It is the opposite of wet.          _____

# Y as a Vowel

**Directions:** Read the rhyming story. Choose the words from the box to fill in the blanks.

| Larry | Mary |
|-------|-------|
| money | funny |
| honey | bunny |

_____ and _____ are friends. Larry is

selling _____ . Mary needs _____ to

buy the honey. "I want to feed it to my _____ ," said

Mary. Larry laughed and said, "That is _____ . Everyone

knows that bunnies do not eat honey."

# Y as a Vowel

**Directions:** Read the story. Choose the words from the box to fill in the blanks.

| try | my | Why | cry | shy | fly |
|-----|----|----|-----|-----|-----|

Sam is very _____. Ann asks, "Would you like to

_____ my kite?" Sam starts to _____ .

Ann asks, "_____ are you crying?"

Sam says, "I am afraid to _____ ."

"Oh, _____ ! You are a good kite flyer," cries Ann.

# Days of the Week

**Directions:** Write the day of the week that answers each question.

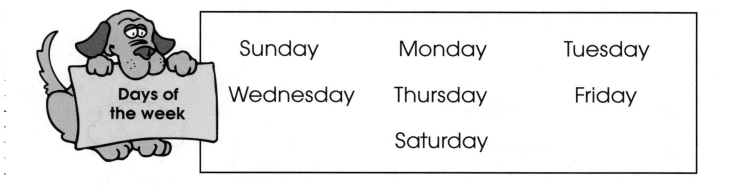

| Sunday | Monday | Tuesday |
| Wednesday | Thursday | Friday |
| | Saturday | |

1. What is the first day of the week?

   _____

2. What is the last day of the week?

   _____

3. What day comes after Tuesday?

   _____

4. What day comes between Wednesday and Friday?

   _____

5. What is the third day of the week?

   _____

6. What day comes before Saturday?

   _____

7. What day comes after Sunday?

   _____

# Compound Words

**Compound words** are formed by putting together two smaller words.

**Directions:** Help the cook brew her stew. Mix words from the first column with words from the second column to make new words. Write your new words on the lines at the bottom.

| grand | brows |
|-------|-------|
| snow  | light |
| eye   | stairs |
| down  | string |
| rose  | book  |
| shoe  | mother |
| note  | ball  |
| moon  | bud   |

1. _____

2. _____

3. _____

4. _____

5. _____

6. _____

7. _____

8. _____

# Compound Words

**Compound words** are two words that are put together to make one new word.

**Directions:** Read the sentences. Fill in the blank with a compound word from the box.

| raincoat | bedroom | lunchbox | hallway | sandbox |
|---|---|---|---|---|

1. A box with sand is a

_____.

2. The way through a hall is a

_____.

3. A box for lunch is a

_____.

4. A coat for the rain is a

_____.

5. A room with a bed is a

_____.

# Compound Words

**Directions:** Draw a line under the compound word in each sentence. On the line, write the two words that make up the compound word.

1. A firetruck came to help put out the fire.

   _____

2. I will be nine years old on my next birthday.

   _____

3. We built a treehouse at the back.

   _____

4. Dad put a scarecrow in his garden.

   _____

5. It is fun to make footprints in the snow.

   _____

6. I like to read the comics in the newspaper.

   _____

7. Cowboys ride horses and use lassos.

   _____

# Contractions

**Contractions** are a short way to write two words, such as **isn't**, **I've** and **weren't**. **Example: it is = it's**

**Directions:** Draw a line from each word pair to its contraction.

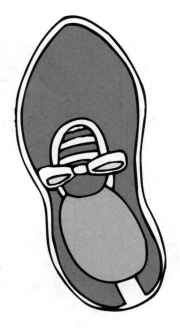 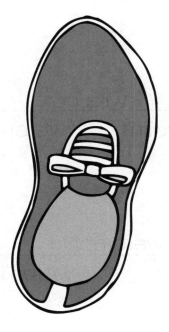

| | |
|---|---|
| I am | she's |
| it is | they're |
| you are | we're |
| we are | he's |
| they are | I'm |
| she is | it's |
| he is | you're |

# Contractions

**Directions:** Circle the contraction that would replace the underlined words.

**Example: were not = weren't**

1. The boy _____was not_____ sad.

         wasn't       weren't

2. We _____were not_____ working.

     wasn't       weren't

3. Jen and Caleb _____have not_____ eaten lunch yet.

          haven't    hasn't

4. The mouse _____has not_____ been here.

        haven't     hasn't

# Contractions

**Directions:** Match the words with their contractions.

| | |
|---|---|
| would not | I've |
| was not | he'll |
| he will | wouldn't |
| could not | wasn't |
| I have | couldn't |

**Directions:** Make the words at the end of each line into contractions to complete the sentences.

1. He _____ know the answer.          **did not**

2. _____ a long way home.          **It is**

3. _____ my house.          **Here is**

4. _____ not going to school today.          **We are**

5. _____ take the bus home tomorrow.          **They will**

# Syllables

Words are made up of parts called **syllables**. Each syllable has a vowel sound. One way to count syllables is to clap as you say the word.

**Example:** cat        1 clap        1 syllable
            table       2 claps       2 syllables
            butterfly   3 claps       3 syllables

**Directions:** "Clap out" the words below. Write how many syllables each word has.

movie _____        dog _____

piano _____        basket _____

tree _____         swimmer _____

bicycle _____      rainbow _____

sun _____          paper _____

cabinet _____      picture _____

football _____     run _____

television _____   enter _____

# Syllables

Dividing a word into syllables can help you read a new word. You also might divide syllables when you are writing if you run out of space on a line.
Many words contain two consonants that are next to each other. A word can usually be divided between the consonants.

**Directions:** Divide each word into two syllables. The first one is done for you.

kitten _____ kit   ten _____

lumber _____

batter _____

winter _____

funny _____

harder _____

dirty _____

sister _____

little _____

dinner _____

# Syllables

One way to help you read a word you don't know is to divide it into parts called **syllables**. Every syllable has a vowel sound.

**Directions:** Say the words. Write the number of syllables. The first one is done for you.

straw • ber • ry

bird _____1_____

apple _____

balloon _____

basketball _____

breakfast _____

block _____

candy _____

popcorn _____

yellow _____

understand _____

rabbit _____

elephant_____

family _____

fence _____

ladder _____

open _____

puddle _____

Saturday_____

wind _____

butterfly _____

# Syllables

When a double consonant is used in the middle of a word, the word can usually be divided between the consonants.

**Directions:** Look at the words in the word box. Divide each word into two syllables. Leave space between each syllable. One is done for you.

| | | | |
|---|---|---|---|
| butter | puppy | kitten | yellow |
| dinner | chatter | ladder | happy |
| pillow | letter | mitten | summer |

**but   ter**
_____        _____        _____

_____        _____        _____

_____        _____        _____

_____        _____        _____

Many words are divided between two consonants that are not alike.

**Directions:** Look at the words in the word box. Divide each word into two syllables. One is done for you.

| | | | |
|---|---|---|---|
| window | doctor | number | carpet |
| mister | winter | pencil | candle |
| barber | sister | picture | under |

**win   dow**
_____        _____        _____

_____        _____        _____

_____        _____        _____

# Syllables

**Directions:** Write 1 or 2 on the line to tell how many syllables are in each word. If the word has 2 syllables, draw a line between the syllables. **Example: sup|per**

dog         _____         timber      _____

bedroom     _____         cat         _____

slipper     _____         street      _____

tree        _____         chalk       _____

batter      _____         blanket     _____

chair       _____         marker      _____

fish        _____         brush       _____

master      _____         rabbit      _____

# Suffixes

A **suffix** is a syllable that is added at the end of a word to change its meaning.

**Directions:** Add the suffixes to the root words to make new words. Use your new words to complete the sentences.

help + ful = _____

care + less = _____

build + er = _____

talk + ed = _____

love + ly = _____

loud + er = _____

1. My mother _____ to my teacher about my homework.

2. The radio was _____ than the television.

3. Sally is always _____ to her mother.

4. A _____ put a new garage on our house.

5. The flowers are _____ .

6. It is _____ to cross the street without looking both ways.

# Suffixes

Adding **ing** to a word means that it is happening now. Adding **ed** to a word means it happened in the past.

**Directions:** Look at the words in the word box. Underline the root word in each one. Write a word to complete each sentence.

| | | | | |
|---|---|---|---|---|
| snowing | wished | played | looking | crying |
| talking | walked | eating | going | doing |

1. We like to play. We _____ yesterday.

2. Is that snow? Yes, it is _____.

3. Do you want to go with me? No, I am _____ with my friend.

4. The baby will cry if we leave. The baby is _____.

5. We will walk home from school. We _____ to school this morning.

6. Did you wish for a new bike? Yes, I _____ for one.

7. Who is going to do it while we are away? I am _____ it.

8. Did you talk to your friend? Yes, we are _____ now.

9. Will you look at my book? I am _____ at it now.

10. I like to eat pizza. We are _____ it today.

# Suffixes

**Directions:** Write a word from the word box next to its root word.

| coming | running | sitting |
| lived | rained | swimming |
| visited | carried | racing |
| hurried | | |

run    _____          come    _____

live    _____          carry    _____

hurry    _____          race    _____

swim    _____          rain    _____

visit    _____          sit    _____

**Directions:** Write a word from the word box to finish each sentence.

1. I _____ my grandmother during vacation.

2. Mary went _____ at the lake with her cousin.

3. Jim _____ the heavy package for his mother.

4. It _____ and stormed all weekend.

5. Cars go very fast when they are _____ .

# Suffixes

**Directions:** Read the story. Underline the words that end with **est**, **ed** or **ing**. On the lines below, write the root words for each word you underlined.

The funniest book I ever read was about a girl named Nan. Nan did everything backward. She even spelled her name backward. Nan slept in the day and played at night. She dried her hair before washing it. She turned on the light after she finished her book—which she read from the back to the front! When it rained, Nan waited until she was inside before opening her umbrella. She even walked backward. The silliest part: The only thing Nan did forward was back up!

1. _____

2. _____

3. _____

4. _____

5. _____

6. _____

7. _____

8. _____

9. _____

10. _____

11. _____

12. _____

13. _____

# Prefixes: The Three R's

**Prefixes** are syllables added to the beginning of words that change their meaning. The prefix **re** means "again."

**Directions:** Read the story. Then follow the instructions.

Kim wants to find ways she can save the Earth. She studies the "three R's"—reduce, reuse and recycle. Reduce means to make less. Both reuse and recycle mean to use again.

Add **re** to the beginning of each word below. Use the new words to complete the sentences.

_____ build        _____ fill

_____ read         _____ tell

_____ write        _____ run

1. The race was a tie, so Dawn and Kathy had to _____ it.

2. The block wall fell down, so Simon had to _____ it.

3. The water bottle was empty, so Luna had to _____ it.

4. Javier wrote a good story, but he wanted to _____ it to make it better.

5. The teacher told a story, and students had to _____ it.

6. Toni didn't understand the directions, so she had to

   _____ them.

# Prefixes

**Directions:** Read the story. Change Unlucky Sam to Lucky Sam by taking the **un** prefix off of the **bold** words.

## Unlucky Sam

Sam was **unhappy** about a lot of things in his life. His parents were **uncaring**. His teacher was **unfair**. His big sister was **unkind**. His neighbors were **unfriendly**. He was **unhealthy**, too! How could one boy be as **unlucky** as Sam?

## Lucky Sam

Sam was _____ about a lot of things in his life. His parents were _____ . His teacher was _____ . His big sister was _____ . His neighbors were _____ . He was _____, too! How could one boy be as _____ as Sam?

# Prefixes

**Directions:** Change the meaning of the sentences by adding the prefixes to the **bold** words.

The boy was **lucky** because he guessed the answer **correctly**.

The boy was (un)_____ because he guessed the

answer (in)_____ .

When Mary **behaved**, she felt **happy**.

When Mary (mis)_____ ,

she felt (un)_____ .

Mike wore his jacket **buttoned** because the dance was **formal**.

Mike wore his jacket (un)_____ because the dance

was (in)_____ .

Tim **understood** because he was **familiar** with the book.

Tim (mis)_____ because he was

(un)_____ with the  book.

# READING COMPREHENSION

# Parts of a Book

A book has many parts. The title is the name of the book. The author is the person who wrote the words. The illustrator is the person who drew the pictures. The table of contents is located at the beginning to list what is in the book. The glossary is a little dictionary in the back to help you with unfamiliar words. Books are often divided into smaller sections of information called chapters.

**Directions:** Look at one of your books. Write the parts you see below.

The title of my book is _____

The author is _____

The illustrator is _____

My book has a table of contents.                Yes or No

My book has a glossary.                Yes or No

My book is divided into chapters.                Yes or No

# Recalling Details: Nikki's Pets

**Directions:** Read about Nikki's pets. Then answer the questions.

Nikki has two cats, Tiger and Sniffer, and two dogs, Spot and Wiggles. Tiger is an orange striped cat who likes to sleep under a big tree and pretend she is a real tiger. Sniffer is a gray cat who likes to sniff the flowers in Nikki's garden. Spot is a Dalmatian with many black spots. Wiggles is a big furry brown dog who wiggles all over when he is happy.

1. Which dog is brown and furry? _____

2. What color is Tiger? _____

3. What kind of dog is Spot? _____

4. Which cat likes to sniff flowers? _____

5. Where does Tiger like to sleep? _____

6. Who wiggles all over when he is happy? _____

Nikki's Garden

# Reading for Details

**Directions:** Read the story about baby animals. Answer the questions with words from the story.

Baby cats are called kittens. They love to play and drink lots of milk. A baby dog is a puppy. Puppies chew on old shoes. They run and bark. A lamb is a baby sheep. Lambs eat grass. A baby duck is called a duckling. Ducklings swim with their wide, webbed feet. Foals are baby horses. A foal can walk the day it is born! A baby goat is a kid. Some people call children kids, too!

1. A baby cat is called a _____.

2. A baby dog is a _____.

3. A _____ is a baby sheep.

4. _____ swim with their webbed feet.

5. A _____ can walk the day it is born.

6. A baby goat is a _____.

# Reading for Details

**Directions:** Read the story about bike safety. Answer the questions below the story.

Mike has a red bike. He likes his bike. Mike wears a helmet. Mike wears knee pads and elbow pads. They keep him safe. Mike stops at signs. Mike looks both ways. Mike is safe on his bike.

1. What color is Mike's bike? _____

2. Which sentence in the story tells why Mike wears pads and a helmet? Write it here.

   _____

3. What else does Mike do to keep safe?

   He _____ at signs and _____ both ways.

# Following Directions: Cows Give Us Milk

**Directions:** Read the story. Answer the questions. Try the recipe.

Cows live on a farm. The farmer milks the cow to get milk. Many things are made from milk. We make ice cream, sour cream, cottage cheese and butter from milk. Butter is fun to make! You can learn to make your own butter. First, you need cream. Put the cream in a jar and shake it. Then you need to pour off the liquid. Next, you put the butter in a bowl. Add a little salt and stir! Finally, spread it on crackers and eat!

1. What animal gives us milk?_____

2. What 4 things are made from milk?

_____  _____  _____  _____

3. What did the story teach you to make?_____

4. Put the steps in order. Place 1, 2, 3, 4 by the sentence.

_____ Spread the butter on crackers and eat!

_____ Shake cream in a jar.

_____ Start with cream.

_____ Add salt to the butter.

# Following Directions: How to Treat a Ladybug

**Directions:** Read about how to treat ladybugs. Then follow the instructions.

Ladybugs are shy. If you see a ladybug, sit very still. Hold out your arm. Maybe the ladybug will fly to you. If it does, talk softly. Do not touch it. It will fly away when it is ready.

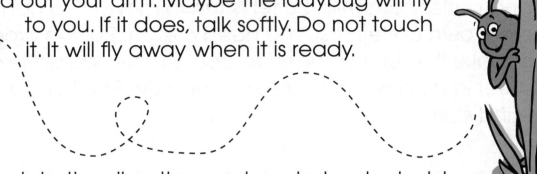

1. Complete the directions on how to treat a ladybug.

   a. Sit very still.

   b. _____

   c. Talk softly.

   d. _____

2. Ladybugs are red. They have black spots. Color the ladybug.

# Sequencing: Story Events

Spencer likes to make new friends. Today, he made friends with the dog in the picture.

**Directions:** Number the sentences in order to find out what Spencer did today.

_____ Spencer kissed his mother good-bye.

_____ Spencer saw the new dog next door.

_____ Spencer went outside.

_____ Spencer said hello.

_____ Spencer got dressed and ate breakfast.

_____ Spencer woke up.

# Sequencing: Yo-Yo Trick

**Directions:** Read about the yo-yo trick.

   Wind up the yo-yo string. Hold the yo-yo in your hand. Now, hold your palm up. Throw the yo-yo downward on the string. Hold your palm down. Now, swing the yo-yo forward. Make it "walk." This yo-yo trick is called "walk the dog."

**Directions:** Number the directions in order.

_____ Swing the yo-yo forward and make it "walk."

_____ Hold your palm up and drop the yo-yo.

_____ Turn your palm down as the yo-yo reaches the ground.

# Sequencing: Follow a Recipe

Here is a recipe for chocolate peanut butter cookies. When you use a recipe, you must follow the directions carefully. The sentences below are not in the correct order.

**Directions:** Write number 1 to show what you would do first. Then number each step to show the correct sequence.

_____ Melt the chocolate almond bark in a microsafe bowl.

_____ Eat!

_____ While the chocolate is melting, spread peanut butter on a cracker and place another cracker on top.

_____ Let the melted candy drip off the cracker into the bowl before you place it on wax paper.

_____ Let it cool!

_____ Carefully use a fork or spoon to dip the crackers into the melted chocolate.

Try the recipe with an adult.

Do you like to cook? _____

# Sequencing: Story Events

Mari was sick yesterday.

**Directions:** Number the events in 1, 2, 3 order to tell the story about Mari.

_____ She went to the doctor's office.

_____ Mari felt much better.

_____ Mari felt very hot and tired.

_____ Mari's mother went to the drugstore.

_____ The doctor wrote down something.

_____ The doctor looked in Mari's ears.

_____ Mari took a pill.

_____ The doctor gave Mari's mother the piece of paper.

_____ Mari drank some water with her pill.

# Sequencing: Making Clay

**Directions:** Read about making clay. Then follow the instructions.

It is fun to work with clay. Here is what you need to make it:

1 cup salt
2 cups flour
3/4 cup water

Mix the salt and flour. Then add the water. DO NOT eat the clay. It tastes bad. Use your hands to mix and mix. Now, roll it out. What can you make with your clay?

1. Circle the main idea:

   Do not eat clay.

   Mix salt, flour and water to make clay.

2. Write the steps for making clay.

   a. _____

   b. _____

   c. Mix the clay.

   d. _____

3. Write why you should not eat clay. _____

   _____

# Sequencing: A Visit to the Zoo

**Directions:** Read the story. Then follow the instructions.

One Saturday morning in May, Gloria and Anna went to the zoo. First, they bought tickets to get into the zoo. Second, they visited the Gorilla Garden and had fun watching the gorillas stare at them. Then they went to Tiger Town and watched the tigers as they slept in the sunshine. Fourth, they went to Hippo Haven and laughed at the hippos cooling off in their pool. Next, they visited Snake Station and learned about poisonous and nonpoisonous snakes. It was noon, and they were hungry, so they ate lunch at the Parrot Patio.

Write **first**, **second**, **third**, **fourth**, **fifth** and **sixth** to put the events in order.

_____ They went to Hippo Haven.

_____ Gloria and Anna bought zoo tickets.

_____ They watched the tigers sleep.

_____ They ate lunch at Parrot Patio.

_____ The gorillas stared at them.

_____ They learned about poisonous and nonpoisonous snakes.

# Same/Different: Stuffed Animals

Kate and Oralia like to collect and trade stuffed animals.

**Directions:** Draw two stuffed animals that are alike and two that are different.

### Alike

### Different

   

# Same/Different: Shell Homes

**Directions:** Read about shells. Then answer the questions.

Shells are the homes of some animals. Snails live in shells on the land. Clams live in shells in the water. Clam shells open. Snail shells stay closed. Both shells keep the animals safe.

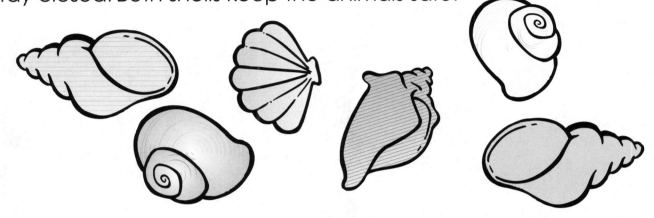

1. (Circle the correct answer.) Snails live in shells on the

   water.          land.

2. (Circle the correct answer.)
   Clam shells are different from snail shells because

   they open.

   they stay closed.

3. Write one way all shells are the same._____

   _____

# Same/Different: Venn Diagram

A **Venn diagram** is a diagram that shows how two things are the same and different.

**Directions:** Choose two outdoor sports. Then follow the instructions to complete the Venn diagram.

1. Write the first sport name under the first circle. Write some words that describe the sport. Write them in the first circle.

2. Write the second sport name under the second circle. Write some words that describe the sport. Write them in the circle.

3. Where the 2 circles overlap, write some words that describe both sports.

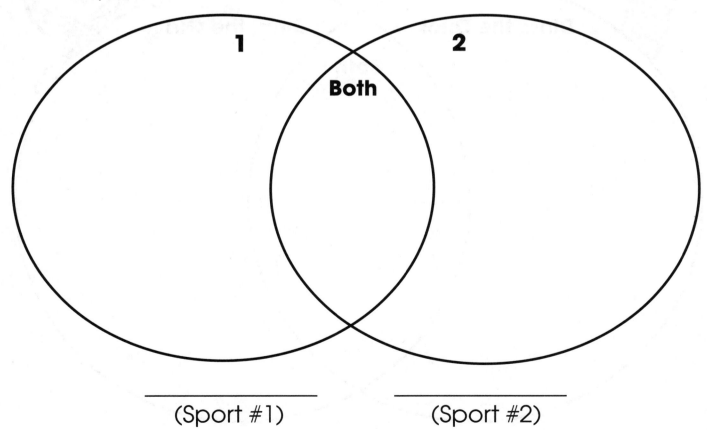

(Sport #1)          (Sport #2)

# Same/Different: Dina and Dina

**Directions:** Read the story. Then complete the Venn diagram, telling how Dina, the duck, is the same or different than Dina, the girl.

One day in the library, Dina found a story about a duck named Dina!

My name is Dina. I am a duck, and I like to swim. When I am not swimming, I walk on land or fly. I have two feet and two eyes. My feathers keep me warm. Ducks can be different colors. I am gray, brown and black. I really like being a duck. It is fun.

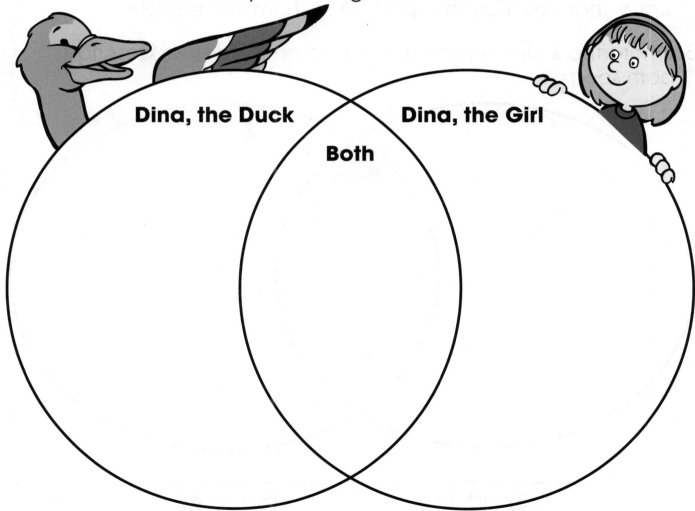

**Dina, the Duck**

**Both**

**Dina, the Girl**

# Same/Different: Cats and Tigers

**Directions:** Read about cats and tigers. Then complete the Venn diagram, telling how they are the same and different.

   Tigers are a kind of cat. Pet cats and tigers both have fur. Pet cats are small and tame. Tigers are large and wild.

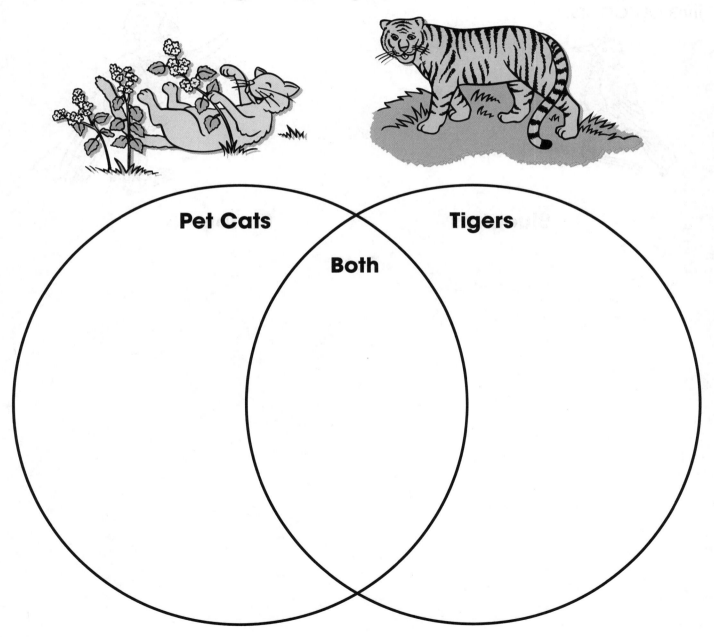

**Pet Cats**          **Tigers**

**Both**

# Same/Different: Bluebirds and Parrots

**Directions:** Read about parrots and bluebirds. Then complete the Venn diagram, telling how they are the same and different.

Bluebirds and parrots are both birds. Bluebirds and parrots can fly. They both have beaks. Parrots can live inside a cage. Bluebirds must live outdoors.

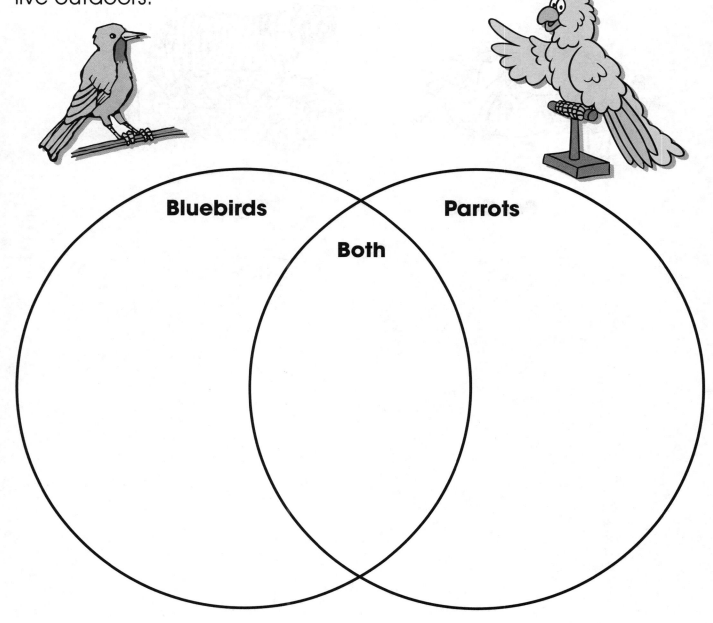

**Bluebirds**          **Parrots**

**Both**

# Similes

A **simile** is a figure of speech that compares two different things. The words **like** or **as** are used in similes.

**Directions:** Draw a line to the picture that goes with each set of words.

as hard as a

as hungry as a

as quiet as a

as soft as a

as easy as

as light as a

as tiny as an

# Classifying

**Classifying** is putting similar things into groups.

**Directions:** Write each word from the word box on the correct line.

| baby | donkey | whale | family | fox |
|------|--------|-------|--------|-----|
| uncle | goose | grandfather | kangaroo | policeman |

people                                        animals

_____          _____

_____          _____

_____          _____

_____          _____

_____          _____

# Classifying: Words

Dapper Dog is going camping.

**Directions:** Draw an **X** on the word in each row that does not belong in that group.

| 1. | flashlight | candle | radio | fire |
| 2. | shirt | pants | coat | bat |
| 3. | cow | car | bus | train |
| 4. | beans | hot dog | ball | bread |
| 5. | gloves | hat | book | boots |
| 6. | fork | butter | cup | plate |
| 7. | book | ball | bat | milk |
| 8. | dogs | bees | flies | ants |

# Classifying: Animal Habitats

**Directions:** Read the story. Then write each animal's name under **Water** or **Land** to tell where it lives.

Animals live in different habitats. A habitat is the place of an animal's natural home. Many animals live on land and others live in water. Most animals that live in water breathe with gills. Animals that live on land breathe with lungs.

| fish | shrimp | giraffe | dog |
| cat | eel | whale | horse |
| bear | deer | shark | jellyfish |

**WATER**

1. _____     4. _____

2. _____     5. _____

3. _____     6. _____

**LAND**

1. _____     4. _____

2. _____     5. _____

3. _____     6. _____

# Comprehension: Types of Tops

The **main idea** is the most important point or idea in a story.

**Directions:** Read about tops. Then answer the questions.

Tops come in all sizes. Some tops are made of wood. Some tops are made of tin. All tops do the same thing. They spin! Do you have a top?

1. Circle the main idea:

   There are many kinds of tops.

   Some tops are made of wood.

2. What are some tops made of? _____

3. What do all tops do? _____

# Comprehension: Singing Whales

**Directions:** Read about singing whales. Then follow the instructions.

Some whales can sing! We cannot understand the words. But we can hear the tune of the humpback whale. Each season, humpback whales sing a different song.

1. Circle the main idea:

   All whales can sing.

   Some whales can sing.

2. Name the kind of whale that sings.

   _____

3. How many different songs does the humpback whale sing each year?

   1                2                3                4

# Comprehension: Sea Horses Look Strange!

**Directions:** Read about sea horses. Then answer the questions.

Sea horses are fish, not horses. A sea horse's head looks like a horse's head. It has a tail like a monkey's tail. A sea horse looks very strange!

1. (Circle the correct answer.)
   A sea horse is a kind of

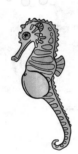

   horse.

   monkey.

   fish.

2. What does a sea horse's head look like?

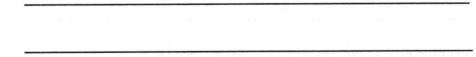

   _____

3. What makes a sea horse look strange?

   a. _____

   b. _____

# Comprehension: How to Stop a Dog Fight

**Directions:** Read about how to stop a dog fight. Then answer the questions.

Sometimes dogs fight. They bark loudly. They may bite. Do not try to pull apart fighting dogs. Turn on a hose and spray them with water. This will stop the fight.

1. Name some things dogs may do if they are mad.

_____

_____

2. Why is it unwise to pull on dogs that are fighting?

_____

_____

3. Do you think dogs like to get wet?

_____

# Comprehension: The Puppet Play

**Directions:** Read the play out loud with a friend. Then answer the questions.

**Pip:** Hey, Pep. What kind of turkey eats very fast?

**Pep:** Uh, I don't know.

**Pip:** A gobbler!

**Pep:** I have a good joke for you, Pip. What kind of burger does a polar bear eat?

**Pip:** Uh, a cold burger?

**Pep:** No, an iceberg-er!

**Pip:** Hey, that was a great joke!

1. Who are the characters in the play? _____

_____

2. Who are the jokes about? _____

_____

3. What are the characters in the play doing? _____

_____

# Comprehension: Snakes!

**Directions:** Read about snakes. Then answer the questions.

There are many facts about snakes that might surprise someone. A snake's skin is dry. Most snakes are shy. They will hide from people. Snakes eat mice and rats. They do not chew them up. Snakes' jaws drop open to swallow their food whole.

1. How does a snake's skin feel? _____

2. Most snakes are _____.

3. What do snakes eat?

   a. _____

   b. _____

Name _____

# Comprehension: Sean's Basketball Game

**Directions:** Read about Sean's basketball game. Then answer the questions.

Sean really likes to play basketball. One sunny day, he decided to ask his friends to play basketball at the park, but there were six people—Sean, Aki, Lance, Kate, Zac and Oralia. A basketball team only allows five to play at a time. So, Sean decided to be the coach. Sean and his friends had fun.

1. How many kids wanted to play basketball? _____

2. Write their names in ABC order:

_____  _____  _____

_____  _____  _____

3. How many players can play on a basketball team

at a time? _____

4. Where did they play basketball? _____

5. Who decided to be the coach? _____

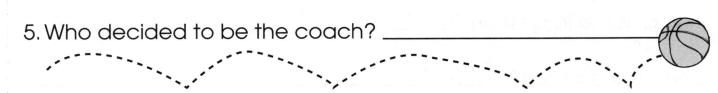

# Comprehension: Amazing Ants

**Directions:** Read about ants. Then answer the questions.

Ants are insects. Ants live in many parts of the world and make their homes in soil, sand, wood and leaves. Most ants live for about 6 to 10 weeks. But the queen ant, who lays the eggs, can live for up to 15 years!

The largest ant is the bulldog ant. This ant can grow to be 5 inches long, and it eats meat! The bulldog ant can be found in Australia.

1. Where do ants make their homes? _____

_____

2. How long can a queen ant live? _____

_____

3. What is the largest ant? _____

4. What does it eat? _____

# Predicting: A Rainy Game

**Predicting** is telling what is likely to happen based on the facts.

**Directions:** Read the story. Then check each sentence below that tells how the story could end.

One cloudy day, Juan and his baseball team, the Bears, played the Crocodiles. It was the last half of the fifth inning, and it started to rain. The coaches and umpires had to decide what to do.

_____ They kept playing until nine innings were finished.

_____ They ran for cover and waited until the rain stopped.

_____ Each player grabbed an umbrella and returned to the field to finish the game.

_____ They canceled the game and played it another day.

_____ They acted like crocodiles and slid around the wet bases.

_____ The coaches played the game while the players sat in the dugout.

# Predicting: Dog Derby

**Directions:** Read the story. Then answer the questions.

Marcy had a great idea for a game to play with her dogs, Marvin and Mugsy. The game was called "Dog Derby." Marcy would stand at one end of the driveway and hold on to the dogs by their collars. Her friend Mitch would stand at the other end of the driveway. When he said, "Go!" Marcy would let go of the dogs and they would race to Mitch. The first one there would get a dog biscuit. If there was a tie, both dogs would get a biscuit.

1. Who do you think will win the race?

_____

Why? _____

_____

2. What do you think will happen when they race again?

_____

_____

# Predicting: Dog-Gone!

**Directions:** Read the story. Then follow the instructions.

Scotty and Simone were washing their dog, Willis. His fur was wet. Their hands were wet. Willis did NOT like to be wet. Scotty dropped the soap. Simone picked it up and let go of Willis. Uh-oh!

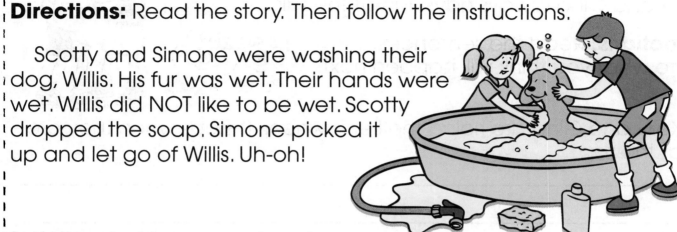

1. Write what happened next.

_____

_____

_____

2. Draw what happened next.

# Predicting Outcomes

Kelly and Gina always have fun at the fair.

**Directions:** Read the sentences.
Write what you think will happen next.

1. Kelly and Gina are riding the Ferris wheel. It stops when they are at the top.

   _____

   _____

   _____

2. As they walk into the animal barn, a little piglet runs towards them.

   _____

   _____

   _____

3. Snow cones are their favorite way to cool off. The ones they bought are made from real snow.

   _____

   _____

   _____

4. They play a "toss the ring over the bottle" game, but when the ring goes around the bottle, it disappears.

   _____

   _____

   _____

# Fact and Opinion: Games!

A **fact** is something that can be proven. An **opinion** is a feeling or belief about something and cannot be proven.

**Directions:** Read these sentences about different games. Then write **F** next to each fact and **O** next to each opinion.

_____ 1. Tennis is cool!

_____ 2. There are red and black markers in a Checkers game.

_____ 3. In football, a touchdown is worth six points.

_____ 4. Being a goalie in soccer is easy.

_____ 5. A yo-yo moves on a string.

_____ 6. June's sister looks like the queen on the card.

_____ 7. The six kids need three more players for a baseball team.

_____ 8. Table tennis is more fun than court tennis.

_____ 9. Hide-and-Seek is a game that can be played outdoors or indoors.

_____ 10. Play money is used in many board games.

# Fact and Opinion: Recycling

**Directions:** Read about recycling. Then follow the instructions.

What do you throw away every day? What could you do with these things? You could change an old greeting card into a new card. You could make a puppet with an old paper bag. Old buttons make great refrigerator magnets. You can plant seeds in plastic cups. Cardboard tubes make perfect rockets. So, use your imagination!

1. Write **F** next to each fact and **O** next to each opinion.

_____ Cardboard tubes are ugly.

_____ Buttons can be made into refrigerator magnets.

_____ An old greeting card can be changed into a new card.

_____ Paper-bag puppets are cute.

_____ Seeds can be planted in plastic cups.

_____ Rockets can be made from cardboard tubes.

2. What could you do with a cardboard tube? _____

_____

# Fact and Opinion: An Owl Story

**Directions:** Read the story. Then follow the instructions.

My name is Owen Owl, and I am a bird. I go to Nocturnal School. Our teacher is Mr. Screech Owl. In his class I learned that owls are birds and can sleep all day and hunt at night. Some of us live in nests in trees. In North America, it is against the law to harm owls. I like being an owl!

Write **F** next to each fact and **O** next to each opinion.

_____ 1. No one can harm owls in North America.

_____ 2. It would be great if owls could talk.

_____ 3. Owls sleep all day.

_____ 4. Some owls sleep in nests.

_____ 5. Mr. Screech Owl is a good teacher.

_____ 6. Owls are birds.

_____ 7. Owen Owl would be a good friend.

_____ 8. Owls hunt at night.

_____ 9. Nocturnal School is a good school for smart owls.

_____ 10. This story is for the birds.

# Making Inferences: Ryan's Top

**Directions:** Read about Ryan's top. Then follow the instructions.

Ryan got a new top. He wanted to place it where it would be safe. He asked his dad to put it up high. Where can his dad put the top?

1. Write where Ryan's dad can put the top. _____

_____

Draw a place Ryan's dad can put the top.

# Making Inferences

**Directions:** Read the story. Then answer the questions.

Jeff is baking cookies. He wears special clothes when he bakes. He puts flour, sugar, eggs and butter into a bowl. He mixes everything together. He puts the cookies in the oven at 11:15 A.M. It takes 15 minutes for the cookies to bake. Jeff wants something cold and white to drink when he eats his cookies.

1. Is Jeff baking a cake?     Yes  No

2. What are two things Jeff might wear when he bakes?

   hat     boots     apron     tie     raincoat     roller skates

3. What didn't Jeff put in the cookies?

   flour          eggs          milk          butter          sugar

4. What do you think Jeff does after he mixes the cookies but before he bakes them?_____

   _____

   _____

5. What time will the cookies be done? _____

6. What will Jeff drink with his cookies? _____

7. Why do you think Jeff wanted to bake cookies? _____

   _____

   _____

# Making Inferences

**Directions:** Read the story. Then answer the questions.

Mrs. Sweet looked forward to a visit from her niece, Candy. In the morning, she cleaned her house. She also baked a cherry pie. An hour before Candy was to arrive, the phone rang. Mrs. Sweet said, "I understand." When she hung up the phone, she looked very sad.

1. Who do you think called Mrs. Sweet?

_____

_____

2. How do you know that?

_____

_____

3. Why is Mrs. Sweet sad?

_____

_____

# Making Inferences: Using Pictures

**Directions:** Draw a picture for each idea. Then write two sentences that tell about it.

You and a friend are playing your favorite game.

_____

_____

You and a friend are sharing your favorite food.

_____

_____

# Making Inferences: Visualizing

**Directions:** Read the story about Melinda. Then draw pictures that describe each part of the story.

**Beginning:** It was Halloween. Melinda's costume was a black cat with super-duper, polka-dot sunglasses.

**Middle:** Her little brown dog, Marco, yelped and ran under a big red chair when he saw her come into the room.

**End:** Melinda took off her black cat mask and sunglasses. Then she held out a dog biscuit. She picked Marco up and hugged him. Then he was happy.

**Name** _____

# Making Inferences: Point of View

Juniper has three problems to solve. She needs your help.

**Directions:** Read each problem. Write what you think she should do.

1. Juniper is watching her favorite TV show when the power goes out.

_____

_____

_____

_____

2. Juniper is riding her bike to school when the front tire goes flat.

_____

_____

_____

_____

3. Juniper loses her father while shopping in the supermarket.

_____

_____

_____

_____

# Making Inferences: Sequencing

**Directions:** Draw three pictures to tell a story about each topic.

1. Feeding a pet

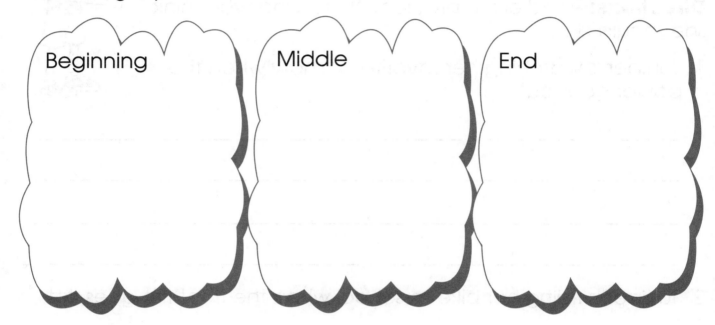

Beginning       Middle       End

2. Playing with a friend

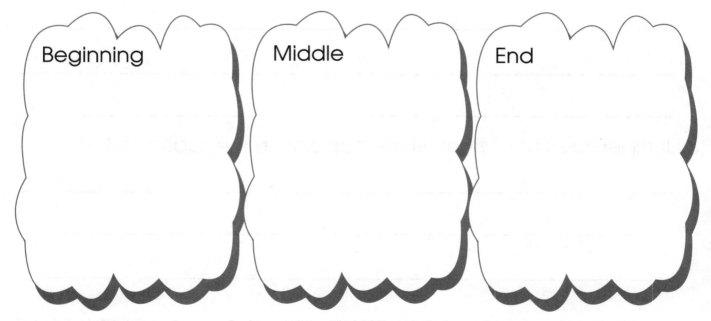

Beginning       Middle       End

# Making Deductions: Find the Books

**Directions:** Use the clues to help the children find their books. Draw a line from each child's name to the correct book.

Brett  Aki  Lorenzo  Kate  Zac  Oralia

| CHILDREN | BOOKS |
|----------|-------|
| Brett | jokes |
| Aki | cakes |
| Lorenzo | monsters |
| Kate | games |
| Zac | flags |
| Oralia | space |

## Clues

1. Lorenzo likes jokes.

2. Kate likes to bake.

3. Oralia likes far away places.

4. Aki does not like monsters or flags.

5. Zac does not like space or monsters.

6. Brett does not like games, jokes or cakes.

# Making Deductions: Sports

Children all over the world like to play sports. They like many different kinds of sports: football, soccer, basketball, softball, in-line skating, swimming and more.

**Directions:** Read the clues. Draw dots and **X**'s on the chart to match the children with their sports.

|        | swimming | football | soccer | basketball | baseball | in-line skating |
|--------|----------|----------|--------|------------|----------|-----------------|
| J.J.   |          |          |        |            |          |                 |
| Zoe    |          |          |        |            |          |                 |
| Andy   |          |          |        |            |          |                 |
| Amber  |          |          |        |            |          |                 |
| Raul   |          |          |        |            |          |                 |
| Sierra |          |          |        |            |          |                 |

## Clues
1. Zoe hates football.
2. Andy likes basketball.
3. Raul likes to pitch in his favorite sport.
4. J.J. likes to play what Zoe hates.
5. Amber is good at kicking the ball to her teammates.
6. Sierra needs a pool for her favorite sport.

# Fiction/Nonfiction: Heavy Hitters

**Fiction** is a make-believe story. **Nonfiction** is a true story.

**Directions:** Read the stories about two famous baseball players. Then write **fiction** or **nonfiction** in the baseball bats.

In 1998, Mark McGwire played for the St. Louis Cardinals. He liked to hit home runs. On September 27, 1998, he hit home run number 70, to set a new record for the most home runs hit in one season. The old record was set in 1961 by Roger Maris, who later played for the St. Louis Cardinals (1967 to 1968), when he hit 61 home runs.

The Mighty Casey played baseball for the Mudville Nine and was the greatest of all baseball players. He could hit the cover off the ball with the power of a hurricane. But, when the Mudville Nine was behind 4 to 2 in the championship game, Mighty Casey struck out with the bases loaded. There was no joy in Mudville that day, because the Mudville Nine had lost the game.

**Name** _____

# Nonfiction: Tornado Tips

**Directions:** Read about tornadoes. Then follow the instructions.

A tornado begins over land with strong winds and thunderstorms. The spinning air becomes a funnel. It can cause damage. If you are inside, go to the lowest floor of the building. A basement is a safe place. A bathroom or closet in the middle of a building can be a safe place, too. If you are outside, lie in a ditch. Remember, tornadoes are dangerous.

Write five facts about tornadoes.

1. _____

_____

2. _____

_____

3. _____

_____

4. _____

_____

5. _____

_____

# Fiction: Hercules

The setting is where a story takes place. The characters are the people in a story or play.

**Directions:** Read about Hercules. Then answer the questions.

Hercules was born in the warm Atlantic Ocean. He was a very small and weak baby. He wanted to be the strongest hurricane in the world. But he had one problem. He couldn't blow 75-mile-per-hour winds. Hercules blew and blew in the ocean, until one day, his sister, Hola, told him it would be more fun to be a breeze than a hurricane. Hercules agreed. It was a breeze to be a breeze!

1. What is the setting of the story? _____

2. Who are the characters? _____

3. What is the problem? _____

4. How does Hercules solve his problem? _____

_____

# Fiction/Nonfiction: The Fourth of July

**Directions:** Read each story. Then write whether it is fiction or nonfiction.

One sunny day in July, a dog named Stan ran away from home. He went up one street and down the other looking for fun, but all the yards were empty. Where was everybody? Stan kept walking until he heard the sound of band music and happy people. Stan

walked faster until he got to Central Street. There he saw men, women, children and dogs getting ready to walk in a parade. It was the Fourth of July!

Fiction or Nonfiction?_____

Americans celebrate the Fourth of July every year, because it is the birthday of the United States of America. On July 4, 1776, the United States got its independence from Great Britain. Today, Americans celebrate this holiday with parades, picnics and fireworks as they proudly wave the red, white and blue American flag.

Fiction or Nonfiction?_____

# Fiction/Nonfiction: Which Is It?

**Directions:** Read about fiction and nonfiction books. Then follow the instructions.

There are many kinds of books. Some books have make-believe stories about princesses and dragons. Some books contain poetry and rhymes, like Mother Goose. These are fiction.

Some books contain facts about space and plants. And still other books have stories about famous people in history like Abraham Lincoln. These are nonfiction.

Write **F** for fiction and **NF** for nonfiction.

_____ 1. nursery rhyme

_____ 2. fairy tale

_____ 3. true life story of a famous athlete

_____ 4. Aesop's fables

_____ 5. dictionary entry about foxes

_____ 6. weather report

_____ 7. story about a talking tree

_____ 8. story about how a tadpole becomes a frog

_____ 9. story about animal habitats

_____ 10. riddles and jokes

# ENGLISH

# Synonyms

Words that mean the same or nearly the same are called **synonyms**.

**Directions:** Read the sentence that tells about the picture. Draw a circle around the word that means the same as the **bold** word.

The child is **unhappy**.

sad             hungry

The flowers are **lovely**.

pretty         green

The baby was very **tired**.

sleepy         hurt

The **funny** clown made us laugh.

silly            glad

The ladybug is so **tiny**.

small          red

We saw a **scary** tiger.

frightening     ugly

# Synonyms

**Synonyms** are words that have almost the same meaning.

**Directions:** Read the story. Then fill in the blanks with the synonyms.

| funny | unhappy |
| windy | little |

**A New Balloon**

It was a breezy day. The wind blew the small child's balloon away. The child was sad. A silly clown gave him a new balloon.

1. It was a _____ day.

2. The wind blew the _____ child's balloon away.

3. The child was _____ .

4. A _____ clown gave him a new balloon.

# Synonyms

**Directions:** Read each sentence. Fill in the blanks with the synonyms.

| friend | tired | story |
|--------|-------|-------|
| presents | | little |

I want to go to bed because I am very <u>sleepy</u>. _____

On my birthday I like to open my <u>gifts</u>. _____

My <u>pal</u> and I like to play together. _____

My favorite <u>tale</u> is *Cinderella*. _____

The mouse was so <u>tiny</u> that it was hard to catch him. _____

# Antonyms

**Antonyms** are words that mean the opposite of another word.

**Examples:**
   **hot** and **cold**
   **short** and **tall**

**Directions:** Draw a line from each word on the left to its antonym on the right.

sad                white

bottom             stop

black              fat

tall               top

thin               hard

little             found

cold               short

lost               hot

go                 big

soft               happy

# Antonyms

**Antonyms** are words that are opposites.

**Directions:** Read the words next to the pictures. Draw a line to the antonyms.

dark                    empty

hairy                   dry

closed                  happy

dirty                   bald

sad                     clean

full                    light

wet                     open

# Homophones

**Homophones** are words that sound the same but are spelled differently and mean different things.

**Directions:** Write the homophone from the box next to each picture.

| so | see | blew | pear |
|----|-----|------|------|

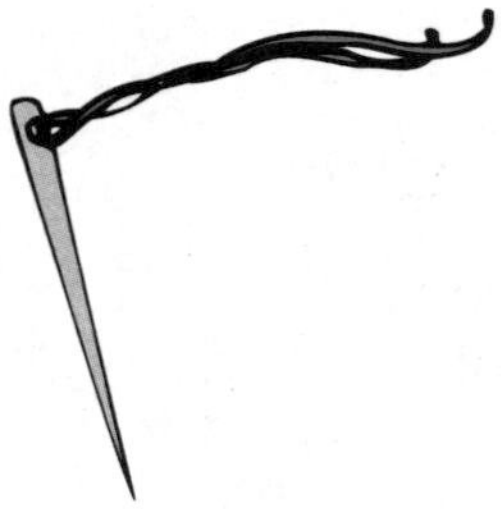

sew _____

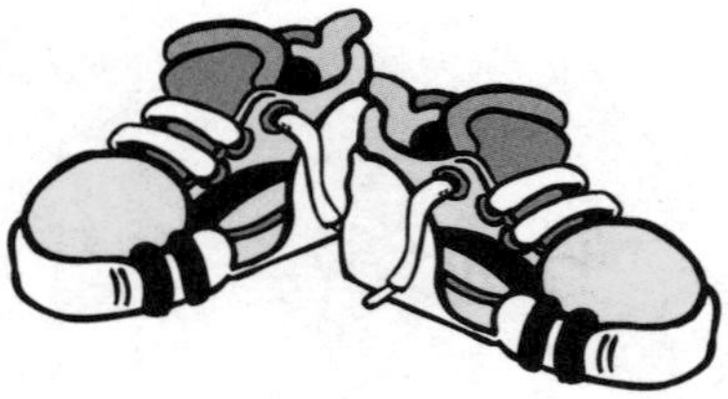

pair _____

sea _____

blue _____

# Homophones

**Directions:** Look at each picture. Circle the correct homophone.

deer   dear

blue   blew

two   to

hi   high

by  bye

new  knew

ate  eight

red  read

# Homophones

**Directions:** Match each word with its homophone.

| | |
|---|---|
| eight | blew |
| buy | whole |
| pail | ate |
| red | pale |
| hole | read |
| blue | hour |
| our | by |

**Directions:** Choose 3 homophone pairs and write sentences using them.

1. _____

2. _____

3. _____

# Nouns

A **noun** is the name of a person, place, or thing.

**Directions:** Read the story and circle all the nouns. Then, write the nouns next to the pictures below.

Our family likes to go to the park.

We play on the swings

We eat cake.

We drink lemonade.

We throw the ball to our dog.

Then we go home.

# Nouns

**Directions:** Look through a magazine. Cut out pictures of nouns and glue them below. Write the name of the noun next to the picture.

# Proper Nouns

**Proper nouns** are the names of specific people, places and pets. Proper nouns begin with a capital letter.

**Directions:** Write the proper nouns on the lines below. Use capital letters at the beginning of each word.

logan, utah

mike smith

_____

lynn cramer

buster

_____

fluffy

chicago, illinois

_____

# Proper Nouns

The days of the week and the months of the year are always capitalized.

**Directions:** Circle the words that are written correctly. Write the words that need capital letters on the lines below.

| sunday | July | Wednesday | may | december |
|--------|------|-----------|-----|----------|
| friday | tuesday | june | august | Monday |
| january | February | March | Thursday | April |
| September | saturday | October | | |

| Days of the Week | Months of the Year |
|------------------|--------------------|
| 1._____ | 1._____ |
| 2._____ | 2._____ |
| 3._____ | 3._____ |
| 4._____ | 4._____ |
| | 5._____ |

# Plural Nouns

**Plural nouns** name more than one person, place or thing.

**Directions:** Read the words in the box. Write the words in the correct column.

| hats | girl | cows | kittens | cake |
| spoons | glass | book | horse | trees |

_____     _____

_____     _____

_____     _____

_____     _____

_____     _____

# Plural Nouns

To make a noun plural, you usually add an **s** or **es** to the word. In some words ending in **y**, the **y** changes to an **i** before adding **es**. For example, **baby** changes to **babies**.

**Directions**: Look at the lists of plural nouns. Write the word that means one next to it. The first one has been done for you.

foxes    **fox** _____

bushes _____

dresses _____

chairs _____

shoes _____

stories _____

puppies _____

matches _____

cars _____

glasses _____

balls _____

candies _____

wishes _____

boxes _____

ladies _____

bunnies _____

desks _____

dishes _____

pencils _____

trucks _____

# Ownership

We add **'s** to nouns (people, places or things) to tell who or what owns something.

**Directions:** Read the sentences. Fill in the blanks to show ownership.

**Example:** The doll belongs to **Sara**.

It is **Sara's** doll.

1. Sparky has a red collar.

_____ collar is red.

2. Jimmy has a blue coat.

_____ coat is blue.

3. The tail of the cat is short.

The _____ tail is short.

4. The name of my mother is Karen.

My _____ name is Karen.

# Ownership

**Directions:** Read the sentences. Choose the correct word and write it in the sentences below.

1. The _____ lunchbox is broken.    boys    boy's

2. The _____ played in the cage.    gerbil's    gerbils

3. _____ hair is brown.    Anns    Ann's

4. The _____ ran in the field.    horse's    horses

5. My _____ coat is torn.    sister's    sisters

6. The _____ fur is brown.    cats    cat's

7. Three _____ flew past our window.    birds    bird's

8. The _____ paws are muddy.    dogs    dog's

9. The _____ neck is long.    giraffes    giraffe's

10. The _____ are big and powerful.    lion's    lions

# Pronouns

**Pronouns** are words that can be used instead of nouns. **She**, **he**, **it** and **they** are pronouns.

**Directions:** Read the sentence. Then write the sentence again, using **she**, **he**, **it** or **they** in the blank.

1. Dan likes funny jokes. _____ likes funny jokes.

2. Peg and Sam went to the zoo. _____ went to the zoo.

3. My dog likes to dig in the yard. _____ likes to dig in the yard.

4. Sara is a very good dancer. _____ is a very good dancer.

5. Fred and Ted are twins. _____ are twins.

# Subjects

The **subject** of a sentence is the person, place or thing the sentence is about.

**Directions:** Underline the subject in each sentence.

**Example:** Mom read a book.

(Think: Who is the sentence about? <u>Mom</u>)

1. The bird flew away.

2. The kite was high in the air.

3. The children played a game.

4. The books fell down.

5. The monkey climbed a tree.

# Compound Subjects

Two similar sentences can be joined into one sentence if the predicate is the same. A **compound subject** is made up of two subjects joined together by the word **and**.

**Example:** Jamie can sing.
Sandy can sing.

Jamie **and** Sandy can sing.

**Directions:** Combine the sentences. Write the new sentence on the line.

1. The cats are my pets.
   The dogs are my pets.

_____

2. Chairs are in the store.
   Tables are in the store.

_____

3. Tom can ride a bike.
   Jack can ride a bike.

_____

# Verbs

A **verb** is the action word in a sentence. Verbs tell what something does or that something exists.

**Example: Run, sleep** and **jump** are verbs.

**Directions:** Circle the verbs in the sentences below.

1. We play baseball everyday.


2. Susan pitches the ball very well.


3. Mike swings the bat harder than anyone.


4. Chris slides into home base.


5. Laura hit a home run.

# Verbs

We use verbs to tell when something happens. Sometimes we add an **ed** to verbs that tell us if something has already happened.

**Example:** Today, we will **play**. Yesterday, we **played**.

**Directions:** Write the correct verb in the blank.

1. Today, I will _____ my dog, Fritz.
        wash      washed

2. Last week, Fritz _____ when we said, "Bath time, Fritz."
        cry      cried

3. My sister likes to _____ wash Fritz.
        help      helped

4. One time she _____ Fritz by herself.
        clean      cleaned

5. Fritz will _____ a lot better after his bath.
        look      looked

# Predicates

The **predicate** is the part of the sentence that tells about the action.

**Directions:** Circle the predicate in each sentence.

**Example:**     The boys ran on the playground.

(Think: The boys did what? (Ran))

1. The woman painted a picture.

2. The puppy chases his ball.

3. The students went to school.

4. Butterflies fly in the air.

5. The baby wants a drink.

# Subjects and Predicates

The **subject** part of the sentence is the person, place or thing the sentence is about. The **predicate** is the part of the sentence that tells what the subject does.

**Directions:** Draw a line between the subject and the predicate. Underline the noun in the subject and circle the verb.

**Example:**     The furry <u>cat</u> |  food.

1. Mandi walks to school.

2. The bus drove the children.

3. The school bell rang very loudly.

4. The teacher spoke to the students.

5. The girls opened their books.

# Parts of a Sentence

**Directions:** Draw a circle around the noun, the naming part of the sentence. Draw a line under the verb, the action part of the sentence.

**Example:** (John) <u>drinks</u> juice every morning.

1. Our class skates at the roller-skating rink.

2. Mike and Jan go very fast.

3. Fred eats hot dogs.

4. Sue dances to the music.

5. Everyone likes the skating rink.

# Parts of a Sentence

**Directions:** Look at the pictures. Draw a line from the naming part of the sentence to the action part to complete the sentence.

The boy                          delivered the mail.

A small dog                      threw a football.

The mailman                      fell down.

The goalie                       chased the ball.

# Adjectives

**Adjectives** are words that tell more about a person, place or thing.

**Examples:** cold, fuzzy, dark

**Directions:** Circle the adjectives in the sentences.

1. The juicy apple is on the plate.

2. The furry dog is eating a bone.

3. It was a sunny day.

4. The kitten drinks warm milk.

5. The baby has a loud cry.

# Adjectives

**Directions:** Choose an adjective from the box to fill in the blanks.

| hungry | sunny | busy | funny |
|--------|-------|------|-------|
| fresh | deep | pretty | cloudy |

1. It is a _____ day on Farmer Brown's farm.

2. Farmer Brown is a very _____ man.

3. Mrs. Brown likes to feed the _____ chickens.

4. Every day she collects the _____ eggs.

5. The ducks swim in the _____ pond.

# Adjectives

**Directions:** Think of your own adjectives. Write a story about Fluffy the cat.

1. Fluffy is a _____ cat.

2. The color of his fur is _____ .

3. He likes to chew on my_____ shoes.

4. He likes to eat _____ cat food.

5. I like Fluffy because he is so _____ .

# Articles

**Articles** are small words that help us to better understand nouns. **A** and **an** are articles. We use **an** before a word that begins with a vowel. We use **a** before a word that begins with a consonant.

**Example:** We looked in **a** nest. It had **an** eagle in it.

**Directions:** Read the sentences. Write **a** or **an** in the blank.

1. I found _____ book.

2. It had a story about _____ ant in it.

3. In the story, _____ lion gave three wishes to _____ ant.

4. The ant's first wish was to ride _____ elephant.

5. The second wish was to ride _____ alligator.

6. The last wish was _____ wish for three more wishes.

# Sentences and Non-Sentences

A **sentence** tells a complete idea. It has a noun and a verb. It begins with a capital letter and has punctuation at the end.

**Directions:** Circle the group of words if it is a sentence.

1. Grass is a green plant.

2. Mowing the lawn.

3. Grass grows in fields and lawns.

4. Tickle the feet.

5. Sheep, cows and horses eat grass.

6. We like to play in.

7. My sister likes to mow the lawn.

8. A picnic on the grass.

9. My dog likes to roll in the grass.

10. Plant flowers around.

# Sentences and Non-Sentences

**Directions:** Circle the group of words if it tells a complete idea.

1. A secret is something you know.

2. My mom's birthday gift is a secret.

3. No one else.

4. If you promise not to.

5. I'll tell you a secret.

6. Something nobody knows.

Name _____

# Statements

**Statements** are sentences that tell us something. They begin with a capital letter and end with a period.

**Directions:** Write the sentences on the lines below. Begin each sentence with a capital letter and end it with a period.

1. we like to ride our bikes

_____

2. we go down the hill very fast

_____

3. we keep our bikes shiny and clean

_____

4. we know how to change the tires

_____

# Surprising Sentences

**Surprising sentences** tell a strong feeling and end with an exclamation point. A surprising sentence may be only one or two words showing fear, surprise or pain. **Example: Oh, no!**

**Directions:** Put a period at the end of the sentences that tell something. Put an exclamation point at the end of the sentences that tell a strong feeling. Put a question mark at the end of the sentences that ask a question.

1. The cheetah can run very fast

2. Wow

3. Look at that cheetah go

4. Can you run fast

5. Oh, my

6. You're faster than I am

7. Let's run together

8. We can run as fast as a cheetah

9. What fun

10. Do you think cheetahs get tired

# Commands

**Commands** tell someone to do something. **Example: "Be careful."**
It can also be written as "Be careful!" if it tells a strong feeling.

**Directions:** Put a period at the end of the command sentences.
Use an exclamation point if the sentence tells a strong feeling. Write
your own commands on the lines below.

1. Clean your room

2. Now

3. Be careful with your goldfish

4. Watch out

5. Be a little more careful

_____

_____

# Questions

**Questions** are sentences that ask something. They begin with a capital letter and end with a question mark.

**Directions:** Write the questions on the lines below. Begin each sentence with a capital letter and end it with a question mark.

1. will you be my friend

_____

2. what is your name

_____

3. are you eight years old

_____

4. do you like rainbows

_____

# Making Inferences: Writing Questions

Tommy likes to answer questions. He knows the answers, but you need to write the questions.

**Directions:** Write two questions for each answer.

Answer: It has four legs.

1. _____?

_____?

Answer: It lives on a farm.

2. _____?

_____?

Answer: It is soft.

3. _____?

_____?

# Making Inferences: Point of View

Ellen likes animals. Someday she might want to be an animal doctor.

**Directions:** Write one question you think Ellen would ask each of these animals if she could speak their language.

1. a giraffe _____?

2. a mouse _____?

3. a shark _____?

4. a hippopotamus _____?

5. a penguin _____?

6. a gorilla _____?

7. an eagle _____?

**Directions:** Now, write the answers you think these animals might have given Ellen.

9. a giraffe _____

10. a mouse _____

11. a shark _____

12. a hippopotamus _____

13. a penguin _____

14. a gorilla _____

15. an eagle _____

# Creative Writing

**Directions:** Look at the picture below. Write a story about the picture.

_____

_____

_____

_____

_____

_____

# Is, Are and Am

**Is, are** and **am** are special action words that tell us something is happening now.

Use **am** with **I**. **Example: I am.**
Use **is** to tell about one person or thing. **Example: He is.**
Use **are** to tell about more than one. **Example: We are.**
Use **are** with **you**. **Example: You are.**

**Directions:** Write **is**, **are** or **am** in the sentences below.

1. My friends _____ helping me build a tree house.

2. It_____ in my backyard.

3. We _____ using hammers, wood and nails.

4. It_____ a very hard job.

5. I _____ lucky to have good friends.

# Was and Were

**Was** and **were** tell us about something that already happened.

Use **was** to tell about one person or thing. **Example:** I **was**, he **was**.
Use **were** to tell about more than one person or thing or when using
the word you. **Example:** We **were**, you **were**.

**Directions:** Write **was** or **were** in each sentence.

1. Lily _____ eight years old on her birthday.

2. Tim and Steve _____ happy to be at the party.

3. Megan _____ too shy to sing "Happy Birthday."

4. Ben _____ sorry he dropped his cake.

5. All of the children _____ happy to be invited.

# Go, Going and Went

We use **go** or **going** to tell about now or later. Sometimes we use **going** with the words **am** or **are**. We use **went** to tell about something that already happened.

**Directions:** Write **go**, **going** or **went** in the sentences below.

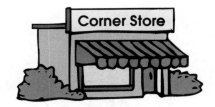

1. Today, I will _____ to the store.

2. Yesterday, we _____ shopping.

3. I am _____ to take Muffy to the vet.

4. Jan and Steve _____ to the party.

5. They are _____ to have a good day.

# Have, Has and Had

We use **have** and **has** to tell about now. We use **had** to tell about something that already happened.

**Directions:** Write **has**, **have** or **had** in the sentences below.

1. We _____ three cats at home.

2. Ginger _____ brown fur.

3. Bucky and Charlie _____ gray fur.

4. My friend Tom _____ one cat, but he died.

5. Tom _____ a new cat now.

# See, Saw and Sees

We use **see** or **sees** to tell about now. We use **saw** to tell about something that already happened.

**Directions:** Write **see**, **sees** or **saw** in the sentences below.

1. Last night, we _____ the stars.

2. John can _____ the stars from his window.

3. He _____ them every night.

4. Last week, he _____ the Big Dipper.

5. Can you _____ it in the night sky, too?

6. If you _____ it, you would remember it!

7. John _____ it often now.

8. How often do you _____ it?

# Eat, Eats and Ate

We use **eat** or **eats** to tell about now. We use **ate** to tell about what already happened.

**Directions:** Write **eat**, **eats** or **ate** in the sentences below.

1. We like to _____ in the lunchroom.

2. Today, my teacher will _____ in a different room.

3. She _____ with the other teachers.

4. Yesterday, we _____ pizza, pears and peas.

5. Today, we will _____ turkey and potatoes.

# Leave, Leaves and Left

We use **leave** and **leaves** to tell about now. We use **left** to tell about what already happened.

**Directions:** Write **leave**, **leaves** or **left** in the sentences below.

1. Last winter, we _____ seeds in the bird feeder everyday.

2. My mother likes to _____ food out for the squirrels.

3. When it rains, she _____ bread for the birds.

4. Yesterday, she _____ popcorn for the birds.

# ABC Order

**Directions:** Put the words in ABC order on the bags.

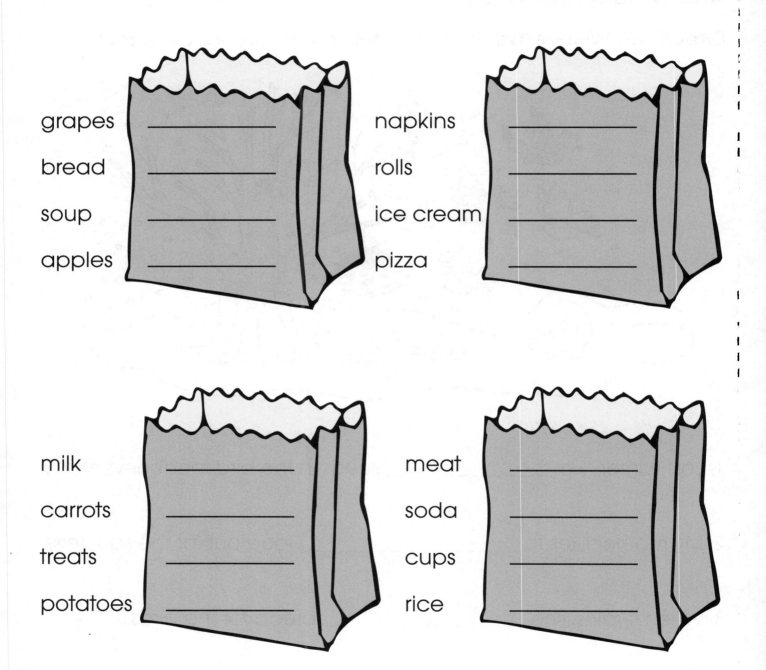

grapes _____

bread _____

soup _____

apples _____

napkins _____

rolls _____

ice cream _____

pizza _____

milk _____

carrots _____

treats _____

potatoes _____

meat _____

soda _____

cups _____

rice _____

# ABC Order

**Directions:** Write these words in order. If two words start with the same letter, look at the second letter in each word.

**Example:** **lamb**    Lamb comes first because **a** comes before **i**
              **light**    in the alphabet.

tree      _____

branch      _____

leaf      _____

dish      _____

dog      _____

bone      _____

rain      _____

umbrella      _____

cloud      _____

mail      _____

stamp      _____

slot      _____

# Learning Dictionary Skills

A dictionary is a book that gives the meaning of words. It also tells how words sound. Words in a dictionary are in ABC order. That makes them easier to find. A picture dictionary lists a word, a picture of the word and its meaning.

**Directions:** Look at this page from a picture dictionary. Then answer the questions.

**baby**

A very young child.

**band**

A group of people who play music.

**bank**

A place where money is kept.

**bark**

The sound a dog makes.

**berry**

A small, juicy fruit.

**board**

A flat piece of wood.

1. What is a small, juicy fruit? _____

2. What is a group of people who play music? _____

3. What is the name for a very young child? _____

4. What is a flat piece of wood called? _____

# Learning Dictionary Skills

**Directions:** Look at this page from a picture dictionary. Then answer the questions.

**safe**

A metal box.

**sea**

A body of water.

**seed**

The beginning of a plant.

**sheep**

An animal that has wool.

**store**

A place where items are sold.

**skate**

A shoe with wheels or a blade on it.

**snowstorm**

A time when much snow falls.

**squirrel**

A small animal with a bushy tail.

**stone**

A small rock.

1. What kind of animal has wool? _____

2. What do you call a shoe with wheels on it? _____

3. When a lot of snow falls, what is it called? _____

4. What is a small animal with a bushy tail? _____

5. What is a place where items are sold? _____

6. When a plant starts, what is it called? _____

# Learning Dictionary Skills

**Directions:** Look at this page from a picture dictionary. Then answer the questions.

**table**

Furniture with legs and a flat top.

**tail**

A slender part that is on the back of an animal.

**teacher**

A person who teaches lessons.

**telephone**

A machine that sends and receives sounds.

**ticket**

A paper slip or card.

**tiger**

An animal with stripes.

1. Who is a person who teaches lessons? _____

2. What is the name of an animal with stripes? _____

3. What is a piece of furniture with legs and a flat top? _____

4. What is the definition of a ticket?

_____

5. What is a machine that sends and receives sounds?

# Learning Dictionary Skills

**Directions:** Write each word from the box in ABC order between each pair of guide words.

| | | | | |
|---|---|---|---|---|
| fierce | fix | fight | first | few |
| fish | fill | flush | flat | finish |

**few**

**flush**

_____          _____

_____          _____

_____          _____

_____          _____

_____          _____

# Number Words

**Directions:** Write the correct number words in the blanks.

| one two three four five six seven eight nine ten |

Add a letter to each of these words to make a number word.

**Example:**

even                          on                          tree

_seven_           _____           _____

Change a letter to make these words into number words.

**Example:**

live                          fix                          line

_five_           _____           _____

Write the number words that sound the same as these:

**Example:**

ate                          to                          for

_eight_           _____           _____

Write the number word you did not use:           _____

# Number Words: Sentences

**Directions:** Change the telling sentences into asking sentences. Change the asking sentences into telling sentences. Begin each one with a capital letter and end it with a period or a question mark.

**Examples:**

Is she eating three cookies?

## She is eating three cookies.

He is bringing one truck.

## Is he bringing one truck?

1. Is he painting two blue birds?

_____

2. Did she find four apples?

_____

3. She will be six on her birthday.

_____

# Short a Words: Rhyming Words

**Short a** is the sound you hear in the word **math**.

**Directions:** Use the **short a** words in the box to write rhyming words.

| | | | |
|---|---|---|---|
| lamp | fat | bat | van |
| path | can | cat | Dan |
| math | stamp | fan | sat |

1. Write four words that rhyme with **mat**.

_____     _____

_____     _____

2. Write two words that rhyme with **bath**.

_____     _____

3. Write two words that rhyme with **damp**.

_____     _____

4. Write four words that rhyme with **pan**.

_____     _____

_____     _____

# Short a Words: Sentences

**Directions:** Use a word from the box to complete each sentence.

| fat | path | lamp | can |
|-----|------|------|-----|
| van | stamp | Dan | math |
| sat | cat | fan | bat |

**Example:**

1. The _____ lamp _____ had a pink shade.

2. The bike _____ led us to the park.

3. I like to add in _____ class.

4. The cat is very _____.

5. The _____ of beans was hard to open.

6. The envelope needed a _____.

7. He swung the _____ and hit the ball.

8. The _____ blew air around.

9. My mom drives a blue _____.

10. I _____ in the backseat.

# Long a Words

**Long a** is the vowel sound which says its own name. **Long a** can be spelled **ai** as in the word **mail**, **ay** as in the word **say** and **a** with a **silent e** at the end of a word as in the word **same**.

**Directions:** Say each word and listen for the **long a** sound. Then write each word and underline the letters that make the **long a** vowel sound.

| | | |
|---|---|---|
| mail | bake | train |
| game | day | sale |
| paint | play | name |
| made | gray | tray |

1. _____

2. _____

3. _____

4. _____

5. _____

6. _____

7. _____

8. _____

9. _____

10. _____

11. _____

12. _____

# Long a Words: Sentence Order

**Directions:** Write the words in order so that each sentence tells a complete idea. Begin each sentence with a capital letter and end it with a period or a question mark.

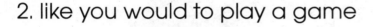

1. plate was on the cake a

_____

2. like you would to play a game

_____

3. gray around the a corner train came

_____

4. was on mail Bob's name the

_____

5. sail for on day we went a nice a

_____

# Short o Words

**Short o** is the vowel sound you hear in the word **pot**.

**Directions:** Say each word and listen for the **short o** sound. Then write each word and underline the letter that makes the **short o** sound.

| | | | |
|---|---|---|---|
| hot | box | sock | mop |
| stop | not | fox | cot |
| Bob | rock | clock | lock |

1. _____

2. _____

3. _____

4. _____

5. _____

6. _____

7. _____

8. _____

9. _____

10. _____

11. _____

12. _____

# Short o Words: Rhyming Words

**Short o** is the vowel sound you hear in the word **got**.

**Directions:** Use the **short o** words in the box to write rhyming words.

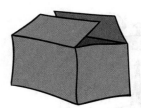

| | | | |
|---|---|---|---|
| hot | rock | lock | cot |
| stop | sock | fox | mop |
| box | mob | clock | Bob |

1. Write the words that rhyme with **dot**.

_____     _____

2. Write the words that rhyme with **socks**.

_____     _____

3. Write the words that rhyme with **hop**.

_____     _____

4. Write the words that rhyme with **dock**.

_____     _____

5. Write the words that rhyme with **cob**.

_____     _____

# Long o Words

**Long o** is the vowel sound which says its own name. **Long o** can be spelled **oa** as in the word **float** or **o** with a **silent e** at the end as in **cone**.

**Directions:** Say each word and listen for the **long o** sound. Then write each word and underline the letters that make the **long o** sound.

| rope | coat | soap | wrote |
|------|------|------|-------|
| note | hope | boat | cone |
| bone | pole | phone | hole |

1. _____

2. _____

3. _____

4. _____

5. _____

6. _____

7. _____

8. _____

9. _____

10. _____

11. _____

12. _____

# Long o Words: Sentences

**Directions:** Draw a line from the first part of the sentence to the part which completes the sentence.

1. Do you know

in the water.

2. The dog

was in the tree.

3. The boat floats

who wrote the note?

4. I hope the phone

has a bone.

5. Carol's ice-cream cone

rings soon for me!

6. The rope swing

a coat in the cold.

7. I had to wear

was melting.

# Animal Words

**Directions:** Write the animal names twice beside each picture.

| fox | rabbit | bear | squirrel | mouse | deer |

**Example:**

 squirrel      squirrel

 _____

 _____

 _____

 _____

 _____

# Animal Words: More Than One

To show more than one of something, we add **s** to most words.

**Example:** one dog – **two dogs**     one book – **two books**

But some words are different. For words that end with **x**, use **es** to show two.

**Example:** one fox – **two foxes**     one box – **two boxes**

The spelling of some words changes a lot when there are two.

**Example:** one mouse – **two mice**

Some words stay the same, even when you mean two of something.

**Example:** one deer – **two deer**     one fish – **two fish**

**Directions:** Complete the sentences below with the correct word.

1. The  run fast.     _____

2. The  are eating.     _____

3. Have you seen any  today?     _____

4. Where do the  live?     _____

5. Did you ever have  for pets? _____

# Animal Words: Kinds of Sentences

Another name for an asking sentence is a **question**.

**Directions:** Use the words in the box to write a telling sentence. Then use the words to write a question.

**Example:**

| a | mouse | I | see |
|------|-------|-------|-----|
| the | bed | under | do |

Telling sentence:

I see a mouse under the bed.

Question:

Do I see a mouse under the bed?

| in | live |
|-------|-------|
| these | woods |
| bears | do |

Telling sentence:

_____

Question:

_____

# Animal Words: Sentences

**Directions:** Read the sentences on each line and draw a line between them. Then write each sentence again on the lines below. Begin each one with a capital letter and put a period or question mark at the end.

**Example:**

why do squirrels hide nuts | they eat them in the winter

## Why do squirrels hide nuts?
## They eat them in the winter.

1. bears sleep in the winter they don't need food then

_____

_____

2. he said he saw a fox do you think he did

_____

_____

# Family Words

**Directions:** This is Andy's **family tree**. It shows all the people in his family. Use the words in the box to finish writing the names in Andy's family tree.

| | |
|---|---|
| grandmother | mother |
| grandfather | father |
| aunt | uncle |
| brother | sister |

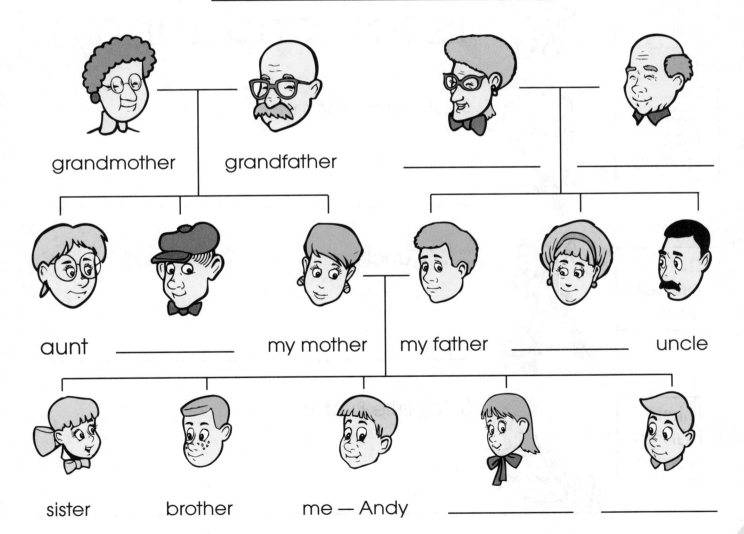

grandmother          grandfather          _____          _____

aunt    _____    my mother  |  my father    _____    uncle

sister          brother          me — Andy          _____

# Family Words

Some words tell how a person looks or feels. These are called **describing** words or **adjectives**.

**Directions:** Help Andy write about the people in his family. Cross out the **describing** word that does not tell about each picture. Write a sentence that uses the other two describing words.

**Example:**

| ~~asleep~~ funny tall |
|---|

My aunt

## is tall and funny.

| fast happy smiling |
|---|

1. My grandmother

_____

| hot broken tired |
|---|

2. My uncle

_____

| thirsty hungry hard |
|---|

3. My little brother

_____

# Family Words: Joining Words

**Joining words** join two ideas to make one long sentence. Three words help do this:

**and** — if both sentences are much the same.
**Example:** I took my dog for a walk, **and** I played with my cat.

**but** — if the second sentence says something different than the first sentence. Sometimes the second sentence tells why you can't do the first sentence.
**Example:** I want to play outside, **but** it is raining.

**or** — if each sentence names a different thing you could do.
**Example:** You could eat your cookie, **or** you could give it to me.

**Directions:** Use the word given to join the two short sentences into one longer sentence.

**(but)**
My aunt lives far away. She calls me often.

My aunt lives far away, but she calls me often.

**1. (and)**
My sister had a birthday. She got a new bike.

_____

_____

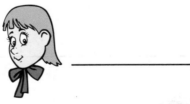

**2. (or)**
We can play outside. We can play inside.

_____

_____

# Family Words: Joining Words

**Directions:** Read each pair of sentences. Then join them with **and**, **but** or **or**.

1. My uncle likes popcorn.
   He does not like peanuts.

_____

_____

2. He could read a book.
   He could tell me his own story.

_____

_____

3. My little brother is sleepy.
   He wants to go to bed.

_____

_____

# Short e Words

**Short e** is the vowel sound you hear in the word **pet**.

**Directions:** Say each word and listen for the **short e** sound. Then write each word and underline the letter that makes the **short e** sound.

| | | | |
|---|---|---|---|
| get | Meg | rest | tent |
| red | spent | test | help |
| bed | pet | head | best |

1. _____

2. _____

3. _____

4. _____

5. _____

6. _____

7. _____

8. _____

9. _____

10. _____

11. _____

12. _____

# Short e Words: Rhyming Words

**Short e** is the vowel sound you hear in the word **egg**.

**Directions:** Use the **short e** words in the box to write rhyming words.

| | | | |
|---|---|---|---|
| get | test | pet | help |
| let | head | spent | red |
| best | tent | rest | bed |

1. Write the words that rhyme with **fed**.

_____   _____   _____

2. Write the words that rhyme with **bent**.

_____   _____

3. Write the words that rhyme with **west**.

_____   _____   _____   _____

4. Write the words that rhyme with **bet**.

_____   _____   _____

# Short e Words: Sentences

**Directions:** Write the correct **short e** word in each sentence.

| get | Meg | rest | bed | spent | best |
|-----|-----|------|-----|-------|------|
| test | help | head | pet | red | tent |

1. Of all my crayons, I like the color _____

the _____ !

2. I always make my _____ when I _____ up.

3. My new hat keeps my _____ warm.

4. _____ wanted a dog for a _____ .

5. When we go camping, my job is to _____ put up

the _____ .

6. I have a _____ in math tomorrow, so I want to get

a good night's _____ .

# Long e Words

**Long e** is the vowel sound which says its own name. **Long e** can be spelled **ee** as in the word **teeth, ea** as in the word **meat** or **e** as in the word **me**.

**Directions:** Say each word and listen for the **long e** sound. Then write the words and underline the letters that make the **long e** sound.

| | | | |
|---|---|---|---|
| street | neat | treat | feet |
| sleep | keep | deal | meal |
| mean | clean | beast | feast |

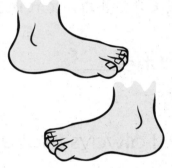

1. _____

2. _____

3. _____

4. _____

5. _____

6. _____

7. _____

8. _____

9. _____

10. _____

11. _____

12. _____

# Long e Words: Rhyming Words

**Long e** is the vowel sound you hear in the word **meet**.

**Directions:** Use the **long e** words in the box to write rhyming words.

| street | feet | neat | treat |
|--------|-------|-------|-------|
| keep | deal | sleep | meal |
| mean | beast | clean | feast |

1. Write the words that rhyme with **beat**.

_____     _____

_____     _____

2. Write the words that rhyme with **deep**.

_____     _____

3. Write the words that rhyme with **feel**.

_____     _____

4. Write the words that rhyme with **bean**.

_____     _____

5. Write the words that rhyme with **least**.

_____     _____

# Long e Words: Sentences

**Directions:** Write a word from the box to complete each sentence.

| | | | |
|---|---|---|---|
| street | feet | neat | treat |
| keep | deal | sleep | meal |
| mean | beast | clean | feast |

1. I went to _____ late last night.

2. One of my favorite stories is "Beauty and

the _____ ."

3. Look both ways when you cross the _____ .

4. It would be _____ to kick someone.

5. I wear socks and shoes on my _____ .

6. The most important _____ of the day

is breakfast.

# Verbs

**Verbs** are words that tell the action in the sentence.

**Directions:** Draw a line from each sentence to its picture. Then finish the sentence with the verb or action word that is under each picture.

**Example:**
He will ___help___ the baby.

**help**

**carry**

1. I can _____ my book.

2. It is time to _____ up.

**cut**

3. That chair might _____ .

**build**

4. They _____ houses.

**clean**

5. I _____ this out myself.

**fix**

6. Is that too heavy to _____ ?

**break**

# Verbs: Sentences

**Directions:** Read the two sentences in each story below. Then write one more sentence to tell what happened next. Use the verbs from the box.

| break | build | fix | clean | cut | carry |
|-------|-------|-----|-------|-----|-------|

 Today is Mike's birthday.

Mike asked four friends to come.

 _____

Edith's dog walked in the mud.

He got mud in the house.

 _____

## Verbs: Sentences

**Directions:** Join each pair of sentences to make one longer sentence. Use one of the **joining** words: **and**, **but** or **or**. In the second part of the sentence, use **he**, **she** or **they** in place of the person's name.

**Example:** I asked Tim to help me. Tim wanted to play.

# I asked Tim to help me, but he wanted to play.

1. Kelly dropped a glass.
   Kelly cut her finger.

_____

_____

2. Linda and Allen got a new dog.
   Linda and Allen named it Baby.

_____

_____

# Verbs: Word Endings

Most **verbs** end with **s** when the sentence tells about one thing. The **s** is taken away when the sentence tells about more than one thing.

**Example:**

One dog walks.          One boy runs.
Two dogs **walk**.          Three boys **run**.

The spelling of some **verbs** changes when the sentence tells about only one thing.

**Example:**

One girl carries her lunch.          The boy fixes his car.
Two girls **carry** their lunches.          Two boys **fix** their cars.

**Directions:** Write the missing verbs in the sentences.

**Example:**

Pam works hard. She and Peter ___work___ all day.

1. The father bird builds a nest.

   The mother and father _____ it together.

2. The girls clean their room. Jenny _____ under her bed.

3. The children cut out their pictures. Henry _____ his slowly.

4. These workers fix things. This man _____ televisions.

5. Two trucks carry horses. One truck _____ pigs.

# Short i Words

**Short i** is the vowel sound you hear in the word **pig**.

**Directions:** Say each word and listen for the **short i** sound. Then write each word and underline the letter that makes the **short i** sound.

| pin | fin | dip | dish |
|-----|------|------|-------|
| kick | rich | ship | wish |
| win | fish | sick | pitch |

1. _____

2. _____

3. _____

4. _____

5. _____

6. _____

7. _____

8. _____

9. _____

10. _____

11. _____

12. _____

# Short i Words: Sentences

**Directions:** Complete the sentences by matching the words to the correct sentence.

1. I made a _____ on a star.                          fin

2. All we could see was the shark's _____ above the water.                                           fish

3. I like to eat vegetables with _____ .                kick

4. We saw lots of _____ in the water.              win

5. The soccer player will _____ the ball and score a goal.                                     dish

6. If you feel _____ , see a doctor.               dip

7. Did Bob _____ the race?                         wish

8. The _____ was full of candy.                    sick

# Long i Words

**Long i** is the vowel sound which says its own name. **Long i** can be spelled **igh** as in **sight**, **i** with a **silent e** at the end as in **mine** and **y** at the end as in **fly**.

**Directions:** Say each word and listen for the **long i** sound. Then write each word and underline the letters that make the **long i** sound.

| | | | |
|---|---|---|---|
| bike | hike | ride | line |
| glide | ripe | nine | pipe |
| fight | high | light | sigh |

1. _____

2. _____

3. _____

4. _____

5. _____

6. _____

7. _____

8. _____

9. _____

10. _____

11. _____

12. _____

# Long i Words: Rhyming Words

**Long i** is the sound you hear in the word **fight**.

**Directions:** Use the **long i** words in the box to write rhyming words.

| | | | |
|---|---|---|---|
| hide | ride | line | my |
| by | nine | high | light |
| sight | fly | | |

1. Write the words that rhyme with **sigh**.

_____ _____ _____ _____

2. Write the words that rhyme with **side**.

_____ _____

3. Write the words that rhyme with **fine**.

_____ _____

4. Write the words that rhyme with **fight**.

_____ _____

# Location Words

**Directions:** Use one of the location words from the box to complete each sentence.

| between | around | inside | outside | beside | across |
|---------|--------|--------|---------|--------|--------|

**Example:**

She will hide ____**under**____ the basket.

1. In the summer, we like to play _____.

2. She can swim _____ the lake.

3. Put the bird _____ its cage so it won't fly away.

4. Sit _____ Bill and me so we can all work together.

5. Your picture is right _____ mine on the wall.

6. The fence goes _____ the house.

# Location Words

**Directions:** Draw a line from each sentence to its picture. Then complete each sentence with the word under the picture.

**Example:**

He is walking **behind** the tree.

**outside**

1. We stay _____ when it rains.

**behind**

**between**

2. She drew a dog _____ his house.

**across**

3. She stands _____ her friends.

**around**

4. They walked _____ the bridge.

**beside**

5. Let the cat go _____ .

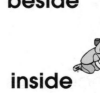

**inside**

6. Draw a circle _____ the fish.

# Short u Words

**Short u** is the sound you hear in the word **bug**.

**Directions:** Say each word and listen for the **short u** sound. Then write each word and underline the letter that makes the **short u** sound.

| dust | must | nut | bug |
| bump | pump | tub | jump |
| cut | hug | rug | cub |

1. _____

2. _____

3. _____

4. _____

5. _____

6. _____

7. _____

8. _____

9. _____

10. _____

11. _____

12. _____

# Short u Words: Sentences

**Directions:** Circle the words in each sentence which are not correct. Then write the correct **short u** words from the box on the lines.

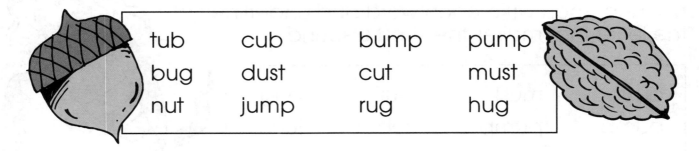

| | | | |
|---|---|---|---|
| tub | cub | bump | pump |
| bug | dust | cut | must |
| nut | jump | rug | hug |

1. The crust made me sneeze. _____

2. I need to take a bath in the cub. _____

3. The mug bite left a big pump on my arm.

_____    _____

4. It is time to get my hair hut. _____

5. The mother bear took care of her shrub. _____

6. We need to jump more gas into the car. _____

# Long u Words

**Long u** is the vowel sound which says its own name. **Long u** is spelled **u** with a silent **e** at the end as in **cute**. The letters **oo** make a sound very much like long **u**. They make the sound you hear in the word **zoo**. The letters **ew** also make the **oo** sound as in the word **grew**.

**Directions:** Say the words and listen for the **u** and **oo** sounds. Then write each word and underline the letters that make the **long u** and **oo** sounds.

| | | | |
|---|---|---|---|
| choose | blew | moon | fuse |
| cube | Ruth | tooth | use |
| flew | loose | goose | noon |

1. _____

2. _____

3. _____

4. _____

5. _____

6. _____

7. _____

8. _____

9. _____

10. _____

11. _____

12. _____

# Long u Words: Sentences

**Directions:** Write the words in the sentences below in the correct order. Begin each sentence with a capital letter and end it with a period or a question mark.

1. the pulled dentist tooth my loose

_____

2. ice cubes I choose in my drink to put

_____

3. a Ruth fuse blew yesterday

_____

4. loose the got in garden goose the

_____

5. flew the goose winter for the south

_____

6. is full there a moon tonight

_____

# Opposite Words

**Directions: Opposites** are words which are different in every way.
Use the opposite word from the box to complete these sentences.

| hard | hot | bottom | quickly | happy |
|------|-----|--------|---------|-------|
| sad  | slowly | cold | soft | top |

**Example:**

My new coat is blue on  top and

red on the bottom .

1. Snow is _____ , but fire is _____ .

2. A rabbit runs_____ , but a turtle

   moves _____ .

3. A bed is _____ , but a floor is _____ .

4. I feel _____ when my friends come

   and _____ when they leave.

# Opposite Words

**Directions:** Draw a line from each sentence to its picture. Then complete each sentence with the word under the picture.

**Example:**

She bought a __new__ bat.

**hard**

1. I like my _____ pillow.

**new**

2. Birthdays make me _____.

**top**

3. Put that book on _____.

 **sad**

4. Jenny runs _____.

 **slowly**

5. A rock makes a _____ seat.

 **quickly**

6. I feel _____ when it rains.

**happy**

7. He eats _____.

 **soft**

# Opposite Words: Sentences

**Directions:** Cross out the word in each box that does not tell about the picture. Write a sentence about the picture using the other two words.

**Example:**

| ~~teeth~~ | garden | digs |
|---|---|---|

**She digs in her garden.**

| swims | quickly | five |
|---|---|---|

_____

_____

| soft | fly | happy |
|---|---|---|

_____

_____

| popcorn | bottom | sad |
|---|---|---|

_____

_____

# Opposite Words: Sentences

**Directions:** Look at each picture. Then write a sentence that uses the word under the picture and tells how something is the same as the picture.

**Example:**

**cold**

My hands are as cold as ice.

**hard**

_____

**slow**

_____

**soft**

_____

**happy**

_____

# Opposite Words: Completing a Story

**Directions:** Write opposite words in the blanks to complete the story.

| | | | | |
|---|---|---|---|---|
| hot | hard | top | cold | bottom |
| soft | quickly | happy | slowly | sad |

One day, Grandma came for a visit. She gave my sister Jenny and me a box of chocolate candy. We said, "Thank you!" Then Jenny _____ took the _____ off the box. The pieces all looked the same! I couldn't tell which pieces were _____ inside and which were _____ ! I only liked the _____ ones. Jenny didn't care. She was _____ to get any kind of candy!

I _____ looked at all the pieces. I didn't know which one to pick. Just then Dad called us. Grandma was going home. He wanted us to say good-bye to her. I hurried to the front door where they were standing. Jenny came a minute later.

I told Grandma I hoped I would see her soon. I always feel _____ when she leaves. Jenny stood behind me and didn't say anything. After Grandma went home, I found out why. Jenny had most of our candy in her mouth! Only a few pieces were left in the _____ of the box! Then I was _____ ! That Jenny!

# Time Words

The time between breakfast and lunch is **morning**.

The time between lunch and dinner is **afternoon**.

The time between dinner and bedtime is **evening**.

**Directions:** Write a time word from the box to complete each sentence. Use each word only once.

| evening | morning | today | tomorrow | afternoon |
|---------|---------|-------|----------|-----------|

1. What did you eat for breakfast

   this _____?

2. We came home from school in the _____ .

3. I help wash the dinner dishes in

   the _____ .

4. I feel a little tired _____ .

5. If I rest tonight, I will feel better _____ .

# Time Words: Sentences

**Directions:** Write a sentence for these time words.
Tell something you do at that time.

**Example:**

day

# Every day I walk to school.

morning

_____

_____

afternoon

_____

_____

evening

_____

_____

# MATH

# Less Than, Greater Than

**Directions:** The open mouth points to the larger number. The small point goes to the smaller number. Draw the symbol < or > to the correct number.

**Example:**  5 $>$ 3

This means that 5 is greater than 3, and 3 is less than 5.

12 $\bigcirc$ 2          16 $\bigcirc$ 6

16 $\bigcirc$ 15         1 $\bigcirc$ 2

7 $\bigcirc$ 1           19 $\bigcirc$ 5

9 $\bigcirc$ 6           11 $\bigcirc$ 13

# Counting by 2's

**Directions:** Each basket the players make is worth 2 points. Help your team win by counting by 2's to beat the other team's score.

**2**

___

___

**8**

___

___

___

**16**

**20**

___

___

___

**28**

___

**32**

```
┌──────────────────────────┐
│      Final Score         │
│   Home        Visitor    │
│  ┌──────┐                │
│  │      │       30       │
│  └──────┘                │
└──────────────────────────┘
```

*Winner!*

┌─────────┐
│         │
└─────────┘

# Counting: 2's, 5's, 10's

**Directions:** Write the missing numbers.

Count by 2's:

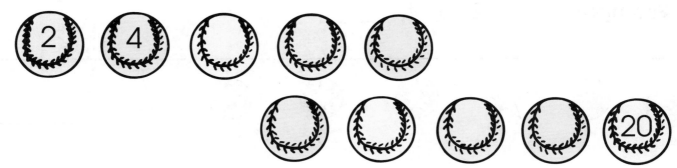

Count by 5's:

Count by 10's:

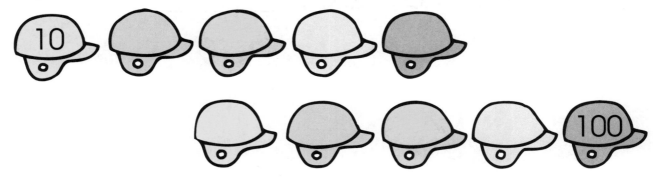

# Patterns

**Directions:** Write or draw what comes next in the pattern.

**Example:** 1, 2, 3, 4, __5__

---

1.  _____

2. A, 1, B, 2, C _____

3. 2, 4, 6, 8, _____

4. A, C, E, G, _____

5. 5, 10, 15, 20, _____

# Finding Patterns: Numbers

Mia likes to count by twos, threes, fours, fives, tens and hundreds.

**Directions:** Complete the number patterns.

1. 5, ____, ____, 20, ____, ____, 35, ____, ____, 50

2. 100, ____, ____, 400, ____, ____, ____, 800, ____

3. ____, 4, 6, ____, ____, 12, ____, 16, ____, ____

4. 10, ____, ____, 40, ____, ____, 70, ____, 90

5. 4, ____, 12, ____, ____, 24, ____, 32, ____, 40

6. ____, 6, 9, ____, ____, 18, ____, 24, ____, 30

**Directions:** Make up two of your own number patterns.

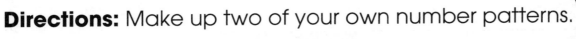

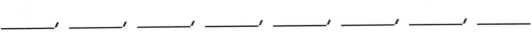

# Finding Patterns: Shapes

**Directions:** Complete each row by drawing the correct shape.

_____

_____

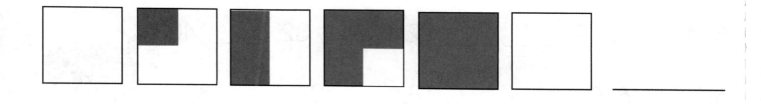

_____

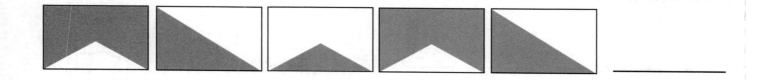

_____

# Ordinal Numbers

Ordinal numbers indicate order in a series, such as **first**, **second** or **third**.

**Directions:** Follow the instructions to color the train cars. The first car is the engine.

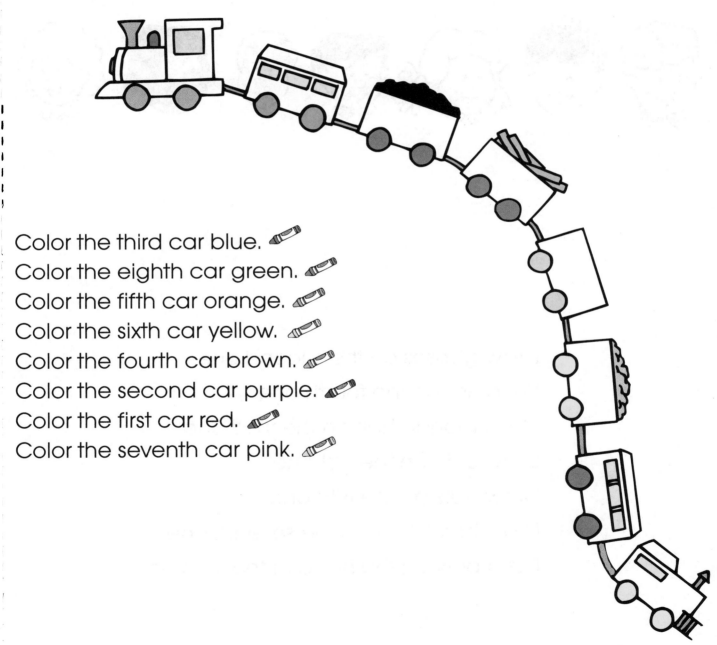

Color the third car blue.

Color the eighth car green.

Color the fifth car orange.

Color the sixth car yellow.

Color the fourth car brown.

Color the second car purple.

Color the first car red.

Color the seventh car pink.

# Ordinal Numbers

**Directions:** Follow the instructions.

Draw glasses on the second one.

Put a hat on the fourth one.

Color blonde hair on the third one.

Draw a tie on the first one.

Draw ears on the fifth one.

Draw black hair on the seventh one.

Put a bow on the head of the sixth one.

# Addition

Addition is "putting together" or adding two or more numbers to find the sum.

**Directions:** Add.

**Example:**

```
  2
+5
  7
```

| | | | | | |
|---|---|---|---|---|---|
| 3<br>+4 | 6<br>+2 | 7<br>+1 | 8<br>+2 | 5<br>+4 | 3<br>+1 |
| 8<br>+2 | 9<br>+5 | 10<br>+3 | 6<br>+6 | 4<br>+9 | 7<br>+7 |
| 9<br>+3 | 8<br>+7 | 6<br>+5 | 7<br>+9 | 7<br>+6 | 9<br>+9 |

# Addition: Commutative Property

The commutative property of addition states that even if the order of the numbers is changed in an addition sentence, the sum will stay the same.

**Example:** $2 + 3 = 5$
$3 + 2 = 5$

**Directions:** Look at the addition sentences below. Complete the addition sentences by writing the missing numerals.

$5 + 4 = 9$          $3 + 1 = 4$          $2 + 6 = 8$
$4 + \underline{\phantom{0}} = 9$          $1 + \underline{\phantom{0}} = 4$          $6 + \underline{\phantom{0}} = 8$

$6 + 1 = 7$          $4 + 3 = 7$          $1 + 9 = 10$
$1 + \underline{\phantom{0}} = 7$          $3 + \underline{\phantom{0}} = 7$          $9 + \underline{\phantom{0}} = 10$

**Now try these:**

$6 + 3 = 9$          $10 + 2 = 12$          $8 + 3 = 11$
$\underline{\phantom{0}} + \underline{\phantom{0}} = 9$          $\underline{\phantom{0}} + \underline{\phantom{0}} = 12$          $\underline{\phantom{0}} + \underline{\phantom{0}} = 11$

Look at these sums. Can you think of two number sentences that would show the commutative property of addition?

$\underline{\phantom{0}} + \underline{\phantom{0}} = 7$          $\underline{\phantom{0}} + \underline{\phantom{0}} = 11$          $\underline{\phantom{0}} + \underline{\phantom{0}} = 9$

$\underline{\phantom{0}} + \underline{\phantom{0}} = 7$          $\underline{\phantom{0}} + \underline{\phantom{0}} = 11$          $\underline{\phantom{0}} + \underline{\phantom{0}} = 9$

# Adding 3 or More Numbers

**Directions:** Add all the numbers to find the sum. Draw pictures to help or break up the problem into two smaller problems.

**Example:**

$$\begin{array}{r} 1 \\ 2 \\ +3 \\ \hline 6 \end{array} \bigcirc \begin{array}{l} \bigcirc\bigcirc \\ \bigcirc\bigcirc\bigcirc \end{array}$$

$$\begin{array}{r} +\begin{array}{r}2\\5\end{array} \\ +\begin{array}{r}2\\4\end{array} \end{array} \Big\rangle \begin{array}{r} 7 \\ +6 \\ \hline 13 \end{array}$$

$$\begin{array}{r} 3 \\ 6 \\ +2 \\ \hline \end{array} \qquad \begin{array}{r} 8 \\ 5 \\ +4 \\ \hline \end{array} \qquad \begin{array}{r} 3 \\ 1 \\ +5 \\ \hline \end{array} \qquad \begin{array}{r} 8 \\ 2 \\ +9 \\ \hline \end{array}$$

$$\begin{array}{r} 2 \\ 8 \\ 4 \\ +3 \\ \hline \end{array} \qquad \begin{array}{r} 3 \\ 6 \\ 5 \\ +2 \\ \hline \end{array} \qquad \begin{array}{r} 4 \\ 1 \\ 2 \\ +5 \\ \hline \end{array} \qquad \begin{array}{r} 6 \\ 7 \\ 3 \\ +1 \\ \hline \end{array}$$

# Subtraction

Subtraction is "taking away" or subtracting one number from another to find the difference.

**Directions:** Subtract.

**Example:**

$$\begin{array}{r} 4 \\ -3 \\ \hline \end{array}$$

$$\begin{array}{r} 5 \\ -3 \\ \hline \end{array} \qquad \begin{array}{r} 6 \\ -1 \\ \hline \end{array} \qquad \begin{array}{r} 4 \\ -3 \\ \hline \end{array} \qquad \begin{array}{r} 3 \\ -1 \\ \hline \end{array} \qquad \begin{array}{r} 2 \\ -0 \\ \hline \end{array} \qquad \begin{array}{r} 1 \\ -1 \\ \hline \end{array}$$

$$\begin{array}{r} 9 \\ -2 \\ \hline \end{array} \qquad \begin{array}{r} 7 \\ -4 \\ \hline \end{array} \qquad \begin{array}{r} 10 \\ -5 \\ \hline \end{array} \qquad \begin{array}{r} 14 \\ -6 \\ \hline \end{array} \qquad \begin{array}{r} 15 \\ -9 \\ \hline \end{array} \qquad \begin{array}{r} 12 \\ -3 \\ \hline \end{array}$$

$$\begin{array}{r} 18 \\ -8 \\ \hline \end{array} \qquad \begin{array}{r} 13 \\ -5 \\ \hline \end{array} \qquad \begin{array}{r} 14 \\ -7 \\ \hline \end{array} \qquad \begin{array}{r} 11 \\ -4 \\ \hline \end{array} \qquad \begin{array}{r} 17 \\ -9 \\ \hline \end{array} \qquad \begin{array}{r} 16 \\ -8 \\ \hline \end{array}$$

# Addition and Subtraction

Addition is "putting together" or adding two or more numbers to find the sum. Subtraction is "taking away" or subtracting one number from another to find the difference.

**Directions:** Add or subtract. Circle the answers that are less than 10.

**Examples:**

$$\begin{array}{r} 3 \\ +1 \\ \hline (4) \end{array}$$
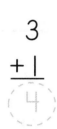

$$\begin{array}{r} 3 \\ -1 \\ \hline (2) \end{array}$$
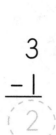

| | | | | |
|---|---|---|---|---|
| $\begin{array}{r} 9 \\ +3 \\ \hline \end{array}$ | $\begin{array}{r} 6 \\ -2 \\ \hline \end{array}$ | $\begin{array}{r} 12 \\ -1 \\ \hline \end{array}$ | $\begin{array}{r} 18 \\ +1 \\ \hline \end{array}$ | $\begin{array}{r} 15 \\ -6 \\ \hline \end{array}$ |
| $\begin{array}{r} 7 \\ +6 \\ \hline \end{array}$ | $\begin{array}{r} 16 \\ -9 \\ \hline \end{array}$ | $\begin{array}{r} 10 \\ -3 \\ \hline \end{array}$ | $\begin{array}{r} 14 \\ +5 \\ \hline \end{array}$ | $\begin{array}{r} 16 \\ -8 \\ \hline \end{array}$ |
| $\begin{array}{r} 8 \\ +7 \\ \hline \end{array}$ | $\begin{array}{r} 12 \\ +2 \\ \hline \end{array}$ | $\begin{array}{r} 13 \\ -4 \\ \hline \end{array}$ | $\begin{array}{r} 17 \\ +2 \\ \hline \end{array}$ | $\begin{array}{r} 9 \\ +9 \\ \hline \end{array}$ |

# Place Value: Ones, Tens

The place value of a digit or numeral is shown by where it is in the number. For example, in the number **23**, **2** has the place value of **tens**, and **3** is **ones**.

**Directions:** Add the tens and ones and write your answers in the blanks.

**Example:**

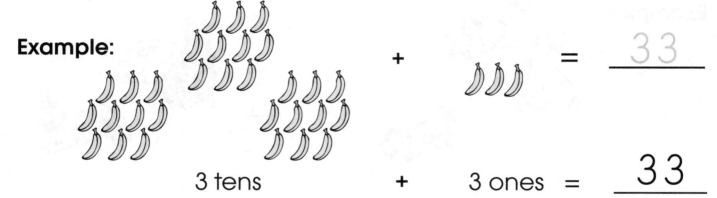

|  |  |  |  |  |
|---|---|---|---|---|
| | + | | = | 33 |

3 tens + 3 ones = **33**

|  |  |
|---|---|
| **tens   ones** | **tens   ones** |
| 7 tens + 5 ones = _____ | 4 tens + 0 ones = _____ |
| 2 tens + 3 ones = _____ | 8 tens + 1 one   = _____ |
| 5 tens + 2 ones = _____ | 1 ten + 1 one   = _____ |
| 5 tens + 4 ones = _____ | 6 tens + 3 ones = _____ |
| 9 tens + 5 ones = _____ | |

**Directions:** Draw a line to the correct number.

| | |
|---|---|
| 6 tens + 7 ones | 73 |
| 4 tens + 2 ones | 67 |
| 8 tens + 0 ones | 51 |
| 7 tens + 3 ones | 80 |
| 5 tens + 1 one | 42 |

Name ____________________

# Place Value: Ones, Tens

**Directions:** Write the numbers for the tens and ones. Then add.

**Example:**

2 tens + 7 ones

20 + 7

27

6 tens + 2 ones

____ + ____

_____

3 tens + 4 ones

____ + ____

_____

8 tens + 3 ones

____ + ____

_____

5 tens + 0 ones

____ + ____

_____

# 2-Digit Addition

**Directions:** Study the example. Follow the steps to add.

**Example:**
$$\begin{array}{r} 33 \\ +41 \\ \hline \end{array}$$

**Step 1:** Add the ones.

| tens | ones |
|:---:|:---:|
| 3 | 3 |
| +4 | 1 |
|  | 4 |

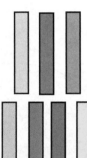 

**Step 2:** Add the tens.

| tens | ones |
|:---:|:---:|
| 3 | 3 |
| +4 | 1 |
| 7 | 4 |

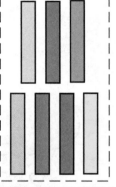

| tens | ones |
|:---:|:---:|
| 4 | 2 |
| +2 | 4 |
| 6 | 6 |

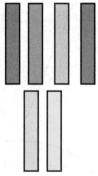 

| tens | ones |
|:---:|:---:|
| 5 | 0 |
| +4 | 7 |
| 9 | 7 |

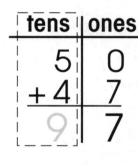 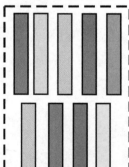

| | | | | | | | |
|:---:|:---:|:---:|:---:|:---:|:---:|:---:|:---:|
| 24 | 15 | 38 | 11 | 37 | 72 | 33 | 10 |
| +62 | +23 | +61 | +26 | +42 | +11 | +51 | +30 |

| | | | | | | | |
|:---:|:---:|:---:|:---:|:---:|:---:|:---:|:---:|
| 25 | 62 | 32 | 25 | 82 | 91 | 16 | 55 |
| +42 | +14 | +44 | +13 | + 6 | + 5 | +71 | + 3 |

# 2-Digit Addition

**Directions:** Add the total points scored in each game. Remember to add **ones** first and **tens** second.

**Example:**

Total __39__

Total _____

Total _____

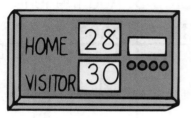

Total _____

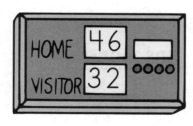

Total _____

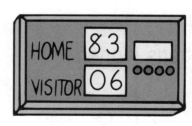

Total _____

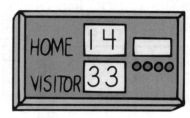

Total _____

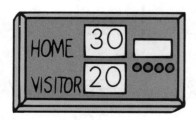

Total _____

Total _____

Total _____

# 2-Digit Addition: Regrouping

Addition is "putting together" or adding two or more numbers to find the sum. Regrouping is using **ten ones** to form **one ten, ten tens** to form **one 100, fifteen ones** to form **one ten** and **five ones** and so on.

**Directions:** Study the examples. Follow the steps to add.

**Example:**

$$\begin{array}{r} 14 \\ + 8 \\ \hline \end{array}$$

**Step 1:** Add the ones.

**Step 2:** Regroup the tens.

**Step 3:** Add the tens.

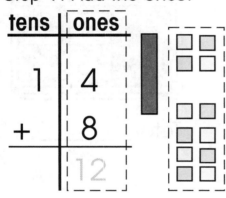

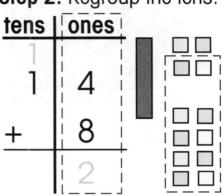

| tens | ones |
|------|------|
| 1 | 6 |
| +3 | 7 |
| 5 | 3 |

| tens | ones |
|------|------|
| 3 | 8 |
| +5 | 3 |
| 9 | 1 |

| tens | ones |
|------|------|
| 2 | 4 |
| +4 | 7 |
| 7 | 1 |

| | | | | | | | |
|---|---|---|---|---|---|---|---|
| 28 | 32 | 54 | 19 | 44 | 25 | 29 | 79 |
| +17 | +38 | +25 | +55 | +48 | +64 | +33 | +15 |

# 2-Digit Addition: Regrouping

**Directions:** Add the total points scored in the game. Remember to add the ones, regroup, and then add the tens.

**Example:**

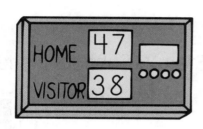

Total ___85___

Total _____

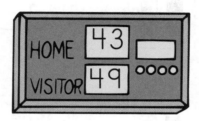

Total _____

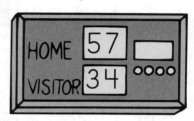

Total _____

Total _____

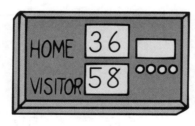

Total _____

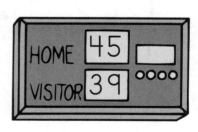

Total _____

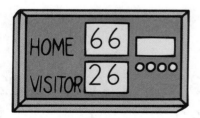

Total _____

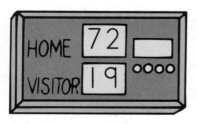

Total _____

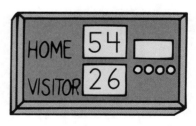

Total _____

# 2-Digit Subtraction

**Directions:** Study the example. Follow the steps to subtract.

**Example:**
$$\begin{array}{r} 28 \\ -14 \\ \hline \end{array}$$

**Step 1:** Subtract the ones.

| tens | ones |
|------|------|
| 2 | 8 |
| -1 | 4 |
| | 4 |

| tens | ones |
|------|------|
| 2 | 4 |
| -1 | 2 |
| 1 | 2 |

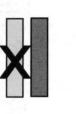

**Step 2:** Subtract the tens.

| tens | ones |
|------|------|
| 2 | 8 |
| -1 | 4 |
| 1 | 4 |

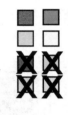

| tens | ones |
|------|------|
| 3 | 8 |
| -1 | 5 |
| 2 | 3 |

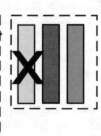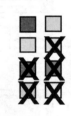

$$\begin{array}{r} 24 \\ -12 \\ \hline \end{array} \qquad \begin{array}{r} 61 \\ -30 \\ \hline \end{array} \qquad \begin{array}{r} 77 \\ -44 \\ \hline \end{array} \qquad \begin{array}{r} 85 \\ -24 \\ \hline \end{array} \qquad \begin{array}{r} 57 \\ -23 \\ \hline \end{array} \qquad \begin{array}{r} 87 \\ -33 \\ \hline \end{array} \qquad \begin{array}{r} 59 \\ -34 \\ \hline \end{array} \qquad \begin{array}{r} 96 \\ -16 \\ \hline \end{array}$$

$$\begin{array}{r} 29 \\ -15 \\ \hline \end{array} \qquad \begin{array}{r} 74 \\ -51 \\ \hline \end{array} \qquad \begin{array}{r} 46 \\ -32 \\ \hline \end{array} \qquad \begin{array}{r} 69 \\ -35 \\ \hline \end{array} \qquad \begin{array}{r} 95 \\ -32 \\ \hline \end{array} \qquad \begin{array}{r} 33 \\ -33 \\ \hline \end{array} \qquad \begin{array}{r} 78 \\ -26 \\ \hline \end{array} \qquad \begin{array}{r} 22 \\ -11 \\ \hline \end{array}$$

# 2-Digit Subtraction: Regrouping

Subtraction is "taking away" or subtracting one number from another to find the difference. Regrouping is using **one ten to form ten ones, one 100 to form ten tens** and so on.

**Directions:** Study the examples. Follow the steps to subtract.

**Example:**    37
           -19

**Step 1:** Regroup.     **Step 2:** Subtract the ones.    **Step 3:** Subtract the tens.

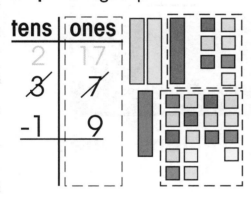

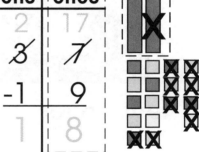

| tens | ones |
|------|------|
| 0 | 12 |
| X | 2 |
| - | 9 |
| | 3 |

| tens | ones |
|------|------|
| 2 | 14 |
| 3 | 4 |
| -1 | 6 |
| 1 | 8 |

| tens | ones |
|------|------|
| 3 | 15 |
| 4 | 5 |
| -2 | 9 |
| 1 | 6 |

|  |  |  |  |  |  |  |  |
|--|--|--|--|--|--|--|--|
| 28 | 46 | 12 | 30 | 52 | 47 | 21 | 45 |
| − 19 | − 18 | − 8 | − 12 | − 25 | − 35 | − 13 | − 25 |

# 2-Digit Subtraction: Regrouping

**Directions:** Study the steps for subtracting. Solve the problems using the steps.

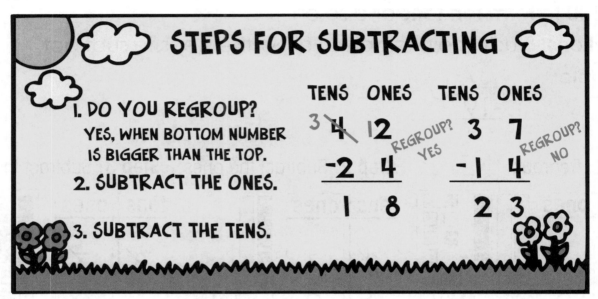

STEPS FOR SUBTRACTING

1. DO YOU REGROUP?
   YES, WHEN BOTTOM NUMBER IS BIGGER THAN THE TOP.

2. SUBTRACT THE ONES.

3. SUBTRACT THE TENS.

|   | TENS | ONES |
|---|------|------|
|   | 3 4̷  | 12   |
| - | 2    | 4    |
|   | 1    | 8    |

REGROUP? YES

|   | TENS | ONES |
|---|------|------|
|   | 3    | 7    |
| - | 1    | 4    |
|   | 2    | 3    |

REGROUP? NO

| tens | ones |
|------|------|
| 4    | 7    |
| - 2  | 8    |

| tens | ones |
|------|------|
| 6    | 4    |
| - 3  | 4    |

| tens | ones |
|------|------|
| 5    | 3    |
| - 3  | 9    |

| 56 | 83 | 43 | 75 | 91 |
|----|----|----|----|----|
| - 27 | - 47 | - 39 | - 53 | - 18 |

| 73 | 35 | 67 | 26 | 68 |
|----|----|----|----|----|
| - 66 | - 14 | - 58 | - 7 | - 45 |

# 2-Digit Addition and Subtraction

Addition is "putting together" or adding two or more numbers to find the sum. Subtraction is "taking away" or subtracting one number from another to find the difference. Regrouping is using **one ten** to form **ten ones**, **one 100** to form **ten tens**, and so on.

**Directions:** Add or subtract using regrouping.

**Example:**

```
tens  ones
  2    15
  3̶    5
 -2    7
       8
```

```
  56      40      35      42      53      97      44      93
- 27    - 16    + 27    - 14    +38    - 48    + 27    - 39
```

```
  56      44      68      73      33      49      77      27
- 17    + 28    - 49    - 24    + 18    + 32    - 68    + 19
```

# 2-Digit Addition and Subtraction

**Directions:** Add or subtract using regrouping.

```
  23        84        69        41
+48       -56       +29       -17
```

```
  52        73        84        57
-28       +18       -27       -39
```

```
  33        64        37        36
-15       +17       +58       -19
```

```
  65        48        33        25
-28       -30       +18       +35
```

# Place Value: Hundreds

The place value of a digit or numeral is shown by where it is in the number. For example, in the number **123, 1** has the place value of **hundreds, 2** is **tens** and **3** is **ones.**

**Directions:** Study the examples. Then write the missing numbers in the blanks.

**Examples:**

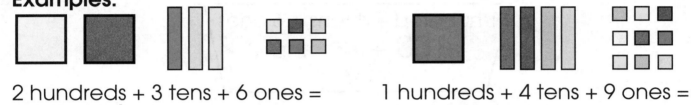

2 hundreds + 3 tens + 6 ones =

| hundreds | tens | ones |     |
| :---: | :---: | :---: | --- |
| 2 | 3 | 6 | = 236 |

1 hundreds + 4 tens + 9 ones =

| hundreds | tens | ones |     |
| :---: | :---: | :---: | --- |
| 1 | 4 | 9 | = 149 |

|  | hundreds | tens | ones | total |
| --- | :---: | :---: | :---: | :---: |
| 3 hundreds + 4 tens + 8 ones = | 3 | 4 | 8 | = _____ |
| _ hundreds + _ ten + _ ones = | 2 | 1 | 7 | = _____ |
| _ hundreds + _ tens + _ ones = | 6 | 3 | 5 | = _____ |
| _ hundreds + _ tens + _ ones = | 4 | 7 | 9 | = _____ |
| _ hundreds + _ tens + _ ones = | 2 | 9 | 4 | = _____ |
| _ hundreds + 5 tens + 6 ones = | 4 | ____ | ____ | = _____ |
| 3 hundreds + 1 ten + 3 ones = | ____ | ____ | ____ | = _____ |
| 3 hundreds + _ tens + 7 ones = | ____ | 5 | ____ | = _____ |
| 6 hundreds + 2 tens + _ ones = | ____ | ____ | 8 | = _____ |

# Place Value: Hundreds

**Directions:** Write the numbers for hundreds, tens and ones. Then add.

**Example:**

1 hundred + 4 tens + 6 ones
**100 +** 40 **+** 6
146

7 hundreds + 3 tens + 5 ones
_____ + _____ + _____
_____

3 hundreds + 1 ten + 9 ones
_____ + _____ + _____
_____

5 hundreds + 8 tens + 0 ones
_____ + _____ + _____
_____

9 hundreds + 0 tens + 7 ones
_____ + _____ + _____
_____

# 3-Digit Addition: Regrouping

**Directions:** Study the examples. Follow the steps to add.

**Example:**

**Step 1:** Add the ones. | **Step 2:** Add the tens. | **Step 3:** Add the hundreds.

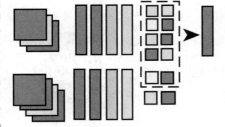

Do you regroup? Yes

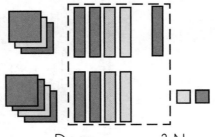

Do you regroup? No

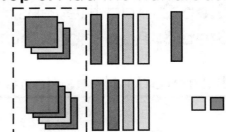

| hundreds | tens | ones | hundreds | tens | ones | hundreds | tens | ones |
|----------|------|------|----------|------|------|----------|------|------|
|          | 1    |      |          | 1    |      |          | 1    |      |
| 3        | 4    | 8    | 3        | 4    | 8    | 3        | 4    | 8    |
| +4       | 4    | 4    | +4       | 4    | 4    | +4       | 4    | 4    |
|          |      | 2    |          | 9    | 2    | 7        | 9    | 2    |

| hundreds | tens | ones | hundreds | tens | ones | hundreds | tens | ones |
|----------|------|------|----------|------|------|----------|------|------|
|          | 1    |      |          | 1    |      |          | 1    |      |
| 2        | 1    | 4    | 3        | 6    | 8    | 1        | 1    | 9    |
| +2       | 3    | 8    | +2       | 1    | 3    | +5       | 6    | 5    |
| 4        | 5    | 2    |          | 8    | 1    |          |      | 4    |

$$
\begin{array}{r} 418 \\ +323 \\ \hline \end{array}
\quad
\begin{array}{r} 471 \\ +319 \\ \hline \end{array}
\quad
\begin{array}{r} 334 \\ +528 \\ \hline \end{array}
\quad
\begin{array}{r} 659 \\ +127 \\ \hline \end{array}
\quad
\begin{array}{r} 736 \\ +145 \\ \hline \end{array}
\quad
\begin{array}{r} 426 \\ +165 \\ \hline \end{array}
\quad
\begin{array}{r} 567 \\ +228 \\ \hline \end{array}
\quad
\begin{array}{r} 327 \\ +354 \\ \hline \end{array}
$$

Name _____

# 3-Digit Addition: Regrouping

**Directions:** Study the example. Follow the steps to add. Regroup when needed.

**Step 1:** Add the ones.
**Step 2:** Add the tens.
**Step 3:** Add the hundreds.

| hundreds | tens | ones |
|----------|------|------|
| 3 | 4 | 8 |
| +4 | 5 | 4 |
| 8 | 0 | 2 |

10 = 1 ten + 0 ones

```
 348      172      575      623      369      733
+214     +418     +329     +268     +533     +229
```

```
 411      423      639      624      272      393
+299     +169     +177     +368     +469     +418
```

# 3-Digit Subtraction: Regrouping

**Directions:** Study the example. Follow the steps to subtract.

**Step 1:** Regroup ones.
**Step 2:** Subtract ones.
**Step 3:** Subtract tens.
**Step 4:** Subtract hundreds.

$$\begin{array}{r} 423 \\ -114 \\ \hline \end{array} \qquad \begin{array}{r} 562 \\ -349 \\ \hline \end{array}$$

**Example:**

| hundreds | tens | ones |
|----------|------|------|
|          | 5    | 12   |
| 4        | 6̸    | 2̸    |
| −2       | 5    | 3    |
| 2        | 0    | 9    |

$$\begin{array}{r} 478 \\ -239 \\ \hline \end{array} \qquad \begin{array}{r} 651 \\ -333 \\ \hline \end{array}$$

**Directions:** Draw a line to the correct answer. Color the kites.

$$\begin{array}{r} 347 \\ -218 \\ \hline \end{array} \quad \begin{array}{r} 144 \\ -135 \\ \hline \end{array} \quad \begin{array}{r} 963 \\ -748 \\ \hline \end{array} \quad \begin{array}{r} 762 \\ -553 \\ \hline \end{array} \quad \begin{array}{r} 287 \\ -179 \\ \hline \end{array} \quad \begin{array}{r} 427 \\ -398 \\ \hline \end{array}$$

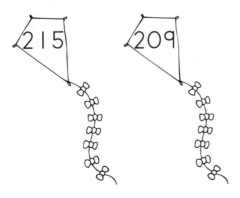
215

209

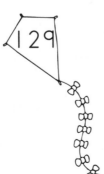
129

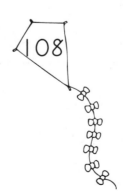
108

29

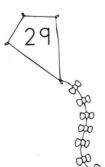

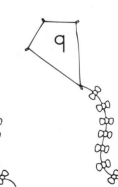
9

# 3-Digit Subtraction: Regrouping

**Directions:** Subtract. Circle the **7**'s that appear in the **tens place**.

```
  492          184
 -221         -129
 -----        -----
  2(7)1
```

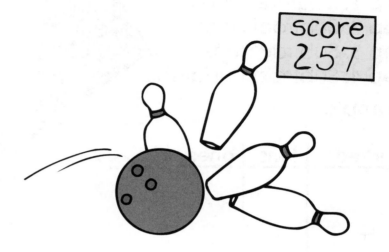

score
257

```
  358          765          584          693          921
 -238         -326         -435         -314         -362
 -----        -----        -----        -----        -----
```

```
  128          744          835          248          635
 -109         -674         -217         -199         -428
 -----        -----        -----        -----        -----
```

# Graphs

A graph is a drawing that shows information about numbers.

**Directions:** Count the apples in each row. Color the boxes to show how many apples have bites taken out of them.

**Example:**

| 1 | 2 | 3 | 4 | 5 | 6 | 7 | 8 |
|---|---|---|---|---|---|---|---|
| ■ | ■ | ■ |   |   |   |   |   |

# Graphs

**Directions:** Count the bananas in each row. Color the boxes to show how many have been eaten by the monkeys.

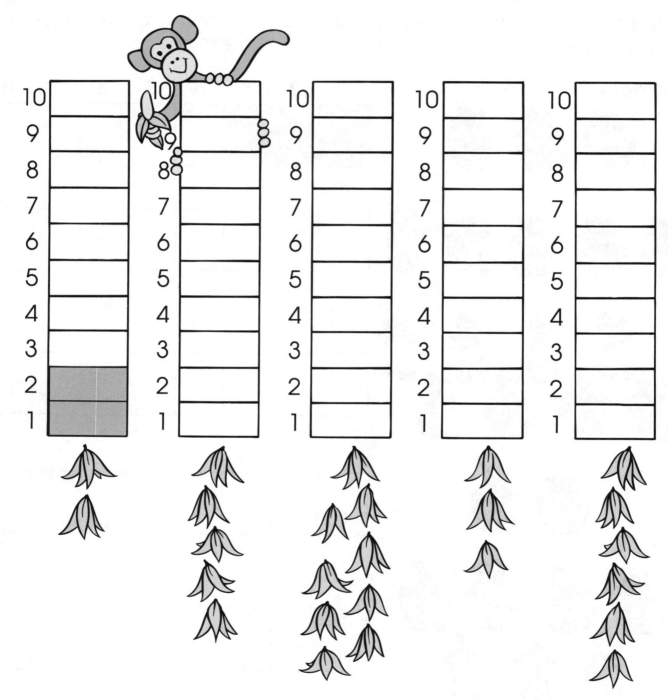

# Graphs

**Directions:** Count the fish. Color the bowls to make a graph that shows the number of fish.

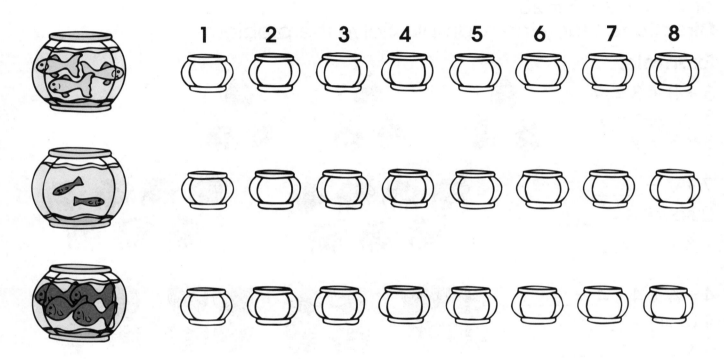

|   1  |   2  |   3  |   4  |   5  |   6  |   7  |   8  |

**Directions:** Use your fishbowl graphs to find the answers to the following questions. Draw a line to the correct bowl.

The most fish

The fewest fish

# Multiplication

Multiplication is a short way to find the sum of adding the same number a certain amount of times. For example, **4 x 7 = 28** instead of **7 + 7 + 7 + 7 = 28**.

**Directions:** Study the example. Solve the problems.

**Example:**

3 + 3 + 3 = 9
3 threes = 9
3 x 3 = 9

7 + 7 = __14__
2 sevens = __14__
2 x 7 = __14__

4 + 4 + 4 + 4 = ____
4 fours = ____
4 x ____ = ____

5 + 5 = ____
2 fives = ____
2 x ____ = ____

2 + 2 + 2 + 2 = ____
4 twos = ____
4 x ____ = ____

6 + 6 = ____
2 sixes = ____
2 x ____ = ____

# Multiplication

Multiplication is repeated addition.

**Directions:** Draw a picture for each problem.
Then write the missing numbers.

**Example:**

Draw 2 groups of three apples.

$$3 + 3 = 6$$

$$\text{or} \quad 2 \times 3 = 6$$

| Draw 3 groups of four hearts. | Draw 2 groups of five boxes. |
|---|---|
|   4 + 4 + 4 = _____  or   3 x _____ = _____ | 5 + _____ = _____  or   2 x _____ = _____ |

Draw 6 groups of two circles.

2 + _____ + _____ + _____ + _____ + _____ = _____

or   6 x _____ = _____

Draw 7 groups of three triangles.

3 + _____ + _____ + _____ + _____ + _____ + _____ = _____

or   _____ x _____ = _____

# Multiplication

**Directions:** Study the example. Draw the groups and write the total.

**Example:**

$3 \times 2$

$2 + 2 + 2$  =  →  6 _____

• • • • • •

$3 \times 4$

___ + ___ + ___ = _____

$2 \times 5$

___ + ___ = _____

$5 \times 3$

___ + ___ + ___ + ___ + ___ = _____

# Multiplication

**Directions:** Solve the problems.

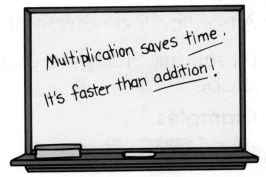

Multiplication saves time.
It's faster than addition!

9 + 9 = _18_

2 nines = ____

2 x 9 = ____

7 + 7 = ____

2 sevens = ____

2 x _7_ = ____

4 + 4 + 4 + 4 = ____

_4_ fours = ____

____ x 4 = ____

8 + 8 + 8 + 8 + 8 = ____

____ eights = ____

____ x 8 = ____

5 + 5 + 5 = ____

____ fives = ____

____ x 5 = ____

9 + 9 = ____

____ nines = ____

____ x 9 = ____

6 + 6 + 6 = ____

____ sixes = ____

____ x 6 = ____

3 + 3 = ____

____ threes = ____

____ x 3 = ____

7 + 7 + 7 + 7 = ____

____ sevens = ____

____ x 7 = ____

2 + 2 = ____

____ twos = ____

____ x 2 = ____

# Fractions: Half, Third, Fourth

A fraction is a number that names part of a whole, such as $\frac{1}{2}$ or $\frac{1}{3}$.

**Directions:** Study the examples. Color the correct fraction of each shape.

**Examples:**

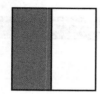

shaded part    1
equal parts    2
$\frac{1}{2}$ (one-half) shaded

shaded part    1
equal parts    3
$\frac{1}{3}$ (one-third) shaded

shaded part    1
equal parts    4
$\frac{1}{4}$ (one-fourth) shaded

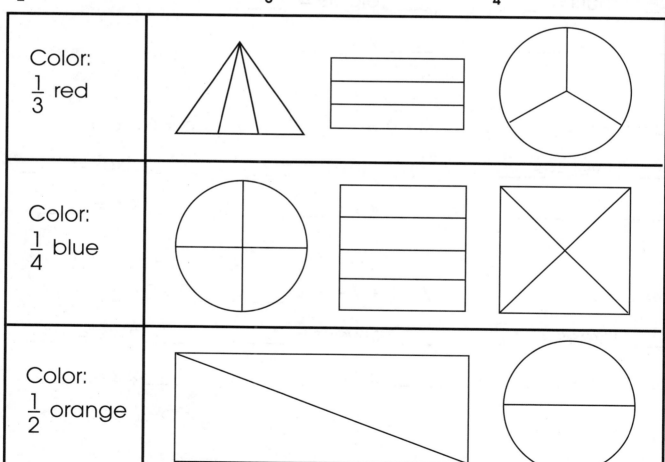

Color: $\frac{1}{3}$ red

Color: $\frac{1}{4}$ blue

Color: $\frac{1}{2}$ orange

# Fractions: Half, Third, Fourth

**Directions:** Study the examples. Circle the fraction that shows the shaded part. Then circle the fraction that shows the white part.

**Examples:**

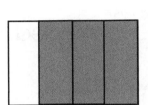

shaded   white       shaded   white       shaded   white

$\frac{1}{4}$ $\frac{1}{3}$ $\boxed{\frac{1}{2}}$   $\frac{1}{3}$ $\boxed{\frac{1}{2}}$ $\frac{1}{4}$        $\frac{1}{2}$ $\boxed{\frac{2}{3}}$ $\frac{3}{4}$   $\frac{2}{3}$ $\frac{1}{2}$ $\boxed{\frac{1}{3}}$        $\frac{1}{4}$ $\frac{1}{2}$ $\boxed{\frac{3}{4}}$   $\boxed{\frac{1}{4}}$ $\frac{2}{3}$ $\frac{1}{2}$

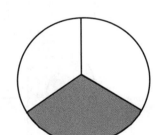

shaded                    white

$\frac{1}{4}$ $\frac{1}{3}$ $\frac{1}{2}$        $\frac{2}{4}$ $\frac{2}{3}$ $\frac{2}{2}$

shaded                    white

$\frac{3}{4}$ $\frac{1}{3}$ $\frac{3}{2}$        $\frac{1}{2}$ $\frac{1}{4}$ $\frac{1}{3}$

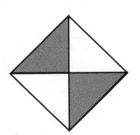

shaded                    white

$\frac{2}{3}$ $\frac{2}{4}$ $\frac{2}{2}$        $\frac{1}{3}$ $\frac{2}{4}$ $\frac{2}{2}$

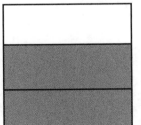

shaded                    white

$\frac{2}{4}$ $\frac{2}{3}$ $\frac{2}{2}$        $\frac{1}{2}$ $\frac{1}{4}$ $\frac{1}{3}$

# Fractions: Half, Third, Fourth

**Directions:** Draw a line from the fraction to the correct shape.

$\frac{1}{4}$ shaded

$\frac{2}{4}$ shaded

$\frac{1}{2}$ shaded

$\frac{1}{3}$ shaded

$\frac{2}{3}$ shaded

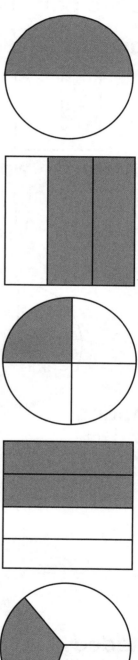

# Geometry

Geometry is mathematics that has to do with lines and shapes.

**Directions:** Color the shapes.

Color the triangles blue.
Color the circles red.
Color the squares green.
Color the rectangles pink.

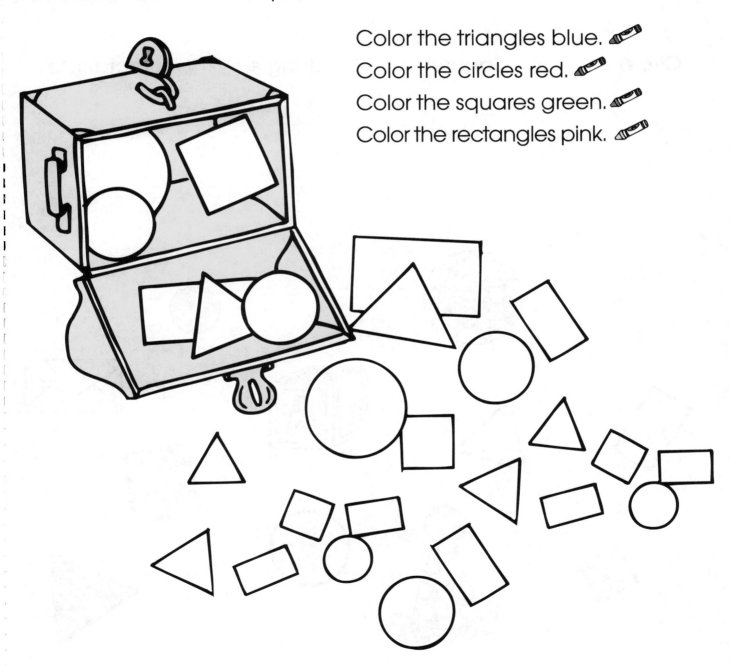

# Geometry

**Directions:** Draw a line from the word to the shape.

Use a red line for circles. ✏  Use a yellow line for rectangles. ✏
Use a blue line for squares. ✏  Use a green line for triangles. ✏

**Circle**          **Square**          **Triangle**          **Rectangle**

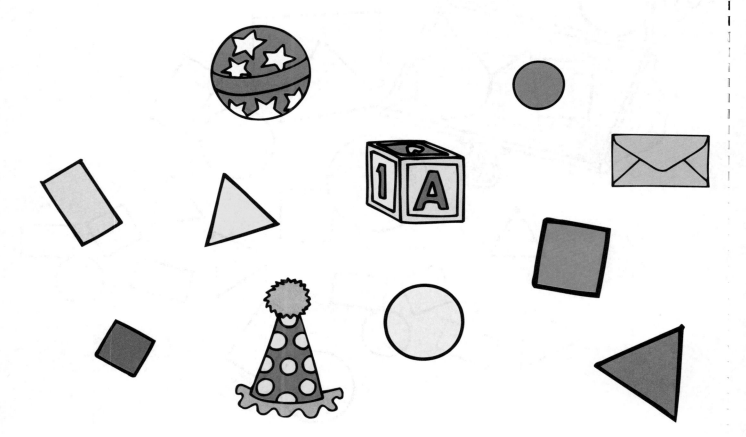

# Geometry

**Directions:** Cut out the tangram below. Mix up the pieces. Try to put it back together into a square.

Page left blank for cutting exercise on reverse.

# Measurement: Inches

**Directions:** Cut out the ruler. Measure each object to the nearest inch.

_____ inches

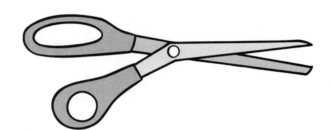

_____ inches

_____ inches

# Measurement

**Directions:** Measure objects around your house. Write the measurement to the nearest inch.

can of soup          _____ inches

pen                  _____ inches

toothbrush           _____ inches

paper clip           _____ inches

small toy            _____ inches

cut out

8
7
6
5
4
3
2
1

Page left blank for cutting exercise on reverse.

# Measurement: Inches

An inch is a unit of length in the standard measurement system.

**Directions:** Use a ruler to measure each object to the nearest inch.

1 inch

about ___1___ inches

about _____ inches

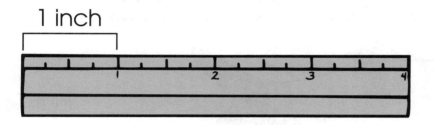

about _____ inches

about _____ inches

about _____ inches

about _____ inches

about _____ inches

# Measurement: Inches

**Directions:** Use the ruler to measure the fish to the nearest inch.

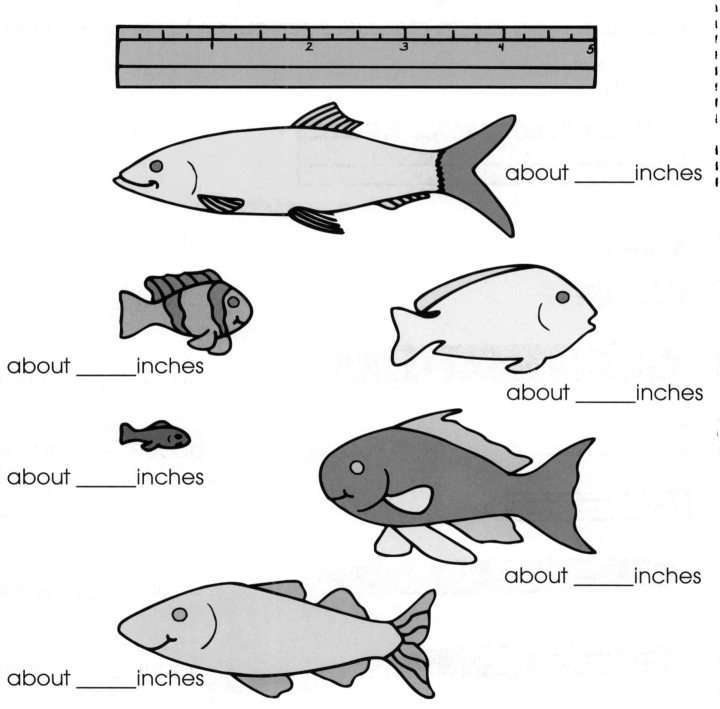

about _____ inches

about _____ inches

about _____ inches

about _____ inches

about _____ inches

about _____ inches

# Measurement: Centimeters

A centimeter is a unit of length in the metric system. There are 2.54 centimeters in an inch.

**Directions:** Use a centimeter ruler to measure the crayons to the nearest centimeter.

**Example:** The first crayon is about 7 centimeters long.

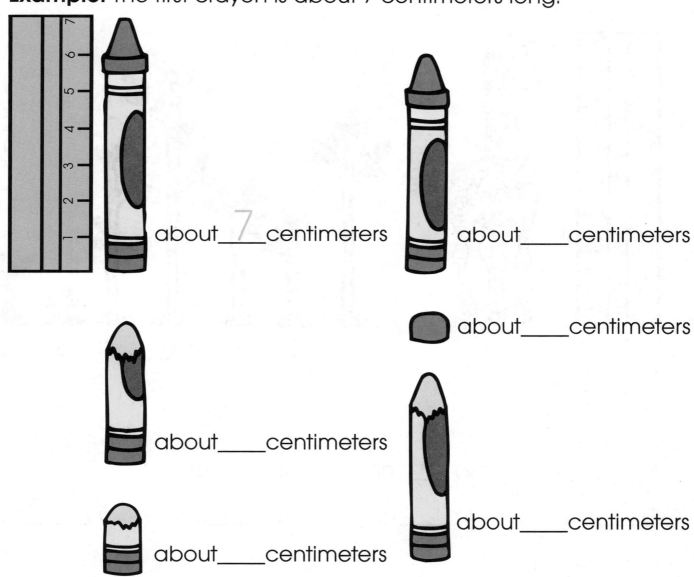

about __7__ centimeters

about ____ centimeters

about ____ centimeters

about ____ centimeters

about ____ centimeters

about ____ centimeters

# Measurement: Centimeters

**Directions:** The giraffe is about 8 centimeters high. How many centimeters (cm) high are the trees? Write your answers in the blanks.

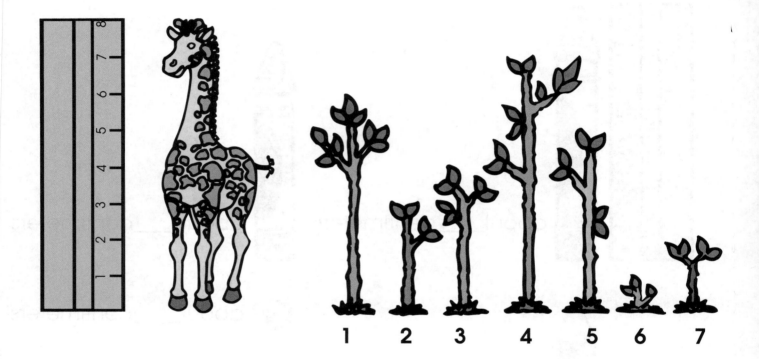

1)_____cm          2)_____cm          3)_____cm

4)_____cm          5)_____cm          6)_____cm          7)_____cm

# Time: Hour, Half-Hour

An hour is sixty minutes. The short hand of a clock tells the hour. It is written **0:00**, such as **5:00**. A half-hour is thirty minutes. When the long hand of the clock is pointing to the six, the time is on the half-hour. It is written **:30**, such as **5:30**.

**Directions:** Study the examples.
Tell what time it is on each clock.

**Examples:**

  **9:00**

The minute hand is on the 12.
The hour hand is on the 9.
It is 9 o'clock.

  **4:30**

The minute hand is on the 6.
The hour hand is *between* the 4 and 5.
It is 4:30.

_____  _____  _____  _____  _____

_____  _____  _____  _____  _____

# Time: Hour, Half-Hour

**Directions:** Draw lines between the clocks that show the same time.

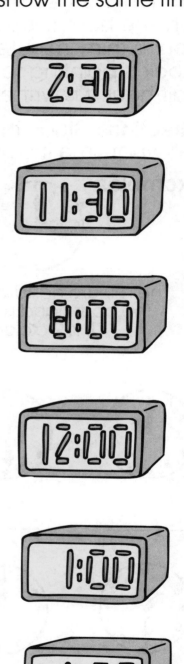

# Time: Counting by 5's

The minute hand of a clock takes 5 minutes to move from one number to the next. Start at the 12 and count by fives to tell how many minutes it is past the hour.

**Directions:** Study the examples. Tell what time is on each clock.

**Examples:**

  9:10 _____     8:25 _____

_____   _____   _____

_____   _____   _____

_____   _____   _____

# Time: Quarter-Hours

Time can also be shown as fractions. 30 minutes = $\frac{1}{2}$ hour.

**Directions:** Shade the fraction of each clock and tell how many minutes you have shaded.

**Example:**

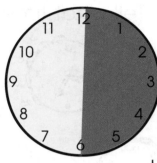

$\frac{1}{2}$ hour

<u>30</u> minutes

$\frac{1}{4}$ hour

____ minutes

$\frac{2}{4}$ hour

____ minutes

$\frac{3}{4}$ hour

____ minutes

$\frac{1}{2}$ hour

____ minutes

# Money: Penny, Nickel

Penny **1¢**        Nickel **5¢**

**Directions:** Count the coins and write the amount.

**Example:**

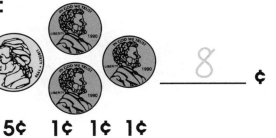

_____ ¢

**5¢   1¢   1¢   1¢**

_____ ¢

_____ ¢

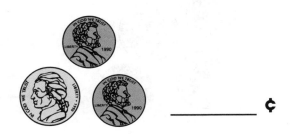

_____ ¢

_____ ¢

# Money: Penny, Nickel, Dime

 Penny **1¢**     Nickel **5¢**     Dime **10¢**

**Directions:** Count the coins and write the amount.

     __16__ ¢

     _____ ¢

     _____ ¢

     _____ ¢

     _____ ¢

# Money: Penny, Nickel, Dime

**Directions:** Draw a line from the toy to the amount of money it costs.

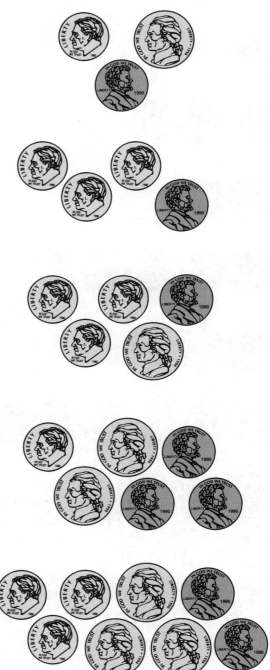

# Money: Penny, Nickel, Dime

**Directions:** Draw a line to match the amounts of money.

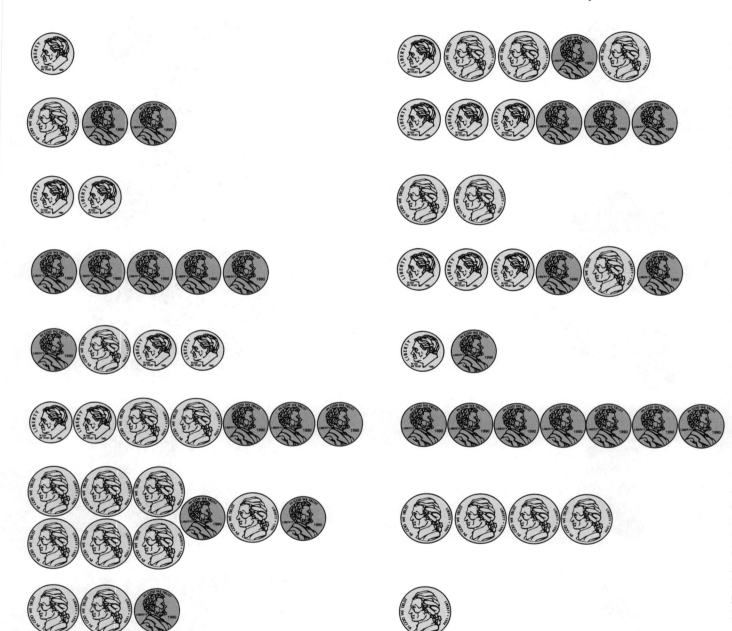

# Money: Quarter

A quarter is worth 25¢.

**Directions:** Count the coins and write the amounts.

 _____ ¢

 _____ ¢

 _____ ¢

 _____ ¢

 _____ ¢

 _____ ¢

  _____ ¢

 _____ ¢

**Math**

# Money: Decimal

A decimal is a number with one or more places to the right of a decimal point, such as 6.5 or 2.25. Money amounts are written with two places to the right of the decimal point.

| 25¢ | 10¢ | 5¢ | 1¢ |
| $.25 | $.10 | $.05 | $.01 |

**Directions:** Count the coins and circle the amount shown.

**Example:**

(\$.17)    23¢    \$.07          \$.50    51¢    61¢

\$.28    36¢    42¢          37¢    43¢    \$.47

# Money: Decimal

**Directions:** Draw a line from the coins to the correct amount in each column.

3¢                                                                $.55

55¢                                                               $.41

31¢                                                               $.37

37¢                                                               $.31

41¢                                                               $.03

# Money: Dollar

One dollar equals 100 cents. It is written $1.00.

**Directions:** Count the money and write the amounts.

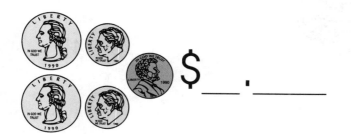 $____.____

 $____.____

 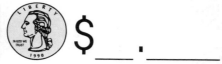 $____.____

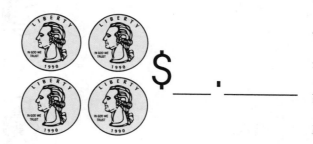 $____.____

 $____.____

 $____.____

 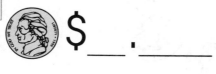 $____.____

 $____.____

# Adding Money

**Directions:** Write the amount of money using decimals. Then add to find the total amount.

**Example:**

$$\begin{array}{r} \$1.00 \\ .05 \\ +\ .02 \\ \hline \$1.07 \end{array}$$

$$\begin{array}{r} \$\underline{\ \ }.\underline{\ \ } \\ \$\underline{\ \ }.\underline{\ \ } \\ \$\underline{\ \ }.\underline{\ \ } \\ +\$\underline{\ \ }.\underline{\ \ } \\ \hline \underline{\ \ }.\underline{\ \ } \end{array}$$

$$\begin{array}{r} \$\underline{\ \ }.\underline{\ \ } \\ \$\underline{\ \ }.\underline{\ \ } \\ \$\underline{\ \ }.\underline{\ \ } \\ +\$\underline{\ \ }.\underline{\ \ } \\ \hline \underline{\ \ }.\underline{\ \ } \end{array}$$

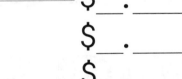 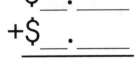  

$$\begin{array}{r} \$\underline{\ \ }.\underline{\ \ } \\ \$\underline{\ \ }.\underline{\ \ } \\ +\$\underline{\ \ }.\underline{\ \ } \\ \hline \underline{\ \ }.\underline{\ \ } \end{array}$$

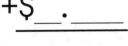

$$\begin{array}{r} \$\underline{\ \ }.\underline{\ \ } \\ \$\underline{\ \ }.\underline{\ \ } \\ \$\underline{\ \ }.\underline{\ \ } \\ +\$\underline{\ \ }.\underline{\ \ } \\ \hline \underline{\ \ }.\underline{\ \ } \end{array}$$

 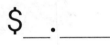 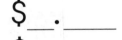   

# Money: Practice

**Directions:** Draw a line from each food item to the correct amount of money.

$1.59

$.89

$1.27

$1.09

$.77

$1.95

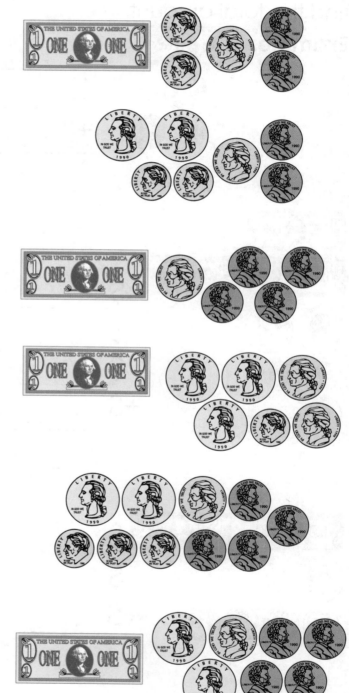

# Problem-Solving

**Directions:** Tell whether you should add or subtract. "In all" is a clue to add. "Left" is a clue to subtract. Draw pictures to help you.

**Example:**
Jane's dog has 5 bones. He ate 3 bones. How many bones are left?

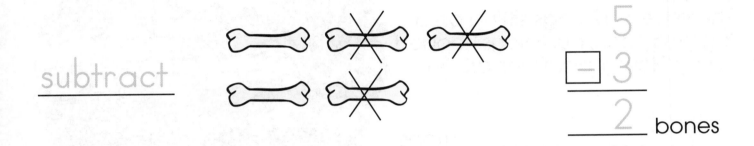

subtract

$$\begin{array}{r} 5 \\ \boxed{-}\ 3 \\ \hline 2 \end{array}$$ bones

Lucky the cat had 5 mice. She got 4 more for her birthday. How many mice did she have in all?

_____

☐☐

_____ mice

Sam bought 6 fish. She gave 2 fish to a friend. How many fish does she have left?

_____

☐☐

_____ fish

# Problem-Solving: Addition, Subtraction, Multiplication

**Directions:** Tell if you add, subtract or multiply. Then write the answer.

**Example:**
There were 12 frogs sitting on a log by a pond, but 3 frogs hopped away. How many frogs are left?

Subtract _____ 9 ___ frogs

There are 9 flowers growing by the pond.
Each flower has 2 leaves.
How many leaves are there?

_____ _____ leaves

A tree had 7 squirrels playing in it.
Then 8 more came along.
How many squirrels are there in all?

_____ _____ squirrels

There were 27 birds living in the trees around the pond, but 9 flew away.
How many birds are left?

_____ _____ birds

# Problem-Solving: Time

**Directions:** Solve each problem.

Tracy wakes up at 7:00. She has 30 minutes before her bus comes. What time does her bus come?

____ : _____

Vera walks her dog for 15 minutes after supper. She finishes supper at 6:30. When does she get home from walking her dog?

____ : _____

Chip practices the piano for 30 minutes when he gets home from school. He gets home at 3:30. When does he stop practicing?

____ : _____

Tanya starts mowing the grass at 4:30. She finishes at 5:00. For how many minutes does she mow the lawn?

_____ minutes

Don does his homework for 45 minutes. He starts his work at 7:15. When does he stop working?

____ : _____

# Problem-Solving: Money

**Directions:** Read each problem. Use the pictures to help you solve the problems.

Ben bought a ball. He had 11¢ left.
How much money did he have at the start?

_____ ¢

Tara has 75¢. She buys a car.
How much money does she have left?

_____ ¢

Leah wants to buy a doll and a ball. She has 80¢.
How much more money does she need?

_____ ¢

Jacob has 95¢. He buys the car and the ball.
How much more money does he need to
buy a doll for his sister?

_____ ¢

Kim paid three quarters, one dime
and three pennies for a hat.
How much did it cost?

_____ ¢

# Answer Key

## Page 6

### All About Me!

**Directions:** Fill in the blanks to tell all about you!

Name **Answers will vary.**
(First)          (Last)

Address _____

City _____ State _____

Phone number _____

Age _____

Places I have visited: **Answers will vary.**
_____
_____

My favorite vacation: **Answers will vary.**
_____
_____

## Page 7

### Review: Beginning Consonants: b, c, d, f, g, h, j

**Directions:** Fill in the beginning consonant for each word.

Example: __c__ at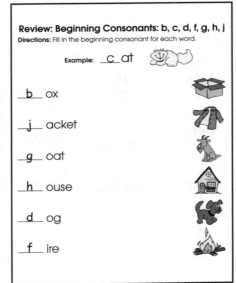

__b__ ox

__j__ acket

__g__ oat

__h__ ouse

__d__ og

__f__ ire

## Page 8

### Beginning Consonants: k, l, m, n, p, q, r

**Directions:** Write the letter that makes the beginning sound for each picture.

__m__   __q__   __r__   __n__

__m__   __l__   __k__   __r__

__q__   __l__   __n__   __m__

__l__   __k__   __r__   __p__

## Page 9

### Beginning Consonants: s, t, v, w, x, y, z

**Directions:** Write the letter under each picture that makes the beginning sound.

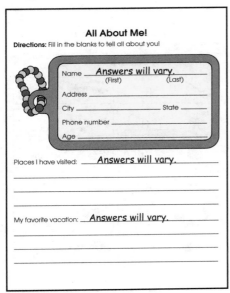

__s__   __z__

__x__

__v__

__y__

__w__   __t__

## Page 10

### Ending Consonants: b, d, f, g

**Directions:** Fill in the ending consonants for each word.

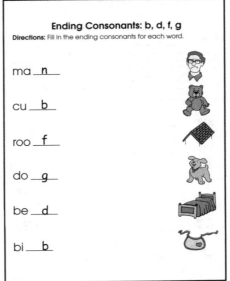

ma __n__

cu __b__

roo __f__

do __g__

be __d__

bi __b__

## Page 11

### Ending Consonants: k, l, m, n, p, r

**Directions:** Fill in the ending consonant for each word.

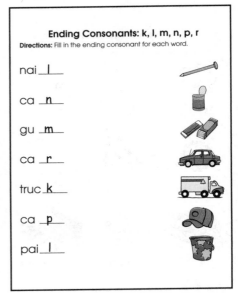

nai __l__

ca __n__

gu __m__

ca __r__

truc __k__

ca __p__

pai __l__

# Answer Key

## Page 12

**Ending Consonants: s, t, x**

**Directions:** Fill in the ending consonant for each word.

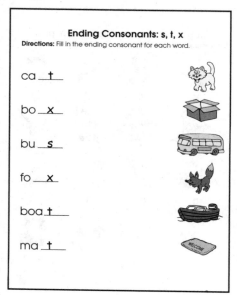

ca __t__

bo __x__

bu __s__

fo __x__

boa __t__

ma __t__

## Page 13

**Consonant Blends**

**Consonant blends** are two or three consonant letters in a word whose sounds combine, or blend. **Examples:** br. fr. gr. pr. tr

**Directions:** Look at each picture. Say its name. Write the blend you hear at the beginning of each word.

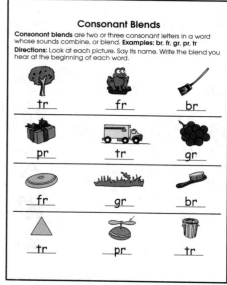

| tr | fr | br |
| pr | tr | gr |
| fr | gr | br |
| tr | pr | tr |

## Page 14

**Blends: fl, br, pl, sk, sn**

**Blends** are two consonants put together to form a single sound.

**Directions:** Look at the pictures and say their names. Write the letters for the beginning sound in each word.

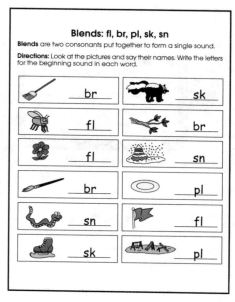

| __br__ | __sk__ |
| __fl__ | __br__ |
| __fl__ | __sn__ |
| __br__ | __pl__ |
| __sn__ | __fl__ |
| __sk__ | __pl__ |

## Page 15

**Blends: bl, sl, cr, cl**

**Directions:** Look at the pictures and say their names. Write the letters for the beginning sound in each word.

__cl__ own    __bl__ anket    __cr__ ayon

__cl__ ock    __sl__ ide    __cl__ oud

__sl__ ed    __cr__ ab    __cr__ ocodile

## Page 16

**Consonant Teams**

**Consonant teams** are two or three consonant letters that have a single sound. **Examples:** sh and tch

**Directions:** Write each word from the word box next to its picture. Underline the consonant team in each word. Circle the consonant team in each word in the box.

| ben(ch) | mat(ch) | sh(oe) | th(imble) |
| sh(ell) | (b)ush | (p)each | wat(ch) |
| (wh)ale | teeth | (ch)air | (wh)eel |

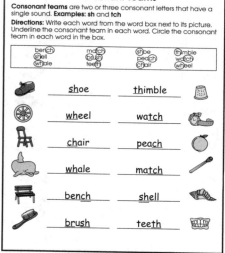

| shoe | thimble |
| wheel | watch |
| chair | peach |
| whale | match |
| bench | shell |
| brush | teeth |

## Page 17

**Consonant Teams**

**Directions:** Read the words in the box. Write a word from the word box to finish each sentence. Circle the consonant team in each word. **Hint:** There are three letters in each team!

| splash | screen | spray | street | scream |
| screw | shrub | split | strong | string |

1. Another word for a bush is a ___(shr)ub___.

2. I tied a ___(str)ing___ to my tooth to help pull it out.

3. I have many friends who live on my ___(str)eet___.

4. We always ___(scr)eam___ when we ride the roller coaster.

5. A ___(scr)een___ helps keep bugs out of the house.

6. It is fun to ___(spl)ash___ in the water.

7. My father uses an ax to ___(spl)it___ the firewood.

8. We will need a ___(scr)ew___ to fix the chair.

9. You must be very ___(str)ong___ to lift this heavy box.

10. The firemen ___(spr)ay___ the fire with water.

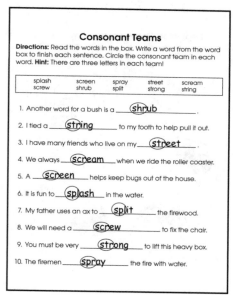

# Answer Key

## Page 18

### Letter Teams: sh, ch, wh, th

**Directions:** Look at the first picture in each row. Circle the pictures that have the same sound.

whistle

shoe

chin

thumb

## Page 19

### Silent Letters

Some words have letters you can't hear at all, such as the **gh** in **night**, the **w** in **wrong**, the **l** in **walk**, the **k** in **knee**, the **b** in **climb** and the **t** in **listen**.

**Directions:** Look at the words in the word box. Write the word under its picture. Underline the silent letters.

| knife | light | calf | wrench | lamb | eight |
| wrist | whistle | comb | thumb | knob | knee |

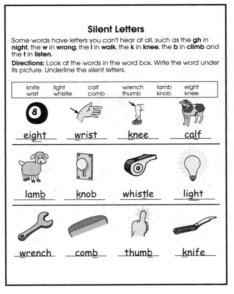

eight     wrist     knee     calf

lamb     knob     whistle     light

wrench     comb     thumb     knife

## Page 20

### Hard and Soft c

When **c** is followed by **e**, **i** or **y**, it usually has a **soft** sound. The **soft c** sounds like **s**. For example, **c**ircle and fen**c**e. When **c** is followed by **a** or **u**, it usually has a **hard** sound. The **hard c** sounds like **k**.

**Example:** **c**up and **c**art

**Directions:** Read the words in the word box. Write the words in the correct lists. Write a word from the word box to finish each sentence.

**Words with soft c**
pencil
dance
cent
mice
circus

**Words with hard c**
circus
popcorn
lucky
tractor
cookie
card

| pencil | cookie |
| dance | cent |
| popcorn | circus |
| lucky | mice |
| tractor | card |

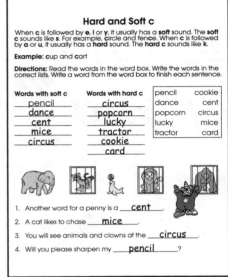

1. Another word for a penny is a __cent__.
2. A cat likes to chase __mice__.
3. You will see animals and clowns at the __circus__.
4. Will you please sharpen my __pencil__?

## Page 21

### Hard and Soft g

When **g** is followed by **e**, **i** or **y**, it usually has a **soft** sound. The **soft g** sounds like **j**. **Example:** chan**g**e and **g**entle. The **hard g** sounds like the **g** in **g**irl or **g**ate.

**Directions:** Read the words in the word box. Write the words in the correct lists. Write a word from the box to finish each sentence.

| engine | glove | cage | magic | frog |
| giant | flag | large | glass | goose |

**Words with soft g**
engine
giant
cage
large
magic

**Words with hard g**
glove
flag
glass
frog
goose

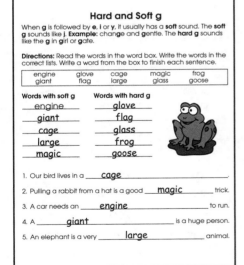

1. Our bird lives in a __cage__.
2. Pulling a rabbit from a hat is a good __magic__ trick.
3. A car needs an __engine__ to run.
4. A __giant__ is a huge person.
5. An elephant is a very __large__ animal.

## Page 22

### Short Vowels

**Vowels** can make **short** or **long** sounds. The short **a** sounds like the **a** in cat. The short **e** is like the **e** in leg. The short **i** sounds like the **i** in pig. The short **o** sounds like the **o** in box. The short **u** sounds like the **u** in cup.

**Directions:** Look at each picture. Write the missing short vowel letter.

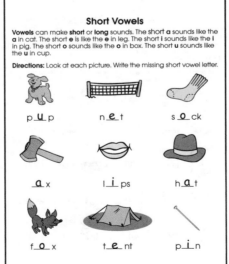

p_u_p     n_e_t     s_o_ck

_a_x     l_i_ps     h_a_t

f_o_x     t_e_nt     p_i_n

## Page 23

### Short Vowels

Vowels can make **short** or **long** sounds. The short **a** sounds like the **a** in cat. The short **e** is like the **e** in leg. The short **i** sounds like the **i** in pig. The short **o** sounds like the **o** in box. The short **u** is like the **u** in cup.

**Directions:** Look at the pictures. Their names all have short vowel sounds. But the vowels are missing! Fill in the missing vowels in each word.

a     e     i     o     u

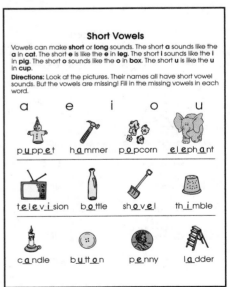

p_u_pp_e_t     h_a_mmer     p_o_pcorn     el_e_ph_a_nt

t_e_l_e_v_i_sion     b_o_ttle     sh_o_v_e_l     th_i_mble

c_a_ndle     b_u_tt_o_n     p_e_nny     l_a_dder

# Answer Key

## Page 24

### Super Silent e

Long vowel sounds have the same sound as their names. When a **Super Silent e** appears at the end of a word, you can't hear it, but it makes the other vowel have a long sound. For example: **tub** has a **short** vowel sound, and **tube** has a **long** vowel sound.

**Directions:** Look at the following pictures. Decide if the word has a short or long vowel sound. Circle the correct word. Watch for the **Super Silent e!**

can (cane)   (tub) tube   rob (robe)   (rat) rate

(pin) pine   (cap) cape   not (note)   (pan) pane

slid (slide)   dim (dime)   tap (tape)   cub (cube)

## Page 25

### Long Vowels

Long vowel sounds have the same sound as their names. When a **Super Silent e** comes at the end of a word, you can't hear it, but it changes the short vowel sound to a long vowel sound.

**Example:** rope, skate, bee, pie, cute

**Directions:** Say the name of the pictures. Listen for the long vowel sounds. Write the missing long vowel sound under each picture.

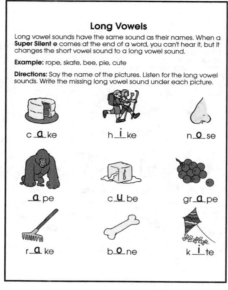

c **a** ke   h **i** ke   n **o** se

**a** pe   c **u** be   gr **a** pe

r **a** ke   b **o** ne   k **i** te

## Page 26

### R-Controlled Vowels

When a vowel is followed by the letter **r**, it has a different sound.

**Example: he** and **her**

**Directions:** Write a word from the word box to finish each sentence. Notice the sound of the vowel followed by an **r**.

| park | chair | horse | bark | bird |
|------|-------|-------|------|------|
| hurt | girl | hair | store | ears |

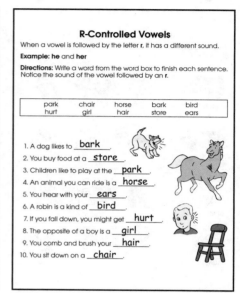

1. A dog likes to __bark__
2. You buy food at a __store__
3. Children like to play at the __park__
4. An animal you can ride is a __horse__
5. You hear with your __ears__
6. A robin is a kind of __bird__
7. If you fall down, you might get __hurt__
8. The opposite of a boy is a __girl__
9. You comb and brush your __hair__
10. You sit down on a __chair__

## Page 27

### R-Controlled Words

**R-Controlled Words** are words in which the **r** that comes after the vowel changes the sound of the vowel. **Examples:** bird, star, burn

**Directions:** Write the correct word in the sentences below.

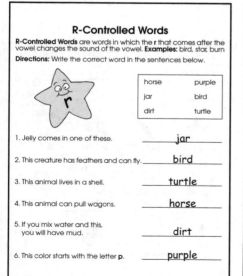

| horse | purple |
|-------|--------|
| jar | bird |
| dirt | turtle |

1. Jelly comes in one of these.   __jar__
2. This creature has feathers and can fly.   __bird__
3. This animal lives in a shell.   __turtle__
4. This animal can pull wagons.   __horse__
5. If you mix water and this, you will have mud.   __dirt__
6. This color starts with the letter **p**.   __purple__

## Page 28

### Double Vowel Words

Usually when two vowels appear together, the first one says its name and the second one is silent.
**Example: bean**

**Directions:** Unscramble the double vowel words below. Write the correct word on the line.

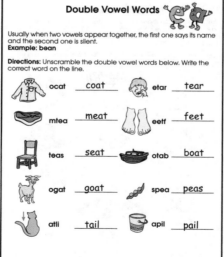

ocat __coat__    etar __tear__

mtea __meat__    eetf __feet__

teas __seat__    otab __boat__

ogat __goat__    spea __peas__

atli __tail__    apil __pail__

## Page 29

### Vowel Teams

The vowel teams **ou** and **ow** can have the same sound. You can hear it in the words **clown** and **cloud**. The vowel teams **au** and **aw** have the same sound. You hear it in the words **because** and **law**.

**Directions:** Look at the pictures. Write the correct vowel team to complete the words. The first one is done for you. You may need to use a dictionary to help you with the correct spelling.

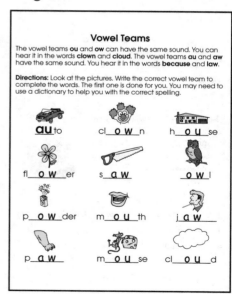

**au** to   cl **o w** n   h **o u** se

fl **o w** er   s **a w**   **o w** l

p **o w** der   m **o u** th   j **a w**

p **a w**   m **o u** se   cl **o u** d

# Answer Key

## Page 30

### Vowel Teams

The vowel team **ea** can have a short **e** sound like in **head**, or a long **e** sound like in **bead**. An **ea** followed by an **r** makes a sound like the one in **ear** or like the one in **heard**.

**Directions:** Read the story. Listen for the sound **ea** makes in the bold words.

Have you ever **read** a book or **heard** a story about a **bear**? You might have **learned** that bears sleep through the winter. Some bears may sleep the whole **season**. Sometimes they look almost **dead**! But they are very much alive. As the cold winter passes and the spring **weather** comes **near**, they wake up. After such a nice rest, they must be **ready** to **eat** a **really** big **meal**!

| words with long ea | words with short ea | ea followed by r |
|---|---|---|
| season | read | heard |
| eat | dead | bear |
| really | weather | learned |
| meal | ready | near |

## Page 31

### Vowel Teams

The vowel team **ie** makes the long **e** sound like in **believe**. The team **ei** also makes the long **e** sound like in **either**. But **ei** can also make a long **a** sound like in **eight**.

**Directions:** Circle the **ei** words with the long **a** sound.

(neighbor)     (veil)
receive        (reindeer)
(reign)        ceiling

The teams **eigh** and **ey** also make the long **a** sound.

**Directions:** Finish the sentences with words from the word box.

| chief | sleigh | obey | weigh | thief | field | ceiling |

1. Eight reindeer pull Santa's ___sleigh___.
2. Rules are for us to ___obey___.
3. The bird got out of its cage and flew up to the ___ceiling___.
4. The leader of an Indian tribe is the ___chief___.
5. How much do you ___weigh___?
6. They caught the ___thief___ who took my bike.
7. Corn grows in a ___field___.

## Page 32

### Letter Teams: oi, oy, ou, ow

**Directions:** Look at the first picture in each row. Circle the pictures that have the same sound.

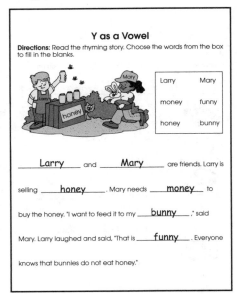

oil

toy

couch

howl

## Page 33

### Letter Teams: ai, ee

**Directions:** Write in the letter team **ai** or **ee** to complete each word.

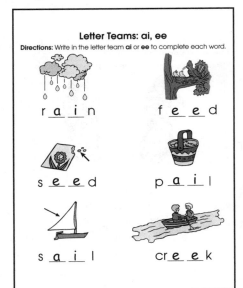

r a i n

f e e d

s e e d

p a i l

s a i l

cr e e k

## Page 34

### Y as a Vowel

When **y** comes at the end of a word, it is a vowel. When **y** is the only vowel at the end of a one-syllable word, it has the sound of a long **i** (like in **my**). When **y** is the only vowel at the end of a word with more than one syllable, it has the sound of a long **e** (like in **baby**).

**Directions:** Look at the words in the word box. If the word has the sound of a long **i**, write it under the word **my**. If the word has the sound of a long **e**, write it under the word **baby**. Write the word from the word box that answers each riddle.

| happy | penny | fry | try | sleepy | dry |
| bunny | why | windy | sky | party | fly |

| my | baby |
|---|---|
| why | happy |
| fry | bunny |
| try | penny |
| sky | windy |
| dry | sleepy |
| fly | party |

1. It takes five of these to make a nickel. ___penny___
2. This is what you call a baby rabbit. ___bunny___
3. It is often blue and you can see it if you look up. ___sky___
4. You might have one of these on your birthday. ___party___
5. It is the opposite of wet. ___dry___
6. You might use this word to ask a question. ___why___

## Page 35

### Y as a Vowel

**Directions:** Read the rhyming story. Choose the words from the box to fill in the blanks.

| Larry | Mary |
| money | funny |
| honey | bunny |

___Larry___ and ___Mary___ are friends. Larry is selling ___honey___. Mary needs ___money___ to buy the honey. "I want to feed it to my ___bunny___," said Mary. Larry laughed and said, "That is ___funny___. Everyone knows that bunnies do not eat honey."

# Answer Key

## Page 36

### Y as a Vowel

**Directions:** Read the story. Choose the words from the box to fill in the blanks.

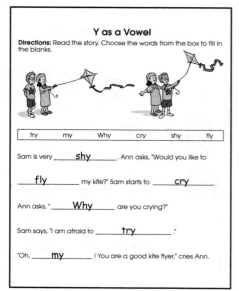

| try | my | Why | cry | shy | fly |
|-----|-----|-----|-----|-----|-----|

Sam is very **shy**. Ann asks, "Would you like to

**fly** my kite?" Sam starts to **cry**.

Ann asks, "**Why** are you crying?"

Sam says, "I am afraid to **try**."

"Oh, **my** ! You are a good kite flyer," cries Ann.

## Page 37

### Days of the Week

**Directions:** Write the day of the week that answers each question.

| Sunday | Monday | Tuesday |
|--------|--------|---------|
| Wednesday | Thursday | Friday |
| | Saturday | |

1. What is the first day of the week?
   **Sunday**

2. What is the last day of the week?
   **Saturday**

3. What day comes after Tuesday?
   **Wednesday**

4. What day comes between Wednesday and Friday?
   **Thursday**

5. What is the third day of the week?
   **Tuesday**

6. What day comes before Saturday?
   **Friday**

7. What day comes after Sunday?
   **Monday**

## Page 38

### Compound Words

**Compound words** are formed by putting together two smaller words.

**Directions:** Help the cook brew her stew. Mix words from the first column with words from the second column to make new words. Write your new words on the lines at the bottom.

| grand | brows |
|-------|-------|
| snow | light |
| eye | stairs |
| down | string |
| rose | book |
| shoe | mother |
| note | ball |
| moon | bud |

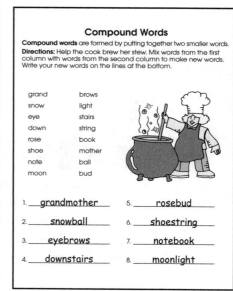

1. **grandmother**
2. **snowball**
3. **eyebrows**
4. **downstairs**
5. **rosebud**
6. **shoestring**
7. **notebook**
8. **moonlight**

## Page 39

### Compound Words

**Compound words** are two words that are put together to make one new word.

**Directions:** Read the sentences. Fill in the blank with a compound word from the box.

| raincoat | bedroom | lunchbox | hallway | sandbox |
|----------|---------|----------|---------|---------|

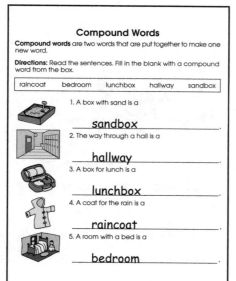

1. A box with sand is a
   **sandbox**

2. The way through a hall is a
   **hallway**

3. A box for lunch is a
   **lunchbox**

4. A coat for the rain is a
   **raincoat**

5. A room with a bed is a
   **bedroom**

## Page 40

### Compound Words

**Directions:** Draw a line under the compound word in each sentence. On the line, write the two words that make up the compound word.

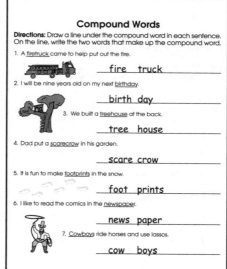

1. A firetruck came to help put out the fire.
   **fire   truck**

2. I will be nine years old on my next birthday.
   **birth   day**

3. We built a treehouse at the back.
   **tree   house**

4. Dad put a scarecrow in his garden.
   **scare   crow**

5. It is fun to make footprints in the snow.
   **foot   prints**

6. I like to read the comics in the newspaper.
   **news   paper**

7. Cowboys ride horses and use lassos.
   **cow   boys**

## Page 41

### Contractions

**Contractions** are a short way to write two words, such as **isn't**, **I've** and **weren't**. Example: **it is = it's**

**Directions:** Draw a line from each word pair to its contraction.

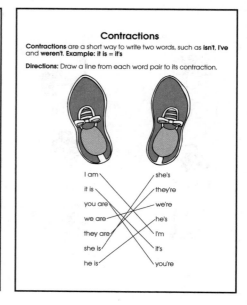

| I am | she's |
|------|-------|
| it is | they're |
| you are | we're |
| we are | he's |
| they are | I'm |
| she is | it's |
| he is | you're |

# Answer Key

## Page 42

### Contractions

**Directions:** Circle the contraction that would replace the underlined words.

**Example: were not = weren't**

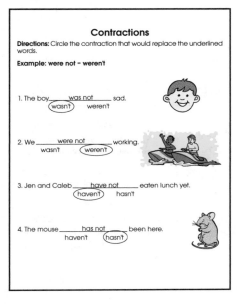

1. The boy _____ was not _____ sad.
   **(wasn't)**   weren't

2. We _____ were not _____ working.
   wasn't   **(weren't)**

3. Jen and Caleb _____ have not _____ eaten lunch yet.
   **(haven't)**   hasn't

4. The mouse _____ has not _____ been here.
   haven't   **(hasn't)**

## Page 43

### Contractions

**Directions:** Match the words with their contractions.

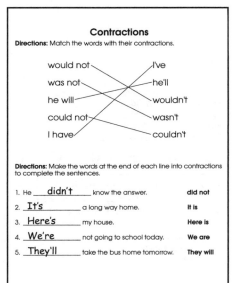

would not ——— wouldn't
was not ——— wasn't
he will ——— he'll
could not ——— couldn't
I have ——— I've

**Directions:** Make the words at the end of each line into contractions to complete the sentences.

1. He **didn't** know the answer.   **did not**
2. **It's** a long way home.   **It is**
3. **Here's** my house.   **Here is**
4. **We're** not going to school today.   **We are**
5. **They'll** take the bus home tomorrow.   **They will**

## Page 44

### Syllables

Words are made up of parts called **syllables**. Each syllable has a vowel sound. One way to count syllables is to clap as you say the word.

**Example:**
| | | |
|---|---|---|
| cat | 1 clap | 1 syllable |
| table | 2 claps | 2 syllables |
| butterfly | 3 claps | 3 syllables |

**Directions:** "Clap out" the words below. Write how many syllables each word has.

| | | | |
|---|---|---|---|
| movie | 2 | dog | 1 |
| piano | 3 | basket | 2 |
| tree | 1 | swimmer | 2 |
| bicycle | 3 | rainbow | 2 |
| sun | 1 | paper | 2 |
| cabinet | 3 | picture | 2 |
| football | 2 | run | 1 |
| television | 4 | enter | 2 |

## Page 45

### Syllables

Dividing a word into syllables can help you read a new word. You also might divide syllables when you are writing if you run out of space on a line.
Many words contain two consonants that are next to each other. A word can usually be divided between the consonants.

**Directions:** Divide each word into two syllables. The first one is done for you.

| | | |
|---|---|---|
| kitten | kit | ten |
| lumber | lum | ber |
| batter | bat | ter |
| winter | win | ter |
| funny | fun | ny |
| harder | hard | er |
| dirty | dir | ty |
| sister | sis | ter |
| little | lit | tle |
| dinner | din | ner |

## Page 46

### Syllables

One way to help you read a word you don't know is to divide it into parts called **syllables**. Every syllable has a vowel sound.

**Directions:** Say the words. Write the number of syllables. The first one is done for you.

straw • ber • ry

| | | | |
|---|---|---|---|
| bird | 1 | rabbit | 2 |
| apple | 2 | elephant | 3 |
| balloon | 2 | family | 3 |
| basketball | 3 | fence | 1 |
| breakfast | 2 | ladder | 2 |
| block | 1 | open | 2 |
| candy | 2 | puddle | 2 |
| popcorn | 2 | Saturday | 3 |
| yellow | 2 | wind | 1 |
| understand | 3 | butterfly | 3 |

## Page 47

### Syllables

When a double consonant is used in the middle of a word, the word can usually be divided between the consonants.

**Directions:** Look at the words in the word box. Divide each word into two syllables. Leave space between each syllable. One is done for you.

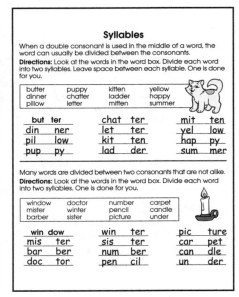

| | | | |
|---|---|---|---|
| butter | puppy | kitten | yellow |
| dinner | chatter | ladder | happy |
| pillow | letter | mitten | summer |

| | | |
|---|---|---|
| but ter | chat ter | mit ten |
| din ner | let ter | yel low |
| pil low | kit ten | hap py |
| pup py | lad der | sum mer |

Many words are divided between two consonants that are not alike.

**Directions:** Look at the words in the word box. Divide each word into two syllables. One is done for you.

| | | | |
|---|---|---|---|
| window | doctor | number | carpet |
| mister | winter | pencil | candle |
| barber | sister | picture | under |

| | | |
|---|---|---|
| win dow | win ter | pic ture |
| mis ter | sis ter | car pet |
| bar ber | num ber | can dle |
| doc tor | pen cil | un der |

# Answer Key

## Page 48

### Syllables

**Directions:** Write 1 or 2 on the line to tell how many syllables are in each word. If the word has 2 syllables, draw a line between the syllables. **Example: sup|per**

| | | | |
|---|---|---|---|
| dog | 1 | tim\|ber | 2 |
| bed\|room | 2 | cat | 1 |
| slip\|per | 2 | street | 1 |
| tree | 1 | chalk | 1 |
| bat\|ter | 2 | blan\|ket | 2 |
| chair | 1 | mark\|er | 2 |
| fish | 1 | brush | 1 |
| mas\|ter | 2 | rab\|bit | 2 |

## Page 49

### Suffixes

A **suffix** is a syllable that is added at the end of a word to change its meaning.

**Directions:** Add the suffixes to the root words to make new words. Use your new words to complete the sentences.

help + ful = __helpful__
care + less = __careless__
build + er = __builder__
talk + ed = __talked__
love + ly = __lovely__
loud + er = __louder__

1. My mother __talked__ to my teacher about my homework.
2. The radio was __louder__ than the television.
3. Sally is always __helpful__ to her mother.
4. A __builder__ put a new garage on our house.
5. The flowers are __lovely__ .
6. It is __careless__ to cross the street without looking both ways.

## Page 50

### Suffixes

Adding **ing** to a word means that it is happening now. Adding **ed** to a word means it happened in the past.

**Directions:** Look at the words in the word box. Underline the root word in each one. Write a word to complete each sentence.

| | | | | |
|---|---|---|---|---|
| snowing | wished | played | looking | crying |
| talking | walked | eating | going | doing |

1. We like to play. We __played__ yesterday.
2. Is that snow? Yes, it is __snowing__ .
3. Do you want to go with me? No, I am __going__ with my friend.
4. The baby will cry if we leave. The baby is __crying__ .
5. We will walk home from school. We __walked__ to school this morning.
6. Did you wish for a new bike? Yes, I __wished__ for one.
7. Who is going to do it while we are away? I am __doing__ it.
8. Did you talk to your friend? Yes, we are __talking__ now.
9. Will you look at my book? I am __looking__ at it now.
10. I like to eat pizza. We are __eating__ it today.

## Page 51

### Suffixes

**Directions:** Write a word from the word box next to its root word.

| | | |
|---|---|---|
| coming | running | sitting |
| lived | rained | swimming |
| visited | carried | racing |
| hurried | | |

| | | | | |
|---|---|---|---|---|
| run | __running__ | come | __coming__ |
| live | __lived__ | carry | __carried__ |
| hurry | __hurried__ | race | __racing__ |
| swim | __swimming__ | rain | __rained__ |
| visit | __visited__ | sit | __sitting__ |

**Directions:** Write a word from the word box to finish each sentence.

1. I __visited__ my grandmother during vacation.
2. Mary went __swimming__ at the lake with her cousin.
3. Jim __carried__ the heavy package for his mother.
4. It __rained__ and stormed all weekend.
5. Cars go very fast when they are __racing__ .

## Page 52

### Suffixes

**Directions:** Read the story. Underline the words that end with **est**, **ed** or **ing**. On the lines below, write the root words for each word you underlined.

The funniest book I ever read was about a girl named Nan. Nan did everything backward. She even spelled her name backward. Nan slept in the day and played at night. She dried her hair before washing it. She turned on the light after she finished her book—which she read from the back to the front! When it rained, Nan waited until she was inside before opening her umbrella. She even walked backward. The silliest part: The only thing Nan did forward was back up!

1. __funny__
2. __name__
3. __spell__
4. __play__
5. __dry__
6. __wash__
7. __turn__
8. __finish__
9. __rain__
10. __wait__
11. __open__
12. __walk__
13. __silly__

## Page 53

### Prefixes: The Three R's

**Prefixes** are syllables added to the beginning of words that change their meaning. The prefix **re** means "again."

**Directions:** Read the story. Then follow the instructions.

Kim wants to find ways she can save the Earth. She studies the "three R's"—reduce, reuse and recycle. Reduce means to make less. Both reuse and recycle mean to use again.

Add **re** to the beginning of each word below. Use the new words to complete the sentences.

__re__ build      __re__ fill
__re__ read      __re__ tell
__re__ write      __re__ run

1. The race was a tie, so Dawn and Kathy had to __rerun__ it.
2. The block wall fell down, so Simon had to __rebuild__ it.
3. The water bottle was empty, so Luna had to __refill__ it.
4. Javier wrote a good story, but he wanted to __rewrite__ it to make it better.
5. The teacher told a story, and students had to __retell__ it.
6. Toni didn't understand the directions, so she had to __reread__ them.

# Answer Key

## Page 54

### Prefixes

**Directions:** Read the story. Change Unlucky Sam to Lucky Sam by taking the **un** prefix off of the **bold** words.

#### Unlucky Sam

Sam was **unhappy** about a lot of things in his life. His parents were **uncaring**. His teacher was **unfair**. His big sister was **unkind**. His neighbors were **unfriendly**. He was **unhealthy**, too! How could one boy be as **unlucky** as Sam?

#### Lucky Sam

Sam was ___happy___ about a lot of things in his life. His parents were ___caring___ . His teacher was ___fair___ . His big sister was ___kind___ . His neighbors were ___friendly___ . He was ___healthy___ , too! How could one boy be as ___lucky___ as Sam?

## Page 55

### Prefixes

**Directions:** Change the meaning of the sentences by adding the prefixes to the **bold** words.

The boy was **lucky** because he guessed the answer **correctly**.

The boy was (un) ___unlucky___ because he guessed the answer (in) ___incorrectly___ .

When Mary **behaved**, she felt **happy**.

When Mary (mis) ___misbehaved___ , she felt (un) ___unhappy___ .

Mike wore his jacket **buttoned** because the dance was **formal**.

Mike wore his jacket (un) ___unbuttoned___ because the dance was (in) ___informal___ .

Tim **understood** because he was **familiar** with the book.

Tim (mis) ___misunderstood___ because he was (un) ___unfamiliar___ with the book.

## Page 57

### Parts of a Book

A book has many parts. The title is the name of the book. The author is the person who wrote the words. The illustrator is the person who drew the pictures. The table of contents is located at the beginning to list what is in the book. The glossary is a little dictionary in the back to help you with unfamiliar words. Books are often divided into smaller sections of information called chapters.

**Directions:** Look at one of your books. Write the parts you see below.

### Answers will vary.

The title of my book is _____

The author is _____

The illustrator is _____

My book has a table of contents.          Yes or No

My book has a glossary.          Yes or No

My book is divided into chapters.          Yes or No

## Page 58

### Recalling Details: Nikki's Pets

**Directions:** Read about Nikki's pets. Then answer the questions.

Nikki has two cats, Tiger and Sniffer, and two dogs, Spot and Wiggles. Tiger is an orange striped cat who likes to sleep under a big tree and pretend she is a real tiger. Sniffer is a gray cat who likes to sniff the flowers in Nikki's garden. Spot is a Dalmatian with many black spots. Wiggles is a big furry brown dog who wiggles all over when he is happy.

1. Which dog is brown and furry? ___Wiggles___
2. What color is Tiger? ___orange with stripes___
3. What kind of dog is Spot? ___Dalmatian___
4. Which cat likes to sniff flowers? ___Sniffer___
5. Where does Tiger like to sleep? ___under a big tree___
6. Who wiggles all over when he is happy? ___Wiggles___

## Page 59

### Reading for Details

**Directions:** Read the story about baby animals. Answer the questions with words from the story.

Baby cats are called kittens. They love to play and drink lots of milk. A baby dog is a puppy. Puppies chew on old shoes. They run and bark. A lamb is a baby sheep. Lambs eat grass. A baby duck is called a duckling. Ducklings swim with their wide, webbed feet. Foals are baby horses. A foal can walk the day it is born! A baby goat is a kid. Some people call children kids, too!

1. A baby cat is called a ___kitten___ .
2. A baby dog is a ___puppy___ .
3. A ___lamb___ is a baby sheep.
4. ___Ducklings___ swim with their webbed feet.
5. A ___foal___ can walk the day it is born.
6. A baby goat is a ___kid___ .

## Page 60

### Reading for Details

**Directions:** Read the story about bike safety. Answer the questions below the story.

Mike has a red bike. He likes his bike. Mike wears a helmet. Mike wears knee pads and elbow pads. They keep him safe. Mike stops at signs. Mike looks both ways. Mike is safe on his bike.

1. What color is Mike's bike? ___red___
2. Which sentence in the story tells why Mike wears pads and a helmet? Write it here.
   ___They keep him safe.___
3. What else does Mike do to keep safe?
   He ___stops___ at signs and ___looks___ both ways.

# Answer Key

## Page 61

### Following Directions: Cows Give Us Milk

**Directions:** Read the story. Answer the questions. Try the recipe.

Cows live on a farm. The farmer milks the cow to get milk. Many things are made from milk. We make ice cream, sour cream, cottage cheese and butter from milk. Butter is fun to make! You can learn to make your own butter. First, you need cream. Put the cream in a jar and shake it. Then you need to pour off the liquid. Next, you put the butter in a bowl. Add a little salt and stir! Finally, spread it on crackers and eat!

1. What animal gives us milk?  __COW__

2. What 4 things are made from milk?
   __ice cream__   __sour cream__   __cottage cheese__   __butter__

3. What did the story teach you to make?  __butter__

4. Put the steps in order. Place 1, 2, 3, 4 by the sentence.

   __4__ Spread the butter on crackers and eat!

   __2__ Shake cream in a jar.

   __1__ Start with cream.

   __3__ Add salt to the butter.

## Page 62

### Following Directions: How to Treat a Ladybug

**Directions:** Read about how to treat ladybugs. Then follow the instructions.

Ladybugs are shy. If you see a ladybug, sit very still. Hold out your arm. Maybe the ladybug will fly to you. If it does, talk softly. Do not touch it. It will fly away when it is ready.

1. Complete the directions on how to treat a ladybug.

   a. Sit very still.

   b. __Hold out your arm.__

   c. Talk softly.

   d. __Do not touch it.__

2. Ladybugs are red. They have black spots. Color the ladybug.

## Page 63

### Sequencing: Packing Bags

**Directions:** Read about packing bags. Then number the objects in the order they should be packed.

Cans are heavy. Put them in first. Then put in boxes. Now, put in the apple. Put the bread in last.

## Page 64

### Sequencing: Yo-Yo Trick

**Directions:** Read about the yo-yo trick.

Wind up the yo-yo string. Hold the yo-yo in your hand. Now, hold your palm up. Throw the yo-yo downward on the string. Hold your palm down. Now, swing the yo-yo forward. Make it "walk." This yo-yo trick is called "walk the dog."

**Directions:** Number the directions in order.

__3__ Swing the yo-yo forward and make it "walk."

__1__ Hold your palm up and drop the yo-yo.

__2__ Turn your palm down as the yo-yo reaches the ground.

## Page 65

### Sequencing: Follow a Recipe

Here is a recipe for chocolate peanut butter cookies. When you use a recipe, you must follow the directions carefully. The sentences below are not in the correct order.

**Directions:** Write number 1 to show what you would do first. Then number each step to show the correct sequence.

__1__ Melt the chocolate almond bark in a microsafe bowl.

__6__ Eat!

__2__ While the chocolate is melting, spread peanut butter on a cracker and place another cracker on top.

__4__ Let the melted candy drip off the cracker into the bowl before you place it on wax paper.

__5__ Let it cool!

__3__ Carefully use a fork or spoon to dip the crackers into the melted chocolate.

Try the recipe with an adult.

Do you like to cook?  __Answers will vary.__

## Page 66

### Sequencing: Story Events

Mari was sick yesterday.

**Directions:** Number the events in 1, 2, 3 order to tell the story about Mari.

__2__ She went to the doctor's office.

__9__ Mari felt much better.

__1__ Mari felt very hot and tired.

__6__ Mari's mother went to the drugstore.

__4__ The doctor wrote down something.

__3__ The doctor looked in Mari's ears.

__7__ Mari took a pill.

__5__ The doctor gave Mari's mother the piece of paper.

__8__ Mari drank some water with her pill.

# Answer Key

## Page 67

### Sequencing: Making Clay

**Directions:** Read about making clay. Then follow the instructions.

It is fun to work with clay. Here is what you need to make it:

1 cup salt
2 cups flour
3/4 cup water

Mix the salt and flour. Then add the water. DO NOT eat the clay. It tastes bad. Use your hands to mix and mix. Now, roll it out. What can you make with your clay?

1. Circle the main idea:

Do not eat clay.

(Mix salt, flour and water to make clay.)

2. Write the steps for making clay.

a. _Mix the salt and flour._

b. _Add the water._

c. Mix the clay.

d. _Roll it out._

3. Write why you should not eat clay. _It tastes bad._

## Page 68

### Sequencing: A Visit to the Zoo

**Directions:** Read the story. Then follow the instructions.

One Saturday morning in May, Gloria and Anna went to the zoo. First, they bought tickets to get into the zoo. Second, they visited the Gorilla Garden and had fun watching the gorillas stare at them. Then they went to Tiger Town and watched the tigers as they slept in the sunshine. Fourth, they went to Hippo Haven and laughed at the hippos cooling off in their pool. Next, they visited Snake Station and learned about poisonous and nonpoisonous snakes. It was noon, and they were hungry, so they ate lunch at the Parrot Patio.

Write **first, second, third, fourth, fifth** and **sixth** to put the events in order.

__Fourth__ They went to Hippo Haven.

__First__ Gloria and Anna bought zoo tickets.

__Third__ They watched the tigers sleep.

__Sixth__ They ate lunch at Parrot Patio.

__Second__ The gorillas stared at them.

__Fifth__ They learned about poisonous and nonpoisonous snakes.

## Page 69

### Same/Different: Stuffed Animals

Kate and Oralia like to collect and trade stuffed animals.

**Directions:** Draw two stuffed animals that are alike and two that are different.

**Alike**

**Different**

Answers will vary.

## Page 70

### Same/Different: Shell Homes

**Directions:** Read about shells. Then answer the questions.

Shells are the homes of some animals. Snails live in shells on the land. Clams live in shells in the water. Clam shells open. Snail shells stay closed. Both shells keep the animals safe.

1. (Circle the correct answer.) Snails live in shells on the

water. (land.)

2. (Circle the correct answer.)
Clam shells are different from snail shells because

(they open.)

they stay closed.

3. Write one way all shells are the same. _They keep animals_ _safe._

## Page 71

### Same/Different: Venn Diagram

A **Venn diagram** is a diagram that shows how two things are the same and different.

**Directions:** Choose two outdoor sports. Then follow the instructions to complete the Venn diagram.

1. Write the first sport name under the first circle. Write some words that describe the sport. Write them in the first circle.

2. Write the second sport name under the second circle. Write some words that describe the sport. Write them in the second circle.

3. Where the 2 circles overlap, write some words that describe both sports.

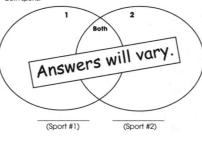

**1**   **2**

**Both**

Answers will vary.

_____ _____
(Sport #1)   (Sport #2)

## Page 72

### Same/Different: Dina and Dina

**Directions:** Read the story. Then complete the Venn diagram, telling how Dina, the duck, is the same or different than Dina, the girl.

One day in the library, Dina found a story about a duck named Dina!

My name is Dina. I am a duck, and I like to swim. When I am not swimming, I walk on land or fly. I have two feet and two eyes. My feathers keep me warm. Ducks can be different colors. I am gray, brown and black. I really like being a duck. It is fun.

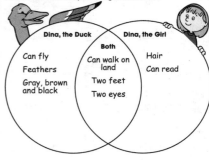

**Dina, the Duck**

Can fly
Feathers
Gray, brown and black

**Both**

Can walk on land
Two feet
Two eyes

**Dina, the Girl**

Hair
Can read

# Answer Key

## Page 73

### Same/Different: Cats and Tigers

**Directions:** Read about cats and tigers. Then complete the Venn diagram, telling how they are the same and different.

Tigers are a kind of cat. Pet cats and tigers both have fur. Pet cats are small and tame. Tigers are large and wild.

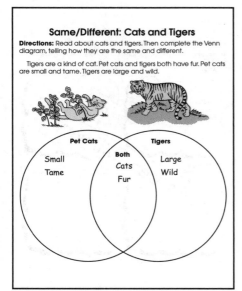

**Pet Cats**
Small
Tame

**Both**
Cats
Fur

**Tigers**
Large
Wild

## Page 74

### Same/Different: Bluebirds and Parrots

**Directions:** Read about parrots and bluebirds. Then complete the Venn diagram, telling how they are the same and different.

Bluebirds and parrots are both birds. Bluebirds and parrots can fly. They both have beaks. Parrots can live inside a cage. Bluebirds must live outdoors.

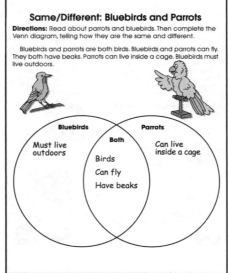

**Bluebirds**
Must live outdoors

**Both**
Birds
Can fly
Have beaks

**Parrots**
Can live inside a cage

## Page 75

### Similes

A **simile** is a figure of speech that compares two different things. The words **like** or **as** are used in similes.

**Directions:** Draw a line to the picture that goes with each set of words.

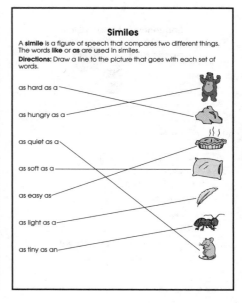

as hard as a

as hungry as a

as quiet as a

as soft as a

as easy as

as light as a

as tiny as an

## Page 76

### Classifying

**Classifying** is putting similar things into groups.

**Directions:** Write each word from the word box on the correct line.

| baby | donkey | whale | family | fox |
| uncle | goose | grandfather | kangaroo | policeman |

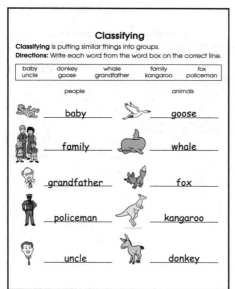

people

baby

family

grandfather

policeman

uncle

animals

goose

whale

fox

kangaroo

donkey

## Page 77

### Classifying: Words

Dapper Dog is going camping.

**Directions:** Draw an **X** on the word in each row that does not belong in that group.

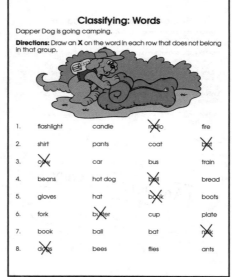

1. flashlight   candle   ~~radio~~   fire
2. shirt   pants   coat   ~~hat~~
3. ~~cow~~   car   bus   train
4. beans   hot dog   ~~ball~~   bread
5. gloves   hat   ~~book~~   boots
6. fork   ~~butter~~   cup   plate
7. book   ball   bat   ~~milk~~
8. ~~dogs~~   bees   flies   ants

## Page 78

### Classifying: Animal Habitats

**Directions:** Read the story. Then write each animal's name under **Water** or **Land** to tell where it lives.

Animals live in different habitats. A habitat is the place of an animal's natural home. Many animals live on land and others live in water. Most animals that live in water breathe with gills. Animals that live on land breathe with lungs.

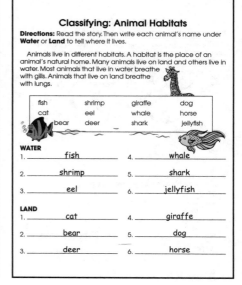

| fish | shrimp | giraffe | dog |
| cat | eel | whale | horse |
| bear | deer | shark | jellyfish |

**WATER**
1. fish
2. shrimp
3. eel
4. whale
5. shark
6. jellyfish

**LAND**
1. cat
2. bear
3. deer
4. giraffe
5. dog
6. horse

# Answer Key

## Page 79

### Comprehension: Types of Tops

The **main idea** is the most important point or idea in a story.

**Directions:** Read about tops. Then answer the questions.

Tops come in all sizes. Some tops are made of wood. Some tops are made of tin. All tops do the same thing. They spin! Do you have a top?

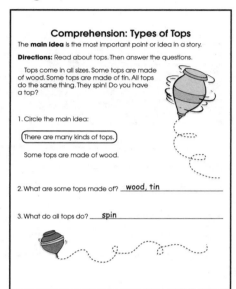

1. Circle the main idea:

   There are many kinds of tops.

   Some tops are made of wood.

2. What are some tops made of? __wood, tin__

3. What do all tops do? __spin__

## Page 80

### Comprehension: Singing Whales

**Directions:** Read about singing whales. Then follow the instructions.

Some whales can sing! We cannot understand the words. But we can hear the tune of the humpback whale. Each season, humpback whales sing a different song.

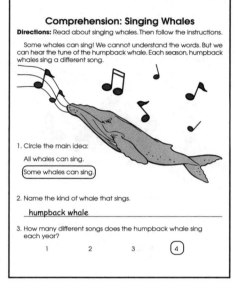

1. Circle the main idea:

   All whales can sing.

   Some whales can sing.

2. Name the kind of whale that sings.

   __humpback whale__

3. How many different songs does the humpback whale sing each year?

   1    2    3    (4)

## Page 81

### Comprehension: Sea Horses Look Strange!

**Directions:** Read about sea horses. Then answer the questions.

Sea horses are fish, not horses. A sea horse's head looks like a horse's head. It has a tail like a monkey's tail. A sea horse looks very strange!

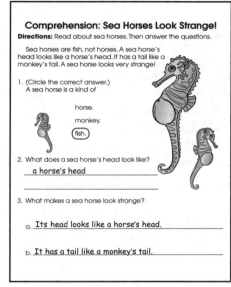

1. (Circle the correct answer.)
   A sea horse is a kind of

   horse.

   monkey.

   (fish.)

2. What does a sea horse's head look like?
   __a horse's head__

3. What makes a sea horse look strange?

   a. __Its head looks like a horse's head.__

   b. __It has a tail like a monkey's tail.__

## Page 82

### Comprehension: How to Stop a Dog Fight

**Directions:** Read about how to stop a dog fight. Then answer the questions.

Sometimes dogs fight. They bark loudly. They may bite. Do not try to pull apart fighting dogs. Turn on a hose and spray them with water. This will stop the fight.

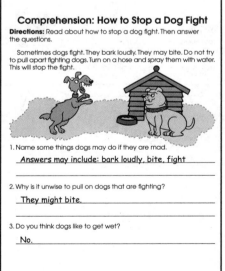

1. Name some things dogs may do if they are mad.
   __Answers may include: bark loudly, bite, fight__

2. Why is it unwise to pull on dogs that are fighting?
   __They might bite.__

3. Do you think dogs like to get wet?
   __No.__

## Page 83

### Comprehension: The Puppet Play

**Directions:** Read the play out loud with a friend. Then answer the questions.

**Pip:** Hey, Pep. What kind of turkey eats very fast?

**Pep:** Uh, I don't know.

**Pip:** A gobbler!

**Pep:** I have a good joke for you, Pip. What kind of burger does a polar bear eat?

**Pip:** Uh, a cold burger?

**Pep:** No, an iceberg-er!

**Pip:** Hey, that was a great joke!

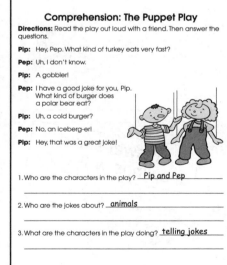

1. Who are the characters in the play? __Pip and Pep__

2. Who are the jokes about? __animals__

3. What are the characters in the play doing? __telling jokes__

## Page 84

### Comprehension: Snakes!

**Directions:** Read about snakes. Then answer the questions.

There are many facts about snakes that might surprise someone. A snake's skin is dry. Most snakes are shy. They will hide from people. Snakes eat mice and rats. They do not chew them up. Snakes' jaws drop open to swallow their food whole.

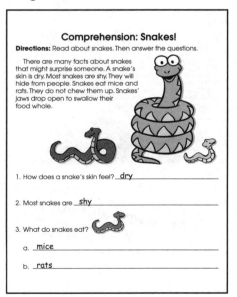

1. How does a snake's skin feel? __dry__

2. Most snakes are __shy__

3. What do snakes eat?

   a. __mice__

   b. __rats__

# Answer Key

## Page 85

### Comprehension: Sean's Basketball Game

**Directions:** Read about Sean's basketball game. Then answer the questions.

Sean really likes to play basketball. One sunny day, he decided to ask his friends to play basketball at the park, but there were six people—Sean, Aki, Lance, Kate, Zac and Oralia. A basketball team only allows five to play at a time. So, Sean decided to be the coach. Sean and his friends had fun.

1. How many kids wanted to play basketball? __six__

2. Write their names in ABC order:

| | | |
|---|---|---|
| Aki | Lance | Sean |
| Kate | Oralia | Zac |

3. How many players can play on a basketball team at a time? __five__

4. Where did they play basketball? __at the park__

5. Who decided to be the coach? __Sean__

## Page 86

### Comprehension: Amazing Ants

**Directions:** Read about ants. Then answer the questions.

Ants are insects. Ants live in many parts of the world and make their homes in soil, sand, wood and leaves. Most ants live for about 6 to 10 weeks. But the queen ant, who lays the eggs, can live for up to 15 years!

The largest ant is the bulldog ant. This ant can grow to be 5 inches long, and it eats meat! The bulldog ant can be found in Australia.

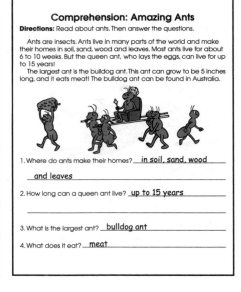

1. Where do ants make their homes? __in soil, sand, wood and leaves__

2. How long can a queen ant live? __up to 15 years__

3. What is the largest ant? __bulldog ant__

4. What does it eat? __meat__

## Page 87

### Predicting: A Rainy Game

**Predicting** is telling what is likely to happen based on the facts.

**Directions:** Read the story. Then check each sentence below that tells how the story could end.

One cloudy day, Juan and his baseball team, the Bears, played the Crocodiles. It was the last half of the fifth inning, and it started to rain. The coaches and umpires had to decide what to do.

- ✓ They kept playing until nine innings were finished.
- ✓ They ran for cover and waited until the rain stopped.
- ___ Each player grabbed an umbrella and returned to the field to finish the game.
- ✓ They canceled the game and played it another day.
- ___ They acted like crocodiles and slid around the wet bases.
- ___ The coaches played the game while the players sat in the dugout.

## Page 88

### Predicting: Dog Derby

**Directions:** Read the story. Then answer the questions.

Marcy had a great idea for a game to play with her dogs, Marvin and Mugsy. The game was called "Dog Derby." Marcy would stand at one end of the driveway and hold on to the dogs by their collars. Her friend Mitch would stand at the other end of the driveway. When he said, "Go!" Marcy would let go of the dogs and they would race to Mitch. The first one there would get a dog biscuit. If there was a tie, both dogs would get a biscuit.

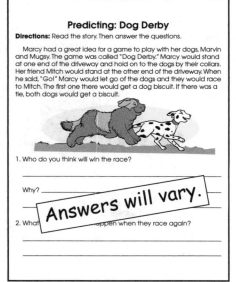

1. Who do you think will win the race?

Why? _Answers will vary._

2. What ___ ppen when they race again?

## Page 89

### Predicting: Dog-Gone!

**Directions:** Read the story. Then follow the instructions.

Scotty and Simone were washing their dog, Willis. His fur was wet. Their hands were wet. Willis did NOT like to be wet. Scotty dropped the soap. Simone picked it up and let go of Willis. Uh-oh!

1. Write what happened next.

_Answers and drawings will vary._

2. Draw ___

## Page 90

### Predicting Outcomes

Kelly and Gina always have fun at the fair

**Directions:** Read the sentences. Write what you think will happen next.

1. Kelly and Gina are riding the Ferris wheel. It stops when they are at the top.

2. As they walk into the animal ___

_Answers will vary._

3. Snow c ___ their favorite way to cool off. The ones they bought are made from real snow.

4. They play a "toss the ring over the bottle" game, but when the ring goes around the bottle, it disappears.

# Answer Key

## Page 91

### Fact and Opinion: Games!

A **fact** is something that can be proven. An **opinion** is a feeling or belief about something and cannot be proven.

**Directions:** Read these sentences about different games. Then write **F** next to each fact and **O** next to each opinion.

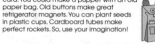

__O__ 1. Tennis is cool!

__F__ 2. There are red and black markers in a Checkers game.

__F__ 3. In football, a touchdown is worth six points.

__O__ 4. Being a goalie in soccer is easy.

__F__ 5. A yo-yo moves on a string.

__O__ 6. June's sister looks like the queen on the card.

__F__ 7. The six kids need three more players for a baseball team.

__O__ 8. Table tennis is more fun than court tennis.

__F__ 9. Hide-and-Seek is a game that can be played outdoors or indoors.

__F__ 10. Play money is used in many board games.

## Page 92

### Fact and Opinion: Recycling

**Directions:** Read about recycling. Then follow the instructions.

What do you throw away every day? What could you do with these things? You could change an old greeting card into a new card. You could make a puppet with an old paper bag. Old buttons make great refrigerator magnets. You can plant seeds in plastic cups. Cardboard tubes make perfect rockets. So, use your imagination!

1. Write **F** next to each fact and **O** next to each opinion.

__O__ Cardboard tubes are ugly.

__F__ Buttons can be made into refrigerator magnets.

__F__ An old greeting card can be changed into a new card.

__O__ Paper-bag puppets are cute.

__F__ Seeds can be planted in plastic cups.

__F__ Rockets can be made from cardboard tubes.

2. What could you do with a cardboard tube? __Make a rocket.__

## Page 93

### Fact and Opinion: An Owl Story

**Directions:** Read the story. Then follow the instructions.

My name is Owen Owl, and I am a bird. I go to Nocturnal School. Our teacher is Mr. Screech Owl. In his class I learned that owls are birds and can sleep all day and hunt at night. Some of us live in nests in trees. In North America, it is against the law to harm owls. I like being an owl!

Write **F** next to each fact and **O** next to each opinion.

__F__ 1. No one can harm owls in North America.

__O__ 2. It would be great if owls could talk.

__F__ 3. Owls sleep all day.

__F__ 4. Some owls sleep in nests.

__O__ 5. Mr. Screech Owl is a good teacher.

__F__ 6. Owls are birds.

__O__ 7. Owen Owl would be a good friend.

__F__ 8. Owls hunt at night.

__O__ 9. Nocturnal School is a good school for smart owls.

__O__ 10. This story is for the birds.

## Page 94

### Making Inferences: Ryan's Top

**Directions:** Read about Ryan's top. Then follow the instructions.

Ryan got a new top. He wanted to place it where it would be safe. He asked his dad to put it up high. Where can his dad put the top?

1. Write where Ryan's dad can put the top. __Answers may include:__

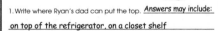
__on top of the refrigerator, on a closet shelf__

Draw a place Ryan's dad can put the top.

Drawings will vary.

## Page 95

### Making Inferences

**Directions:** Read the story. Then answer the questions.

Jeff is baking cookies. He wears special clothes when he bakes. He puts flour, sugar, eggs and butter into a bowl. He mixes everything together. He puts the cookies in the oven at 11:15 A.M. It takes 15 minutes for the cookies to bake. Jeff wants something cold and white to drink when he eats his cookies.

1. Is Jeff baking a cake?   Yes  (No)

2. What are two things Jeff might wear when he bakes?
(hat)   boots   (apron)   tie   raincoat   roller skates

3. What didn't Jeff put in the cookies?
flour   eggs   (milk)   butter   sugar

4. What do you think Jeff does after he mixes the cookies but before he bakes them? __Answers may include: rolling dough into small balls or dropping dough from a teaspoon onto a cookie sheet.__

5. What time will the cookies be done? __11:30 a.m.__

6. What will Jeff drink with his cookies? __milk__

7. Why do you think Jeff wanted to bake cookies? _____
__Answers will vary.__

## Page 96

### Making Inferences

**Directions:** Read the story. Then answer the questions.

Mrs. Sweet looked forward to a visit from her niece, Candy. In the morning, she cleaned her house. She also baked a cherry pie. An hour before Candy was to arrive, the phone rang. Mrs. Sweet said, "I understand." When she hung up the phone, she looked very sad.

Answers may include:

1. Who do you think called Mrs. Sweet?
__Candy called Mrs. Sweet.__

2. How do you know that?
__Mrs. Sweet probably said, "I understand," when Candy said she wouldn't visit today.__

3. Why is Mrs. Sweet sad?
__Her niece, Candy, probably can't come visit today.__

# Answer Key

## Page 97

### Making Inferences: Using Pictures

**Directions:** Draw a picture for each idea. Then write two sentences that tell about it.

You and a friend are playing your favorite game.

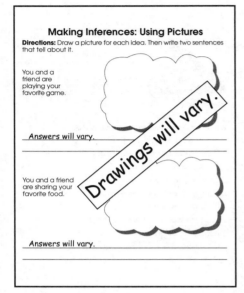

Answers will vary.

You and a friend are sharing your favorite food.

Answers will vary.

## Page 98

### Making Inferences: Visualizing

**Directions:** Read the story about Melinda. Then draw pictures that describe each part of the story.

**Beginning:** It was Halloween. Melinda's costume was a black cat with super-duper, polka-dot sunglasses.

**Middle:** Her little brown dog, Marco, yelped and ran under a big red chair when he saw her come into the room.

**End:** Melinda took off her black cat mask and sunglasses. Then she held out a dog biscuit. She picked Marco up and hugged him. Then he was happy.

## Page 99

### Making Inferences: Point of View

Juniper has three problems to solve. She needs your help.

**Directions:** Read each problem. Write what you think she should do.

1. Juniper is watching her favorite TV show when the power goes out.

2. Juniper is riding her bike to school when she gets a flat.

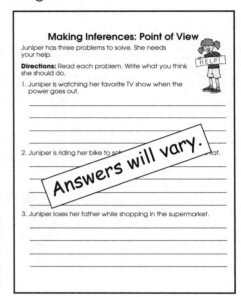

3. Juniper loses her father while shopping in the supermarket.

## Page 100

### Making Inferences: Sequencing

**Directions:** Draw three pictures to tell a story about each topic.

1. Feeding a pet

| Beginning | Middle | End |
|---|---|---|

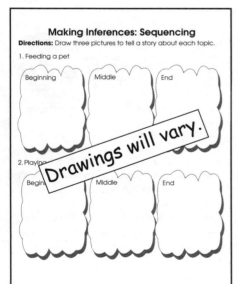

2. Playing

| Beginning | Middle | End |
|---|---|---|

## Page 101

### Making Deductions: Find the Books

**Directions:** Use the clues to help the children find their books. Draw a line from each child's name to the correct book.

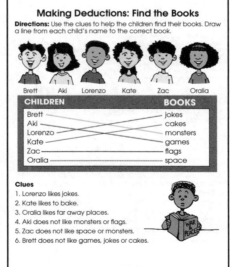

Brett   Aki   Lorenzo   Kate   Zac   Oralia

**CHILDREN** — **BOOKS**

Brett — jokes
Aki — cakes
Lorenzo — monsters
Kate — games
Zac — flags
Oralia — space

**Clues**
1. Lorenzo likes jokes.
2. Kate likes to bake.
3. Oralia likes far away places.
4. Aki does not like monsters or flags.
5. Zac does not like space or monsters.
6. Brett does not like games, jokes or cakes.

## Page 102

### Making Deductions: Sports

Children all over the world like to play sports. They like many different kinds of sports: football, soccer, basketball, softball, in-line skating, swimming and more.

**Directions:** Read the clues. Draw dots and **X**'s on the chart to match the children with their sports.

|  | swimming | football | soccer | basketball | baseball | in-line skating |
|---|---|---|---|---|---|---|
| J.J. | X | ● | X | X | X | X |
| Zoe | X | X | X | X | X | ● |
| Andy | X | X | X | ● | X | X |
| Amber | X | X | ● | X | X | X |
| Raul | X | X | X | X | ● | X |
| Sierra | ● | X | X | X | X | X |

**Clues**
1. Zoe hates football.
2. Andy likes basketball.
3. Raul likes to pitch in his favorite sport.
4. J.J. likes to play what Zoe hates.
5. Amber is good at kicking the ball to her teammates.
6. Sierra needs a pool for her favorite sport.

# Answer Key

## Page 103

### Fiction/Nonfiction: Heavy Hitters

**Fiction** is a make-believe story. **Nonfiction** is a true story.

**Directions:** Read the stories about two famous baseball players. Then write **fiction** or **nonfiction** in the baseball bats.

In 1998, Mark McGwire played for the St. Louis Cardinals. He liked to hit home runs. On September 27, 1998, he hit home run number 70, to set a new record for the most home runs hit in one season. The old record was set in 1961 by Roger Maris, who later played for the St. Louis Cardinals (1967 to 1968), when he hit 61 home runs.

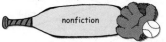

nonfiction

The Mighty Casey played baseball for the Mudville Nine and was the greatest of all baseball players. He could hit the cover off the ball with the power of a hurricane. But, when the Mudville Nine was behind 4 to 2 in the championship game, Mighty Casey struck out with the bases loaded. There was no joy in Mudville that day, because the Mudville Nine had lost the game.

fiction

## Page 104

### Nonfiction: Tornado Tips

**Directions:** Read about tornadoes. Then follow the instructions.

A tornado begins over land with strong winds and thunderstorms. The spinning air becomes a funnel. It can cause damage. If you are inside, go to the lowest floor of the building. A basement is a safe place. A bathroom or closet in the middle of a building can be a safe place, too. If you are outside, lie in a ditch. Remember, tornadoes are dangerous.

**Answers may include:**

Write five facts about tornadoes.

1. A tornado begins over land.

2. Spinning air becomes a funnel.

3. Tornadoes can cause damage.

4. A basement is a safe place to be in a tornado.

5. If you are outside during a tornado, you should lie in a ditch.

## Page 105

### Fiction: Hercules

The setting is where a story takes place. The characters are the people in a story or play.

**Directions:** Read about Hercules. Then answer the questions.

Hercules was born in the warm Atlantic Ocean. He was a very small and weak baby. He wanted to be the strongest hurricane in the world. But he had one problem. He couldn't blow 75-mile-per-hour winds. Hercules blew and blew in the ocean, until one day, his sister, Hola, told him it would be more fun to be a breeze than a hurricane. Hercules agreed. It was a breeze to be a breeze!

1. What is the setting of the story? Atlantic Ocean

2. Who are the characters? Hercules, Hola

3. What is the problem? Hercules couldn't blow 75 mile-per-hour winds.

4. How does Hercules solve his problem? He decides that it is more fun to be a breeze than a hurricane.

## Page 106

### Fiction/Nonfiction: The Fourth of July

**Directions:** Read each story. Then write whether it is fiction or nonfiction.

One sunny day in July, a dog named Stan ran away from home. He went up one street and down the other looking for fun, but all the yards were empty. Where was everybody? Stan kept walking until he heard the sound of band music and happy people. Stan walked faster until he got to Central Street. There he saw men, women, children and dogs getting ready to walk in a parade. It was the Fourth of July!

Fiction or Nonfiction? __Fiction__

Americans celebrate the Fourth of July every year, because it is the birthday of the United States of America. On July 4, 1776, the United States got its independence from Great Britain. Today, Americans celebrate this holiday with parades, picnics and fireworks as they proudly wave the red, white and blue American flag.

Fiction or Nonfiction? __Nonfiction__

## Page 107

### Fiction/Nonfiction: Which Is It?

**Directions:** Read about fiction and nonfiction books. Then follow the instructions.

There are many kinds of books. Some books have make-believe stories about princesses and dragons. Some books contain poetry and rhymes, like Mother Goose. These are fiction.

Some books contain facts about space and plants. And still other books have stories about famous people in history like Abraham Lincoln. These are nonfiction.

Write **F** for fiction and **NF** for nonfiction.

__F__ 1. nursery rhyme

__F__ 2. fairy tale

__NF__ 3. true life story of a famous athlete

__F__ 4. Aesop's fables

__NF__ 5. dictionary entry about foxes

__NF__ 6. weather report

__F__ 7. story about a talking tree

__NF__ 8. story about how a tadpole becomes a frog

__NF__ 9. story about animal habitats

__F__ 10. riddles and jokes

## Page 109

### Synonyms

Words that mean the same or nearly the same are called **synonyms**.

**Directions:** Read the sentence that tells about the picture. Draw a circle around the word that means the same as the **bold** word.

| | |
|---|---|
| The child is **unhappy.** (sad) hungry | The flowers are **lovely.** (pretty) green |
| The baby was very **tired.** (sleepy) hurt | The **funny** clown made us laugh. (silly) glad |
| The ladybug is so **tiny.** (small) red | We saw a **scary** tiger. (frightening) ugly |

# Answer Key

## Page 110

### Synonyms

**Synonyms** are words that have almost the same meaning.

**Directions:** Read the story. Then fill in the blanks with the synonyms.

| funny | unhappy |
|-------|---------|
| windy | little |

**A New Balloon**

It was a breezy day. The wind blew the small child's balloon away. The child was sad. A silly clown gave him a new balloon.

1. It was a **windy** day.

2. The wind blew the **little** child's balloon away.

3. The child was **unhappy**.

4. A **funny** clown gave him a new balloon.

## Page 111

### Synonyms

**Directions:** Read each sentence. Fill in the blanks with the synonyms.

| friend | tired | story |
|--------|-------|-------|
| presents | little | |

I want to go to bed because I am very <u>sleepy</u>. — **tired**

On my birthday I like to open my <u>gifts</u>. — **presents**

My <u>pal</u> and I like to play together. — **friend**

My favorite <u>tale</u> is Cinderella. — **story**

The mouse was so <u>tiny</u> that it was hard to catch him. — **little**

## Page 112

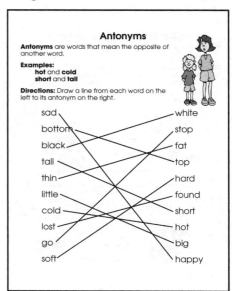

### Antonyms

**Antonyms** are words that mean the opposite of another word.

**Examples:**
**hot** and **cold**
**short** and **tall**

**Directions:** Draw a line from each word on the left to its antonym on the right.

| | |
|------|------|
| sad | white |
| bottom | stop |
| black | fat |
| tall | top |
| thin | hard |
| little | found |
| cold | short |
| lost | hot |
| go | big |
| soft | happy |

## Page 113

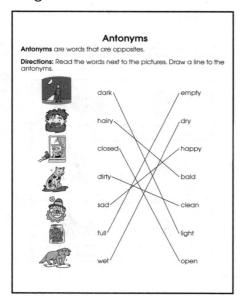

### Antonyms

**Antonyms** are words that are opposites.

**Directions:** Read the words next to the pictures. Draw a line to the antonyms.

| | |
|------|------|
| dark | empty |
| hairy | dry |
| closed | happy |
| dirty | bald |
| sad | clean |
| full | light |
| wet | open |

## Page 114

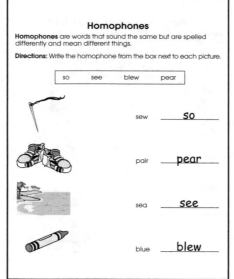

### Homophones

**Homophones** are words that sound the same but are spelled differently and mean different things.

**Directions:** Write the homophone from the box next to each picture.

| so | see | blew | pear |
|----|-----|------|------|

sew — **so**

pair — **pear**

sea — **see**

blue — **blew**

## Page 115

### Homophones

**Directions:** Look at each picture. Circle the correct homophone.

(deer) dear

blue (blew)

(two) to

hi (high)

by (bye)

(new) knew

ate (eight)

(red) read

# Answer Key

## Page 116

### Homophones

**Directions:** Match each word with its homophone.

eight — by
buy — hour
pail — pale
red — read
hole — whole
blue — blew
our — ate

**Directions:** Choose 3 homophone pairs and write sentences using them.

Answers will vary.

1. _____
2. _____
3. _____

## Page 117

### Nouns

A **noun** is the name of a person, place or thing.

**Directions:** Read the story and circle all the nouns. Then write the nouns next to the pictures below.

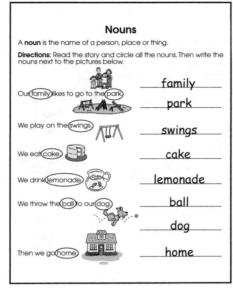

Our (family) likes to go to the (park) — family, park

We play on the (swings) — swings

We eat (cake) — cake

We drink (lemonade) — lemonade

We throw the (ball) to our (dog) — ball, dog

Then we go (home) — home

## Page 118

### Nouns

**Directions:** Look through a magazine. Cut out pictures of nouns and glue them below. Write the name of the noun next to the picture.

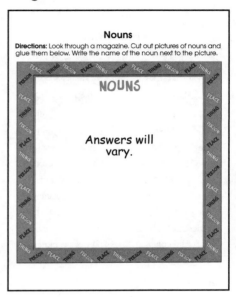

NOUNS

Answers will vary.

## Page 119

### Proper Nouns

**Proper nouns** are the names of specific people, places and pets. Proper nouns begin with a capital letter.

**Directions:** Write the proper nouns on the lines below. Use capital letters at the beginning of each word.

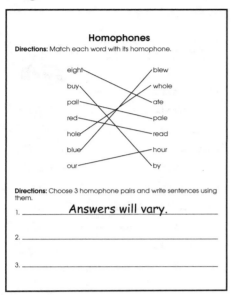

logan, utah — Logan, Utah

mike smith — Mike Smith

lynn cramer — Lynn Cramer

buster — Buster

fluffy — Fluffy

chicago, illinois — Chicago, Illinois

## Page 120

### Proper Nouns

The days of the week and the months of the year are always capitalized.

**Directions:** Circle the words that are written correctly. Write the words that need capital letters on the lines below.

| sunday | (July) | (Wednesday) | may | december |
| friday | tuesday | june | august | (Monday) |
| january | (February) | (March) | (Thursday) | (April) |
| (September) | saturday | (October) | | |

**Days of the Week**

1. Sunday
2. Friday
3. Tuesday
4. Saturday

**Months of the Year**

1. January
2. June
3. May
4. August
5. December

## Page 121

### Plural Nouns

**Plural nouns** name more than one person, place or thing.

**Directions:** Read the words in the box. Write the words in the correct column.

| hats | girl | cows | kittens | cake |
| spoons | glass | book | horse | trees |

one — more than one

girl — hats
glass — spoons
book — cows
horse — kittens
cake — trees

# Answer Key

## Page 122

### Plural Nouns

**Plurals** are words that mean more than one. You usually add an **s** or **es** to the word. In some words ending in **y**, the **y** changes to an **i** before adding **es**. For example, **baby** changes to **babies**.

**Directions:** Look at the following lists of plural words. Write the word that means one next to it. The first one has been done for you.

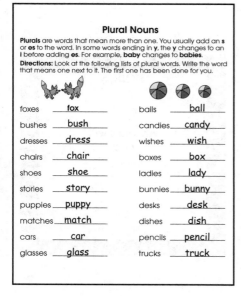

| | | | |
|---|---|---|---|
| foxes | **fox** | balls | **ball** |
| bushes | **bush** | candies | **candy** |
| dresses | **dress** | wishes | **wish** |
| chairs | **chair** | boxes | **box** |
| shoes | **shoe** | ladies | **lady** |
| stories | **story** | bunnies | **bunny** |
| puppies | **puppy** | desks | **desk** |
| matches | **match** | dishes | **dish** |
| cars | **car** | pencils | **pencil** |
| glasses | **glass** | trucks | **truck** |

## Page 123

### Ownership

We add **'s** to nouns (people, places or things) to tell who or what owns something.

**Directions:** Read the sentences. Fill in the blanks to show ownership.

**Example:** The doll belongs to **Sara**.
It is **Sara's** doll.

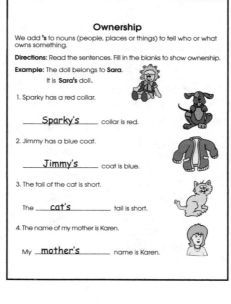

1. Sparky has a red collar.

    **Sparky's** collar is red.

2. Jimmy has a blue coat.

    **Jimmy's** coat is blue.

3. The tail of the cat is short.

The **cat's** tail is short.

4. The name of my mother is Karen.

My **mother's** name is Karen.

## Page 124

### Ownership

**Directions:** Read the sentences. Choose the correct word and write it in the sentences below.

1. The **boy's** lunchbox is broken.  boys  (boy's)
2. The **gerbils** played in the cage.  gerbil's  (gerbils)
3. **Ann's** hair is brown.  Anns  (Ann's)
4. The **horses** ran in the field.  horse's  (horses)
5. My **sister's** coat is torn.  (sister's)  sisters
6. The **cat's** fur is brown.  cats  (cat's)
7. Three **birds** flew past our window.  (birds)  bird's
8. The **dog's** paws are muddy.  dogs  (dog's)
9. The **giraffe's** neck is long.  giraffes  (giraffe's)
10. The **lions** are big and powerful.  lion's  (lions)

## Page 125

### Pronouns

**Pronouns** are words that can be used instead of nouns. **She**, **he**, **it** and **they** are pronouns.

**Directions:** Read the sentence. Then write the sentence again, using **she**, **he**, **it** or **they** in the blank.

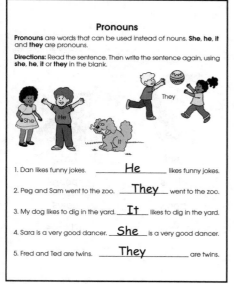

1. Dan likes funny jokes. **He** likes funny jokes.
2. Peg and Sam went to the zoo. **They** went to the zoo.
3. My dog likes to dig in the yard. **It** likes to dig in the yard.
4. Sara is a very good dancer. **She** is a very good dancer.
5. Fred and Ted are twins. **They** are twins.

## Page 126

### Subjects

The **subject** of a sentence is the person, place or thing the sentence is about.

**Directions:** Underline the subject in each sentence.

**Example:** Mom read a book.
(Think: Who is the sentence about? Mom)

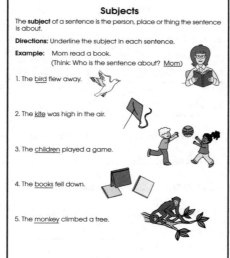

1. The <u>bird</u> flew away.
2. The <u>kite</u> was high in the air.
3. The <u>children</u> played a game.
4. The <u>books</u> fell down.
5. The <u>monkey</u> climbed a tree.

## Page 127

### Compound Subjects

Two similar sentences can be joined into one sentence if the predicate is the same. A **compound subject** is made up of two subjects joined together by the word **and**.

**Example:** Jamie can sing.
Sandy can sing.
Jamie **and** Sandy can sing.

**Directions:** Combine the sentences. Write the new sentence on the line.

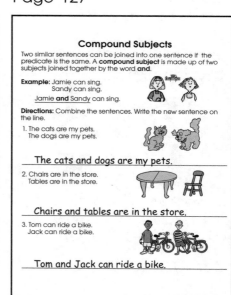

1. The cats are my pets.
   The dogs are my pets.

   The cats and dogs are my pets.

2. Chairs are in the store.
   Tables are in the store.

   Chairs and tables are in the store.

3. Tom can ride a bike.
   Jack can ride a bike.

   Tom and Jack can ride a bike.

# Answer Key

## Page 128

### Verbs

A **verb** is the action word in a sentence. Verbs tell what something does or that something exists.

**Example:** Run, sleep and jump are verbs.

**Directions:** Circle the verbs in the sentences below.

1. We (play) baseball everyday.

2. Susan (pitches) the ball very well.

3. Mike (swings) the bat harder than anyone.

4. Chris (slides) into home base.

5. Laura (hit) a home run.

## Page 129

### Verbs

We use verbs to tell when something happens. Sometimes we add an **ed** to verbs that tell us if something has already happened.

**Example:** Today, we will **play**. Yesterday, we **played**.

**Directions:** Write the correct verb in the blank.

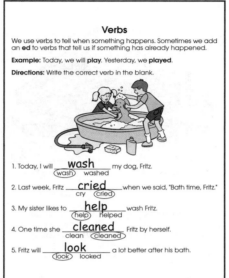

1. Today, I will **wash** my dog, Fritz.
   (wash) washed

2. Last week, Fritz **cried** when we said, "Bath time, Fritz."
   cry (cried)

3. My sister likes to **help** wash Fritz.
   (help) helped

4. One time she **cleaned** Fritz by herself.
   clean (cleaned)

5. Fritz will **look** a lot better after his bath.
   (look) looked

## Page 130

### Predicates

The **predicate** is the part of the sentence that tells about the action.

**Directions:** Circle the predicate in each sentence.

**Example:** The boys ran on the playground.
(Think: The boys did what? (Ran))

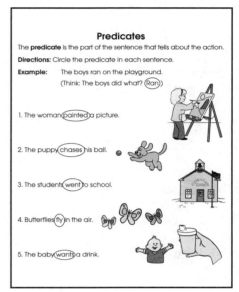

1. The woman (painted) a picture.

2. The puppy (chases) his ball.

3. The students (went) to school.

4. Butterflies (fly) in the air.

5. The baby (wants) a drink.

## Page 131

### Subjects and Predicates

The **subject** part of the sentence is the person, place or thing the sentence is about. The **predicate** is the part of the sentence that tells what the subject does.

**Directions:** Draw a line between the subject and the predicate. Underline the noun in the subject and circle the verb.

**Example:** The furry <u>cat</u> | (ate) food.

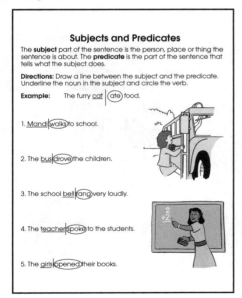

1. <u>Mandi</u> | (walks) to school.

2. The <u>bus</u> | (drove) the children.

3. The school <u>bell</u> | (rang) very loudly.

4. The <u>teacher</u> | (spoke) to the students.

5. The <u>girls</u> | (opened) their books.

## Page 132

### Parts of a Sentence

**Directions:** Draw a circle around the noun, the naming part of the sentence. Draw a line under the verb, the action part of the sentence.

**Example:** (John) <u>drinks</u> juice every morning.

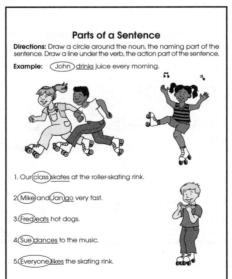

1. Our (class) <u>skates</u> at the roller-skating rink.

2. (Mike) and (Jan) <u>go</u> very fast.

3. (Fred) <u>eats</u> hot dogs.

4. (Sue) <u>dances</u> to the music.

5. (Everyone) <u>likes</u> the skating rink.

## Page 133

### Parts of a Sentence

**Directions:** Look at the pictures. Draw a line from the naming part of the sentence to the action part to complete the sentence.

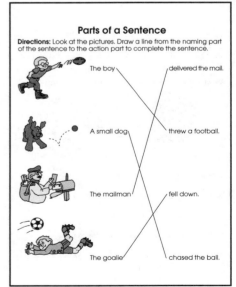

The boy ——— threw a football.

A small dog ——— chased the ball.

The mailman ——— delivered the mail.

The goalie ——— fell down.

# Answer Key

## Page 134

**Adjectives**

**Adjectives** are words that tell more about a person, place or thing.

**Examples:** cold, fuzzy, dark

**Directions:** Circle the adjectives in the sentences.

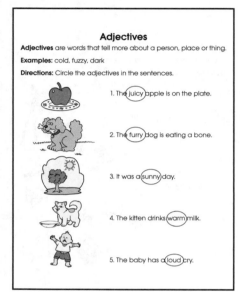

1. The (juicy) apple is on the plate.

2. The (furry) dog is eating a bone.

3. It was a (sunny) day.

4. The kitten drinks (warm) milk.

5. The baby has a (loud) cry.

## Page 135

**Adjectives**

**Directions:** Choose an adjective from the box to fill in the blanks.

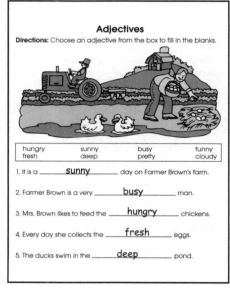

| hungry | sunny | busy | funny |
| fresh | deep | pretty | cloudy |

1. It is a ___sunny___ day on Farmer Brown's farm.

2. Farmer Brown is a very ___busy___ man.

3. Mrs. Brown likes to feed the ___hungry___ chickens.

4. Every day she collects the ___fresh___ eggs.

5. The ducks swim in the ___deep___ pond.

## Page 136

**Adjectives**

**Directions:** Think of your own adjectives. Write a story about Fluffy the cat.

**Answers will vary.**

1. Fluffy is a _____ cat.

2. The color of his fur is _____ .

3. He likes to chew on my _____ shoes.

4. He likes to eat _____ cat food.

5. I like Fluffy because he is so _____ .

## Page 137

**Articles**

**Articles** are small words that help us to better understand nouns. **A** and **an** are articles. We use **an** before a word that begins with a vowel. We use **a** before a word that begins with a consonant.

**Example:** We looked in **a** nest. It had **an** eagle in it.

**Directions:** Read the sentences. Write **a** or **an** in the blank.

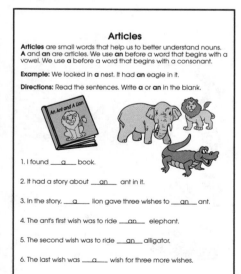

1. I found __a__ book.

2. It had a story about __an__ ant in it.

3. In the story, __a__ lion gave three wishes to __an__ ant.

4. The ant's first wish was to ride __an__ elephant.

5. The second wish was to ride __an__ alligator.

6. The last wish was __a__ wish for three more wishes.

## Page 138

**Sentences and Non-Sentences**

A **sentence** tells a complete idea. It has a noun and a verb. It begins with a capital letter and has punctuation at the end.

**Directions:** Circle the group of words if it is a sentence.

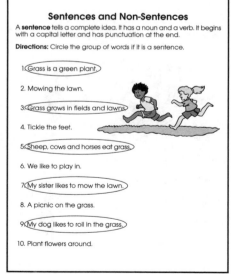

1. (Grass is a green plant.)

2. Mowing the lawn.

3. (Grass grows in fields and lawns.)

4. Tickle the feet.

5. (Sheep, cows and horses eat grass.)

6. We like to play in.

7. (My sister likes to mow the lawn.)

8. A picnic on the grass.

9. (My dog likes to roll in the grass.)

10. Plant flowers around.

## Page 139

**Sentences and Non-Sentences**

**Directions:** Circle the group of words if it tells a complete idea.

1. (A secret is something you know.)

2. (My mom's birthday gift is a secret.)

3. No one else.

4. If you promise not to.

5. (I'll tell you a secret.)

6. Something nobody knows.

# Answer Key

## Page 140

### Statements

**Statements** are sentences that tell us something. They begin with a capital letter and end with a period.

**Directions:** Write the sentences on the lines below. Begin each sentence with a capital letter and end it with a period.

1. we like to ride our bikes

   We like to ride our bikes.

2. we go down the hill very fast

   We go down the hill very fast.

3. we keep our bikes shiny and clean

   We keep our bikes shiny and clean.

4. we know how to change the tires

   We know how to change the tires.

## Page 141

### Surprising Sentences

**Surprising sentences** tell a strong feeling and end with an exclamation point. A surprising sentence may be only one or two words showing fear, surprise or pain. **Example: Oh, no!**

**Directions:** Put a period at the end of the sentences that tell something. Put an exclamation point at the end of the sentences that tell a strong feeling. Put a question mark at the end of the sentences that ask a question.

1. The cheetah can run very fast .
2. Wow !
3. Look at that cheetah go !
4. Can you run fast ?
5. Oh, my !
6. You're faster than I am .
7. Let's run together .
8. We can run as fast as a cheetah .
9. What fun !
10. Do you think cheetahs get tired ?

## Page 142

### Commands

**Commands** tell someone to do something. Example: "Be careful." It can also be written as "Be careful!" if it tells a strong feeling.

**Directions:** Put a period at the end of the command sentences. Use an exclamation point if the sentence tells a strong feeling. Write your own commands on the lines below.

1. Clean your room .
2. Now !
3. Be careful with your goldfish .
4. Watch out !
5. Be a little more careful .

   Answers will vary.

## Page 143

### Questions

**Questions** are sentences that ask something. They begin with a capital letter and end with a question mark.

**Directions:** Write the questions on the lines below. Begin each sentence with a capital letter and end it with a question mark.

1. will you be my friend

   Will you be my friend?

2. what is your name

   What is your name?

3. are you eight years old

   Are you eight years old?

4. do you like rainbows

   Do you like rainbows?

## Page 144

### Making Inferences: Writing Questions

Tommy likes to answer questions. He knows the answers, but you need to write the questions.

**Directions:** Write two questions for each answer.

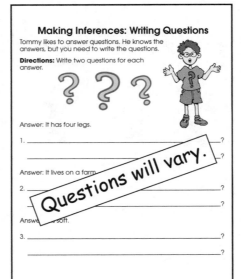

Answer: It has four legs.

1. _____?

Answer: It lives on a farm.

2. _____?

Answer: ___ soft.

3. _____?

Questions will vary.

## Page 145

### Making Inferences: Point of View

Ellen likes animals. Someday she might want to be an animal doctor.

**Directions:** Write one question you think Ellen would ask each of these animals if she could speak their language.

1. a giraffe _____?
2. a mouse _____?
3. a shark _____?
4. a hippopotamus _____?
5. a penguin _____?
6. a gorilla _____?
7. an eagle _____?

Questions will vary.

**Directions:** Now, write the answers you think these animals might have given Ellen.

9. a giraffe _____
10. a mouse _____
11. a shark _____
12. a hippopotamus _____
13. a penguin _____
14. a gorilla _____
15. an eagle _____

Answers will vary.

# Answer Key

## Page 146

### Creative Writing

**Directions:** Look at the picture below. Write a story about the picture.

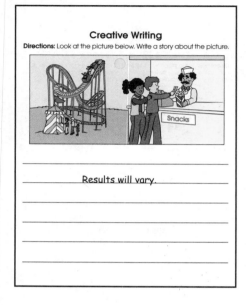

_____

Results will vary.

_____

_____

_____

## Page 147

### Is, Are and Am

**Is**, **are** and **am** are special action words that tell us something is happening now.

Use **am** with I. **Example: I am.**
Use **is** to tell about one person or thing. **Example: He is.**
Use **are** to tell about more than one. **Example: We are.**
Use **are** with you. **Example: You are.**

**Directions:** Write **is**, **are** or **am** in the sentences below.

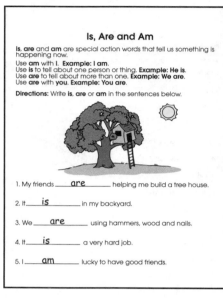

1. My friends ___are___ helping me build a tree house.

2. It ___is___ in my backyard.

3. We ___are___ using hammers, wood and nails.

4. It ___is___ a very hard job.

5. I ___am___ lucky to have good friends.

## Page 148

### Was and Were

**Was** and **were** tell us about something that already happened.

Use **was** to tell about one person or thing. **Example: I was, he was.**
Use **were** to tell about more than one person or thing or when using the word you. **Example: We were, you were.**

**Directions:** Write **was** or **were** in each sentence.

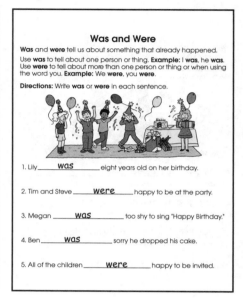

1. Lily ___was___ eight years old on her birthday.

2. Tim and Steve ___were___ happy to be at the party.

3. Megan ___was___ too shy to sing "Happy Birthday."

4. Ben ___was___ sorry he dropped his cake.

5. All of the children ___were___ happy to be invited.

## Page 149

### Go, Going and Went

We use **go** or **going** to tell about now or later. Sometimes we use **going** with the words **am** or **are**. We use **went** to tell about something that already happened.

**Directions:** Write **go**, **going** or **went** in the sentences below.

1. Today, I will ___go___ to the store.

2. Yesterday, we ___went___ shopping.

3. I am ___going___ to take Muffy to the vet.

4. Jan and Steve ___went___ to the party.

5. They are ___going___ to have a good day.

## Page 150

### Have, Has and Had

We use **have** and **has** to tell about now. We use **had** to tell about something that already happened.

**Directions:** Write **has**, **have** or **had** in the sentences below.

1. We ___have___ three cats at home.

2. Ginger ___has___ brown fur.

3. Bucky and Charlie ___have___ gray fur.

4. My friend Tom ___had___ one cat, but he died.

5. Tom ___has___ a new cat now.

## Page 151

### See, Saw and Sees

We use **see** or **sees** to tell about now. We use **saw** to tell about something that already happened.

**Directions:** Write **see**, **sees** or **saw** in the sentences below.

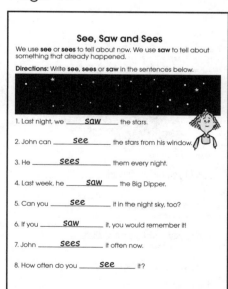

1. Last night, we ___saw___ the stars.

2. John can ___see___ the stars from his window.

3. He ___sees___ them every night.

4. Last week, he ___saw___ the Big Dipper.

5. Can you ___see___ it in the night sky, too?

6. If you ___saw___ it, you would remember it!

7. John ___sees___ it often now.

8. How often do you ___see___ it?

# Answer Key

## Page 152

### Eat, Eats and Ate

We use **eat** or **eats** to tell about now. We use **ate** to tell about what already happened.

**Directions:** Write **eat, eats** or **ate** in the sentences below.

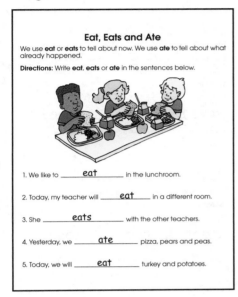

1. We like to _____eat_____ in the lunchroom.

2. Today, my teacher will _____eat_____ in a different room.

3. She _____eats_____ with the other teachers.

4. Yesterday, we _____ate_____ pizza, pears and peas.

5. Today, we will _____eat_____ turkey and potatoes.

## Page 153

### Leave, Leaves and Left

We use **leave** and **leaves** to tell about now. We use **left** to tell about what already happened.

**Directions:** Write **leave, leaves** or **left** in the sentences below.

1. Last winter, we _____left_____ seeds in the bird feeder everyday.

2. My mother likes to _____leave_____ food out for the squirrels.

3. When it rains, she _____leaves_____ bread for the birds.

4. Yesterday, she _____left_____ popcorn for the birds.

## Page 154

### ABC Order

**Directions:** Put the words in ABC order on the bags.

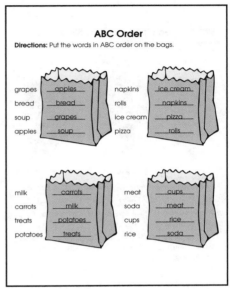

| grapes | apples | napkins | ice cream |
| bread | bread | rolls | napkins |
| soup | grapes | ice cream | pizza |
| apples | soup | pizza | rolls |

| milk | carrots | meat | cups |
| carrots | milk | soda | meat |
| treats | potatoes | cups | rice |
| potatoes | treats | rice | soda |

## Page 155

### ABC Order

**Directions:** Write these words in order. If two words start with the same letter, look at the second letter in each word.

**Example:** lamb    Lamb comes first because **a** comes before **i**
light    in the alphabet.

| tree | branch |
| branch | leaf |
| leaf | tree |

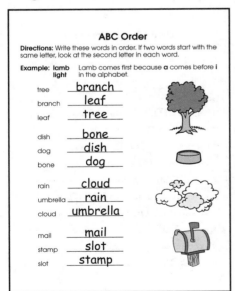

| dish | bone |
| dog | dish |
| bone | dog |

| rain | cloud |
| umbrella | rain |
| cloud | umbrella |

| mail | mail |
| stamp | slot |
| slot | stamp |

## Page 156

### Learning Dictionary Skills

A dictionary is a book that gives the meaning of words. It also tells how words sound. Words in a dictionary are in ABC order. That makes them easier to find. A picture dictionary lists a word, a picture of the word and its meaning.

**Directions:** Look at this page from a picture dictionary. Then answer the questions.

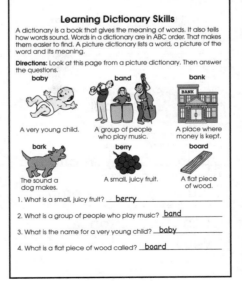

**baby** — A very young child.

**band** — A group of people who play music.

**bank** — A place where money is kept.

**bark** — The sound a dog makes.

**berry** — A small, juicy fruit.

**board** — A flat piece of wood.

1. What is a small, juicy fruit? _____berry_____

2. What is a group of people who play music? _____band_____

3. What is the name for a very young child? _____baby_____

4. What is a flat piece of wood called? _____board_____

## Page 157

### Learning Dictionary Skills

**Directions:** Look at this page from a picture dictionary. Then answer the questions.

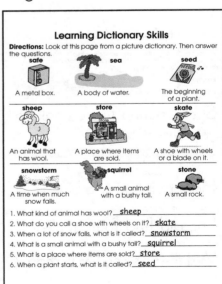

**safe** — A metal box.

**sea** — A body of water.

**seed** — The beginning of a plant.

**sheep** — An animal that has wool.

**store** — A place where items are sold.

**skate** — A shoe with wheels or a blade on it.

**snowstorm** — A time when much snow falls.

**squirrel** — A small animal with a bushy tail.

**stone** — A small rock.

1. What kind of animal has wool? _____sheep_____

2. What do you call a shoe with wheels on it? _____skate_____

3. When a lot of snow falls, what is it called? _____snowstorm_____

4. What is a small animal with a bushy tail? _____squirrel_____

5. What is a place where items are sold? _____store_____

6. When a plant starts, what is it called? _____seed_____

# Answer Key

## Page 158

**Learning Dictionary Skills**

**Directions:** Look at this page from a picture dictionary. Then answer the questions.

**table** — Furniture with legs and a flat top.

**tail** — A slender part that is on the back of an animal.

**teacher** — A person who teaches lessons.

**telephone** — A machine that sends and receives sounds.

**ticket** — A paper slip or card.

**tiger** — An animal with stripes.

1. Who is a person who teaches lessons? __teacher__
2. What is the name of an animal with stripes? __tiger__
3. What is a piece of furniture with legs and a flat top? __table__
4. What is the definition of a ticket?
   __a paper slip or card__
5. What is a machine that sends and receives sounds?
   __telephone__

## Page 159

**Learning Dictionary Skills**

**Directions:** Write each word from the box in ABC order between each pair of guide words.

| fierce | fix | fight | first | few |
| fish | fill | flush | flat | finish |

**few**

| few |
| fierce |
| fight |
| fill |
| finish |

**flush**

| first |
| fish |
| fix |
| flat |
| flush |

## Page 161

**Number Words**

**Directions:** Write the correct number words in the blanks.

| one two three four five six seven eight nine ten |

Add a letter to each of these words to make a number word.

**Example:**

| even | on | tree |
| __seven__ | __one__ | __three__ |

Change a letter to make these words into number words.

**Example:**

| live | fix | line |
| __five__ | __six__ | __nine__ |

Write the number words that sound the same as these:

**Example:**

| ate | to | for |
| __eight__ | __two__ | __four__ |

Write the number word you did not use: __ten__

## Page 162

**Number Words: Sentences**

**Directions:** Change the telling sentences into asking sentences. Change the asking sentences into telling sentences. Begin each one with a capital letter and end it with a period or a question mark.

**Examples:**

Is she eating three cookies?

She is eating three cookies.

He is bringing one truck.

Is he bringing one truck?

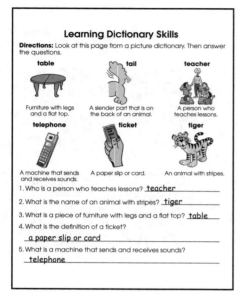

1. Is he painting two blue birds?

He is painting two bluebirds.

2. Did she find four apples?

She did find four apples.

3. She will be six on her birthday.

Will she be six on her birthday?

## Page 163

**Short a Words: Rhyming Words**

**Short a** is the sound you hear in the word **math**.

**Directions:** Use the **short a** words in the box to write rhyming words.

| lamp | fat | bat | van |
| path | can | cat | Dan |
| math | stamp | fan | sat |

1. Write four words that rhyme with **mat**.

__fat__        __bat__

__cat__        __sat__

2. Write two words that rhyme with **bath**.

__path__        __math__

3. Write two words that rhyme with **damp**.

__lamp__        __stamp__

4. Write four words that rhyme with **pan**.

__can__        __fan__

__van__        __Dan__

## Page 164

**Short a Words: Sentences**

**Directions:** Use a word from the box to complete each sentence.

| fat | path | lamp | can |
| van | stamp | Dan | math |
| sat | cat | fan | bat |

**Example:**

1. The __lamp__ had a pink shade.
2. The bike __path__ led us to the park.
3. I like to add in __math__ class.
4. The cat is very __fat__.
5. The __can__ of beans was hard to open.
6. The envelope needed a __stamp__.
7. He swung the __bat__ and hit the ball.
8. The __fan__ blew air around.
9. My mom drives a blue __van__.
10. I __sat__ in the backseat.

# Answer Key

## Page 165

### Long a Words

**Long a** is the vowel sound which says its own name. **Long a** can be spelled **ai** as in the word **mail**, **ay** as in the word **say** and **a** with a **silent e** at the end of a word as in the word **same**.

**Directions:** Say each word and listen for the **long a** sound. Then write each word and underline the letters that make the **long a** vowel sound.

| mail | bake | train |
|------|------|-------|
| game | day | sale |
| paint | play | name |
| made | gray | tray |

1. <u>mail</u>
2. <u>paint</u>
3. <u>game</u>
4. <u>made</u>
5. <u>bake</u>
6. <u>play</u>
7. <u>day</u>
8. <u>gray</u>
9. <u>train</u>
10. <u>name</u>
11. <u>sale</u>
12. <u>tray</u>

## Page 166

### Long a Words: Sentence Order

**Directions:** Write the words in order so that each sentence tells a complete idea. Begin each Sentence with a capital letter and end it with a period or a question mark.

1. plate was on the cake a

The cake was on a plate.

2. like you would to play a game

You would like to play a game.

3. gray around the a corner train came

A gray train came around the corner.

4. was on mail Bob's name the

Bob's name was on the mail.

5. sail for on day we went a nice a

We went for a sail on a nice day.

## Page 167

### Short o Words

**Short o** is the vowel sound you hear in the word **pot**.

**Directions:** Say each word and listen for the **short o** sound. Then write each word and underline the letter that makes the **short o** sound.

| hot | box | sock | mop |
|-----|-----|------|-----|
| stop | not | fox | cot |
| Bob | rock | clock | lock |

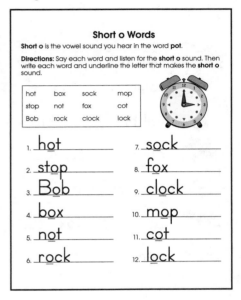

1. <u>hot</u>
2. <u>stop</u>
3. <u>Bob</u>
4. <u>box</u>
5. <u>not</u>
6. <u>rock</u>
7. <u>sock</u>
8. <u>fox</u>
9. <u>clock</u>
10. <u>mop</u>
11. <u>cot</u>
12. <u>lock</u>

## Page 168

### Short o Words: Rhyming Words

**Short o** is the vowel sound you hear in the word **got**.

**Directions:** Use the **short o** words in the box to write rhyming words.

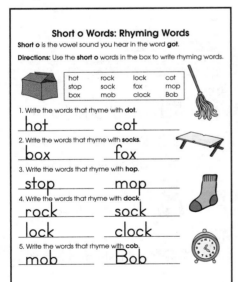

| hot | rock | lock | cot |
|-----|------|------|-----|
| stop | sock | fox | mop |
| box | mob | clock | Bob |

1. Write the words that rhyme with **dot**.
hot    cot

2. Write the words that rhyme with **socks**.
box    fox

3. Write the words that rhyme with **hop**.
stop    mop

4. Write the words that rhyme with **dock**.
rock    sock
lock    clock

5. Write the words that rhyme with **cob**.
mob    Bob

## Page 169

### Long o Words

**Long o** is the vowel sound which says its own name. **Long o** can be spelled **oa** as in the word **float** or **o** with a **silent e** at the end as in **cone**.

**Directions:** Say each word and listen for the **long o** sound. Then write each word and underline the letters that make the **long o** sound.

| rope | coat | soap | wrote |
|------|------|------|-------|
| note | hope | boat | cone |
| bone | pole | phone | hole |

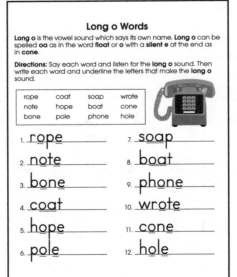

1. <u>rope</u>
2. <u>note</u>
3. <u>bone</u>
4. <u>coat</u>
5. <u>hope</u>
6. <u>pole</u>
7. <u>soap</u>
8. <u>boat</u>
9. <u>phone</u>
10. <u>wrote</u>
11. <u>cone</u>
12. <u>hole</u>

## Page 170

### Long o Words: Sentences

**Directions:** Draw a line from the first part of the sentence to the part which completes the sentence.

1. Do you know — in the water.
2. The dog — was in the tree.
3. The boat floats — who wrote the note?
4. I hope the phone — has a bone.
5. Carol's ice-cream cone — rings soon for me!
6. The rope swing — a coat in the cold.
7. I had to wear — was melting.

# Answer Key

## Page 171

### Animal Words

**Directions:** Write the animal names twice beside each picture.

| fox | rabbit | bear | squirrel | mouse | deer |

**Example:**

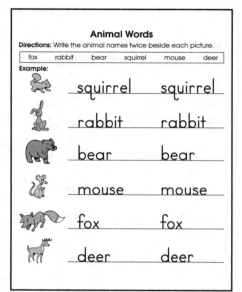

squirrel    squirrel

rabbit    rabbit

bear    bear

mouse    mouse

fox    fox

deer    deer

## Page 172

### Animal Words: More Than One

To show more than one of something, we add **s** to most words.
**Example:** one dog – **two dogs**    one book – **two books**
But some words are different. For words that end with **x**, use **es** to show two.
**Example:** one fox – **two foxes**    one box – **two boxes**
The spelling of some words changes a lot when there are two.
**Example:** one mouse – **two mice**
Some words stay the same, even when you mean two of something.
**Example:** one deer – **two deer**    one fish – **two fish**

**Directions:** Complete the sentences below with the correct word.

1. The _____ run fast.    rabbits

2. The _____ are eating.    deer

3. Have you seen any _____ today?    bears

4. Where do the _____ live?    foxes

5. Did you ever have _____ for pets?    mice

## Page 173

### Animal Words: Kinds of Sentences

Another name for an asking sentence is a **question**.

**Directions:** Use the words in the box to write a telling sentence. Then use the words to write a question.

**Example:**

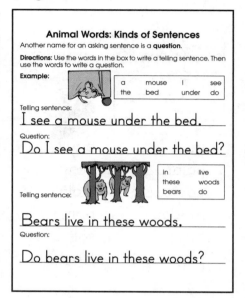

| a | mouse | I | see |
| the | bed | under | do |

Telling sentence:

I see a mouse under the bed.

Question:

Do I see a mouse under the bed?

| in | | live |
| these | | woods |
| bears | | do |

Telling sentence:

Bears live in these woods.

Question:

Do bears live in these woods?

## Page 174

### Animal Words: Sentences

**Directions:** Read the sentences on each line and draw a line between them. Then write each sentence again on the lines below. Begin each one with a capital letter and put a period or question mark at the end.

**Example:**

why do squirrels hide nuts | they eat them in the winter

Why do squirrels hide nuts?
They eat them in the winter.

1. bears sleep in the winter | they don't need food then

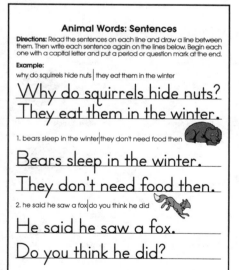

Bears sleep in the winter.
They don't need food then.

2. he said he saw a fox | do you think he did

He said he saw a fox.
Do you think he did?

## Page 175

### Family Words

**Directions:** This is Andy's **family tree**. It shows all the people in his family. Use the words in the box to finish writing the names in Andy's family tree.

| grandmother | mother |
| grandfather | father |
| aunt | uncle |
| brother | sister |

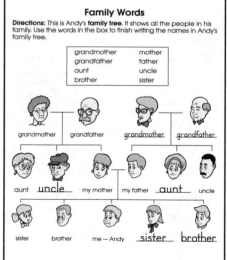

## Page 176

### Family Words

Some words tell how a person looks or feels. These are called **describing** words or **adjectives**.

**Directions:** Help Andy write about the people in his family. Cross out the **describing** word that does not tell about each picture. Write a sentence that uses the other two describing words.

**Example:**

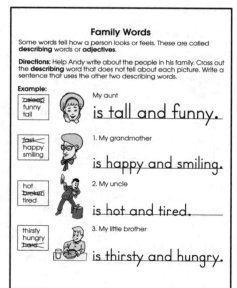

~~asleep~~
funny
tall

My aunt is tall and funny.

~~fast~~
happy
smiling

1. My grandmother is happy and smiling.

hot
~~broken~~
tired

2. My uncle is hot and tired.

thirsty
hungry
~~hard~~

3. My little brother is thirsty and hungry.

# Answer Key

## Page 177

### Family Words: Joining Words

**Joining words** join two ideas to make one long sentence. Three words help do this:

**and** — if both sentences are much the same.
**Example:** I took my dog for a walk, **and** I played with my cat.

**but** — if the second sentence says something different than the first sentence. Sometimes the second sentence tells why you can't do the first sentence.
**Example:** I want to play outside, **but** it is raining.

**or** — if each sentence names a different thing you could do.
**Example:** You could eat your cookie, **or** you could give it to me.

**Directions:** Use the word given to join the two short sentences into one longer sentence.

**(but)**
My aunt lives far away. She calls me often.

My aunt lives far away, but she calls me often.

**1. (and)**
My sister had a birthday. She got a new bike.

My sister had a birthday, and she got a new bike.

**2. (or)**
We can play outside. We can play inside.

We can play outside, or we can play inside.

## Page 178

### Family Words: Joining Words

**Directions:** Read each pair of sentences. Then join them with **and, but** or **or**.

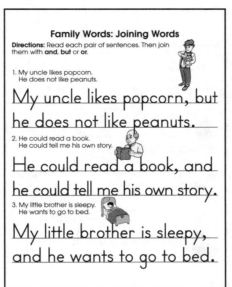

1. My uncle likes popcorn.
   He does not like peanuts.

My uncle likes popcorn, but he does not like peanuts.

2. He could read a book.
   He could tell me his own story.

He could read a book, and he could tell me his own story.

3. My little brother is sleepy.
   He wants to go to bed.

My little brother is sleepy, and he wants to go to bed.

## Page 179

### Short e Words

**Short e** is the vowel sound you hear in the word **pet**.
**Directions:** Say each word and listen for the **short e** sound. Then write each word and underline the letter that makes the **short e** sound.

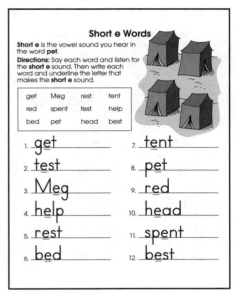

| get | Meg | rest | tent |
|-----|-----|------|------|
| red | spent | test | help |
| bed | pet | head | best |

1. get
2. test
3. Meg
4. help
5. rest
6. bed
7. tent
8. pet
9. red
10. head
11. spent
12. best

## Page 180

### Short e Words: Rhyming Words

**Short e** is the vowel sound you hear in the word **egg**.

**Directions:** Use the **short e** words in the box to write rhyming words.

| get | test | pet | help |
|-----|------|-----|------|
| let | head | spent | red |
| best | tent | rest | bed |

1. Write the words that rhyme with **fed**.

head    red    bed

2. Write the words that rhyme with **bent**.

tent    spent

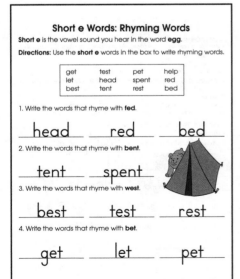

3. Write the words that rhyme with **west**.

best    test    rest

4. Write the words that rhyme with **bet**.

get    let    pet

## Page 181

### Short e Words: Sentences

**Directions:** Write the correct **short e** word in each sentence.

| get | Meg | rest | bed | spent | best |
|-----|-----|------|-----|-------|------|
| test | help | head | pet | red | tent |

1. Of all my crayons, I like the color **red** the **best**!

2. I always make my **bed** when I **get** up.

3. My new hat keeps my **head** warm.

4. **Meg** wanted a dog for a **pet**.

5. When we go camping, my job is to **help** put up the **tent**.

6. I have a **test** in math tomorrow, so I want to get a good night's **rest**.

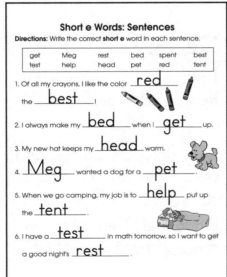

## Page 182

### Long e Words

**Long e** is the vowel sound which says its own name. **Long e** can be spelled **ee** as in the word **teeth**, **ea** as in the word **meat** or **e** as in the word **me**.

**Directions:** Say each word and listen for the **long e** sound. Then write the words and underline the letters that make the **long e** sound.

| street | neat | treat | feet |
|--------|------|-------|------|
| sleep | keep | deal | meal |
| mean | clean | beast | feast |

1. street
2. sleep
3. mean
4. neat
5. keep
6. clean
7. treat
8. deal
9. beast
10. feet
11. meal
12. feast

# Answer Key

## Page 183

### Long e Words: Rhyming Words

**Long e** is the vowel sound you hear in the word **meet**.

**Directions:** Use the **long e** words in the box to write rhyming words.

| street | feet | neat | treat |
|--------|------|------|-------|
| keep | deal | sleep | meal |
| mean | beast | clean | feast |

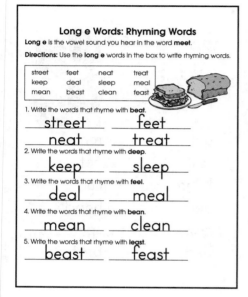

1. Write the words that rhyme with **beat**.

 street     feet

 neat     treat

2. Write the words that rhyme with **deep**.

 keep     sleep

3. Write the words that rhyme with **feel**.

 deal     meal

4. Write the words that rhyme with **bean**.

 mean     clean

5. Write the words that rhyme with **least**.

 beast     feast

## Page 184

### Long e Words: Sentences

**Directions:** Write a word from the box to complete each sentence.

| street | feet | neat | treat |
|--------|------|------|-------|
| keep | deal | sleep | meal |
| mean | beast | clean | feast |

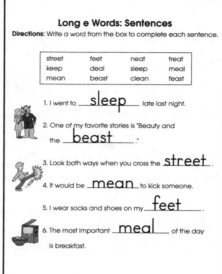

1. I went to **sleep** late last night.

2. One of my favorite stories is "Beauty and the **beast** ."

3. Look both ways when you cross the **street** .

4. It would be **mean** to kick someone.

5. I wear socks and shoes on my **feet** .

6. The most important **meal** of the day is breakfast.

## Page 185

### Verbs

**Verbs** are words that tell the action in the sentence.

**Directions:** Draw a line from each sentence to its picture. Then finish the sentence with the verb or action word that is under each picture.

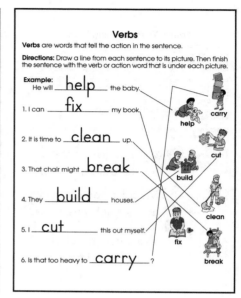

**Example:**

He will **help** the baby.

1. I can **fix** my book.

2. It is time to **clean** up.

3. That chair might **break** .

4. They **build** houses.

5. I **cut** this out myself.

6. Is that too heavy to **carry** ?

carry, help, cut, build, clean, fix, break

## Page 186

### Verbs: Sentences

**Directions:** Read the two sentences in each story below. Then write one more sentence to tell what happened next. Use the verbs from the box.

| break | build | fix | clean | cut | carry |
|-------|-------|-----|-------|-----|-------|

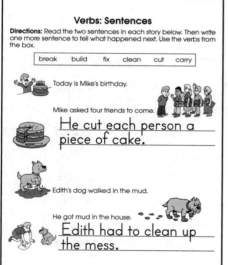

Today is Mike's birthday.

Mike asked four friends to come.

**He cut each person a piece of cake.**

Edith's dog walked in the mud.

He got mud in the house.

**Edith had to clean up the mess.**

## Page 187

### Verbs: Sentences

**Directions:** Join each pair of sentences to make one longer sentence. Use one of the **joining** words: **and**, **but** or **or**. In the second part of the sentence, use **he**, **she** or **they** in place of the person's name.

**Example:** I asked Tim to help me. Tim wanted to play.

**I asked Tim to help me, but he wanted to play.**

1. Kelly dropped a glass.
 Kelly cut her finger.

**Kelly dropped a glass, and she cut her finger.**

2. Linda and Allen got a new dog.
 Linda and Allen named it Baby.

**Linda and Allen got a new dog, and they named it Baby.**

## Page 188

### Verbs: Word Endings

Most **verbs** end with **s** when the sentence tells about one thing. The **s** is taken away when the sentence tells about more than one thing.

**Example:**

One dog walks.     One boy runs.
Two **dogs** walk.     Three **boys** run.

The spelling of some **verbs** changes when the sentence tells about only one thing.

**Example:**

One girl carries her lunch.     The boy fixes his car.
Two girls **carry** their lunches.     Two boys **fix** their cars.

**Directions:** Write the missing verbs in the sentences.

**Example:**

Pam works hard. She and Peter **work** all day.

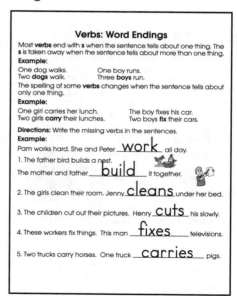

1. The father bird builds a nest.
 The mother and father **build** it together.

2. The girls clean their room. Jenny **cleans** under her bed.

3. The children cut out their pictures. Henry **cuts** his slowly.

4. These workers fix things. This man **fixes** televisions.

5. Two trucks carry horses. One truck **carries** pigs.

# Answer Key

## Page 189

**Short i Words**

**Short i** is the vowel sound you hear in the word **pig**.

**Directions:** Say each word and listen for the **short i** sound. Then write each word and underline the letter that makes the **short i** sound.

| pin | fin | dip | dish |
|-----|-----|------|------|
| kick | rich | ship | wish |
| win | fish | sick | pitch |

1. p<u>i</u>n
2. sh<u>i</u>p
3. f<u>i</u>n
4. w<u>i</u>sh
5. d<u>i</u>p
6. w<u>i</u>n
7. d<u>i</u>sh
8. f<u>i</u>sh
9. k<u>i</u>ck
10. s<u>i</u>ck
11. r<u>i</u>ch
12. p<u>i</u>tch

## Page 190

**Short i Words: Sentences**

**Directions:** Complete the sentences by matching the words to the correct sentence.

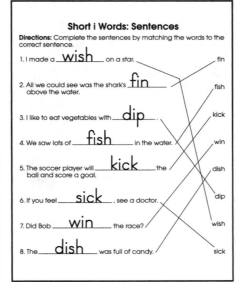

1. I made a **wish** on a star. — fin
2. All we could see was the shark's **fin** above the water. — fish
3. I like to eat vegetables with **dip**. — kick
4. We saw lots of **fish** in the water. — win
5. The soccer player will **kick** the ball and score a goal. — dish
6. If you feel **sick**, see a doctor. — dip
7. Did Bob **win** the race? — wish
8. The **dish** was full of candy. — sick

## Page 191

**Long i Words**

**Long i** is the vowel sound which says its own name. **Long i** can be spelled **igh** as in **sight**, **i** with a **silent e** at the end as in **mine** and **y** at the end as in **fly**.

**Directions:** Say each word and listen for the **long i** sound. Then write each word and underline the letters that make the **long i** sound.

| bike | hike | ride | line |
|------|------|------|------|
| glide | ripe | nine | pipe |
| fight | high | light | sigh |

1. b<u>i</u>ke
2. gl<u>i</u>de
3. f<u>igh</u>t
4. h<u>i</u>ke
5. r<u>i</u>pe
6. h<u>igh</u>
7. r<u>i</u>de
8. n<u>i</u>ne
9. l<u>igh</u>t
10. l<u>i</u>ne
11. p<u>i</u>pe
12. s<u>igh</u>

## Page 192

**Long i Words: Rhyming Words**

**Long i** is the sound you hear in the word **fight**.

**Directions:** Use the **long i** words in the box to write rhyming words.

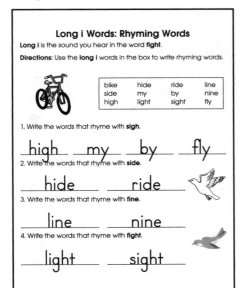

| bike | hide | ride | line |
|------|------|------|------|
| side | my | by | nine |
| high | light | sight | fly |

1. Write the words that rhyme with **sigh**.

high   my   by   fly

2. Write the words that rhyme with **side**.

hide   ride

3. Write the words that rhyme with **fine**.

line   nine

4. Write the words that rhyme with **fight**.

light   sight

## Page 193

**Location Words**

**Directions:** Use one of the location words from the box to complete each sentence.

| between | around | inside | outside | beside | across |
|---------|--------|--------|---------|--------|--------|

**Example:**
She will hide **under** the basket.

1. In the summer, we like to play **outside**.
2. She can swim **across** the lake.
3. Put the bird **inside** its cage so it won't fly away.
4. Sit **between** Bill and me so we can all work together.
5. Your picture is right **beside** mine on the wall.
6. The fence goes **around** the house.

## Page 194

**Location Words**

**Directions:** Draw a line from each sentence to its picture. Then complete each sentence with the word under the picture.

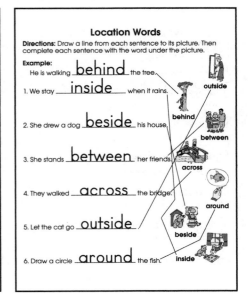

**Example:**
He is walking **behind** the tree.

1. We stay **inside** when it rains. — outside
2. She drew a dog **beside** his house. — behind
3. She stands **between** her friends. — between
4. They walked **across** the bridge. — across
5. Let the cat go **outside**. — around
6. Draw a circle **around** the fish. — beside / inside

# Answer Key

## Page 195

### Short u Words

**Short u** is the sound you hear in the word **bug**.

**Directions:** Say each word and listen for the **short u** sound. Then write each word and underline the letter that makes the **short u** sound.

| | | | |
|---|---|---|---|
| dust | must | nut | bug |
| bump | pump | tub | jump |
| cut | hug | rug | cub |

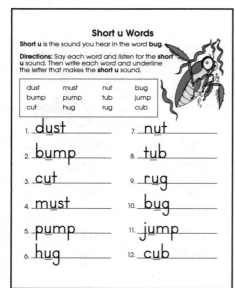

1. d<u>u</u>st
2. b<u>u</u>mp
3. c<u>u</u>t
4. m<u>u</u>st
5. p<u>u</u>mp
6. h<u>u</u>g
7. n<u>u</u>t
8. t<u>u</u>b
9. r<u>u</u>g
10. b<u>u</u>g
11. j<u>u</u>mp
12. c<u>u</u>b

## Page 196

### Short u Words: Sentences

**Directions:** Circle the words in each sentence which are not correct. Then write the correct **short u** words from the box on the lines.

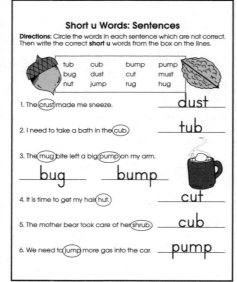

| | | | |
|---|---|---|---|
| tub | cub | bump | pump |
| bug | dust | cut | must |
| nut | jump | rug | hug |

1. The (crust) made me sneeze. — dust
2. I need to take a bath in the (cub). — tub
3. The (mug) bite left a big (pump) on my arm. — bug   bump
4. It is time to get my hair (hut). — cut
5. The mother bear took care of her (shrub). — cub
6. We need to (jump) more gas into the car. — pump

## Page 197

### Long u Words

**Long u** is the vowel sound which says its own name. **Long u** is spelled **u** with a silent **e** at the end as in **cute**. The letters **oo** make a sound very much like long **u**. They make the sound you hear in the word **zoo**. The letters **ew** also make the **oo** sound as in the word **grew**.

**Directions:** Say the words and listen for the **u** and **oo** sounds. Then write each word and underline the letters that make the **long u** and **oo** sounds.

| | | | |
|---|---|---|---|
| choose | blew | moon | fuse |
| cube | Ruth | tooth | use |
| flew | loose | goose | noon |

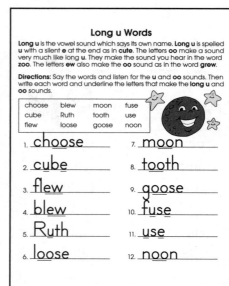

1. ch<u>oo</u>se
2. c<u>u</u>be
3. fl<u>ew</u>
4. bl<u>ew</u>
5. R<u>u</u>th
6. l<u>oo</u>se
7. m<u>oo</u>n
8. t<u>oo</u>th
9. g<u>oo</u>se
10. f<u>u</u>se
11. <u>u</u>se
12. n<u>oo</u>n

## Page 198

### Long u Words: Sentences

**Directions:** Write the words in the sentences below in the correct order. Begin each sentence with a capital letter and end it with a period or a question mark.

1. the pulled dentist tooth my loose

The dentist pulled my loose tooth.

2. ice cubes I choose in my drink to put

I choose to put ice cubes in my drink.

3. a Ruth fuse blew yesterday

Ruth blew a fuse yesterday.

4. loose the got in garden goose the

The goose got loose in the garden.

5. flew the goose winter for the south

The goose flew south for the winter.

6. is full there a moon tonight

Answer may vary.

## Page 199

### Opposite Words

**Directions: Opposites** are words which are different in every way. Use the opposite word from the box to complete these sentences.

| | | | | |
|---|---|---|---|---|
| hard | hot | bottom | quickly | happy |
| sad | slowly | cold | soft | top |

**Example:**

My new coat is blue on top and red on the bottom.

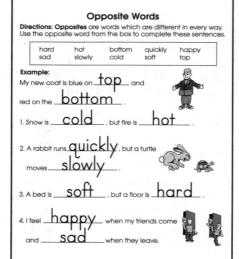

1. Snow is cold , but fire is hot .
2. A rabbit runs quickly, but a turtle moves slowly .
3. A bed is soft , but a floor is hard .
4. I feel happy when my friends come and sad when they leave.

## Page 200

### Opposite Words

**Directions:** Draw a line from each sentence to its picture. Then complete each sentence with the word under the picture.

**Example:**

She bought a new bat.

1. I like my soft pillow.
2. Birthdays make me happy
3. Put that book on top
4. Jenny runs quickly
5. A rock makes a hard seat.
6. I feel sad when it rains.
7. He eats slowly

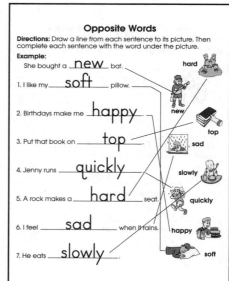

# Answer Key

## Page 201

**Opposite Words: Sentences**

**Directions:** Cross out the word in each box that does not tell about the picture. Write a sentence about the picture using the other two words.

**Example:**

| ~~teeth~~ | garden | digs |

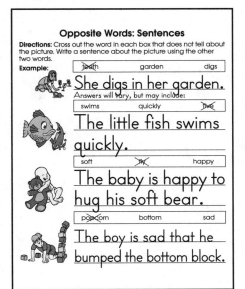

She digs in her garden.

*Answers will vary, but may include:*

| swims | quickly | ~~five~~ |

The little fish swims quickly.

| soft | ~~fly~~ | happy |

The baby is happy to hug his soft bear.

| ~~popcorn~~ | bottom | sad |

The boy is sad that he bumped the bottom block.

## Page 202

**Opposite Words: Sentences**

**Directions:** Look at each picture. Then write a sentence that uses the word under the picture and tells how something is the same as the picture.

**Example:**

cold

My hands are as cold as ice.

*Answers will vary, but may include:*

hard

This cookie is as hard as a rock.

slow

When he walked to school, he was as slow as a turtle.

soft

The chair was as soft as a pillow.

happy

The girl was as happy as a lark.

## Page 203

**Opposite Words: Completing a Story**

**Directions:** Write opposite words in the blanks to complete the story.

| hot | hard | top | cold | bottom |
| soft | quickly | happy | slowly | sad |

One day, Grandma came for a visit. She gave my sister Jenny and me a box of chocolate candy. We said, "Thank you!" Then Jenny **quickly** took the **top** off the box. The pieces all looked the same! I couldn't tell which pieces were **soft** inside and which were **hard** ! I only liked the **soft** ones. Jenny didn't care. She was **happy** to get any kind of candy! I **slowly** looked at all the pieces. I didn't know which one to pick. Just then Dad called us. Grandma was going home. He wanted us to say good-bye to her. I hurried to the front door where they were standing. Jenny came a minute later.

I told Grandma I hoped I would see her soon. I always feel **sad** when she leaves. Jenny stood behind me and didn't say anything. After Grandma went home, I found out why. Jenny had most of our candy in her mouth! Only a few pieces were left in the **bottom** of the box! Then I was **sad** ! That Jenny!

## Page 204

**Time Words**

The time between breakfast and lunch is **morning**.
The time between lunch and dinner is **afternoon**.
The time between dinner and bedtime is **evening**.

**Directions:** Write a time word from the box to complete each sentence. Use each word only once.

| evening | morning | today | tomorrow | afternoon |

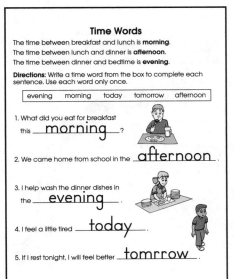

1. What did you eat for breakfast this **morning** ?

2. We came home from school in the **afternoon**

3. I help wash the dinner dishes in the **evening**

4. I feel a little tired **today**

5. If I rest tonight, I will feel better **tomrrow**

## Page 205

**Time Words: Sentences**

**Directions:** Write a sentence for these time words. Tell something you do at that time.

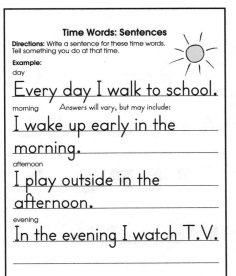

**Example:**

day

Every day I walk to school.

morning          *Answers will vary, but may include:*

I wake up early in the morning.

afternoon

I play outside in the afternoon.

evening

In the evening I watch T.V.

## Page 207

**Less Than, Greater Than**

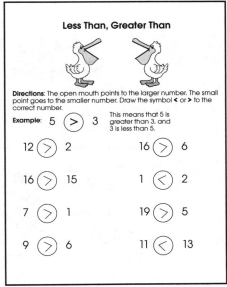

**Directions:** The open mouth points to the larger number. The small point goes to the smaller number. Draw the symbol **<** or **>** to the correct number.

**Example:** 5 ( > ) 3    This means that 5 is greater than 3, and 3 is less than 5.

12 ( > ) 2          16 ( > ) 6

16 ( > ) 15         1 ( < ) 2

7 ( > ) 1           19 ( > ) 5

9 ( > ) 6           11 ( < ) 13

# Answer Key

## Page 208

### Counting by 2's

**Directions:** Each basket the players make is worth 2 points. Help your team win by counting by 2's to beat the other team's score.

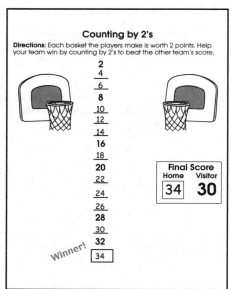

2
4
6
8
10
12
14
16
18
20
22
24
26
28
30
32

*Winner!* 34

**Final Score**

| Home | Visitor |
|------|---------|
| 34 | 30 |

## Page 209

### Counting: 2's, 5's, 10's

**Directions:** Write the missing numbers.

Count by 2's:

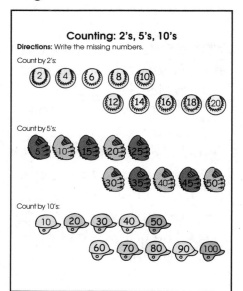

2 4 6 8 10
12 14 16 18 20

Count by 5's:

5 10 15 20 25
30 35 40 45 50

Count by 10's:

10 20 30 40 50
60 70 80 90 100

## Page 210

### Patterns

**Directions:** Write or draw what comes next in the pattern.

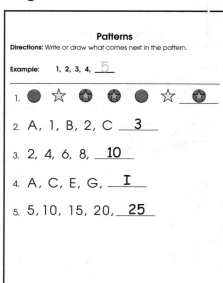

**Example:** 1, 2, 3, 4, __5__

1. ● ☆ ● ● ● ☆ __●__

2. A, 1, B, 2, C __3__

3. 2, 4, 6, 8, __10__

4. A, C, E, G, __I__

5. 5, 10, 15, 20, __25__

## Page 211

### Finding Patterns: Numbers

Mia likes to count by twos, threes, fours, fives, tens and hundreds.

**Directions:** Complete the number patterns.

1. 5, __10__, __15__, 20, __25__, __30__, 35, __40__, __45__, 50

2. 100, __200__, __300__, 400, __500__, __600__, __700__, 800, __900__

3. __2__, 4, 6, __8__, __10__, 12, __14__, 16, __18__, __20__

4. 10, __20__, __30__, 40, __50__, __60__, 70, __80__, 90

5. 4, __8__, 12, __16__, __20__, 24, __28__, 32, __36__, 40

6. __3__, 6, 9, __12__, __15__, 18, __21__, 24, __27__, 30

**Directions:** Make up two of your own number patterns.

___ ___ ___ ___ ___ ___

*Answers will vary.*

## Page 212

### Finding Patterns: Shapes

**Directions:** Complete each row by drawing the correct shape.

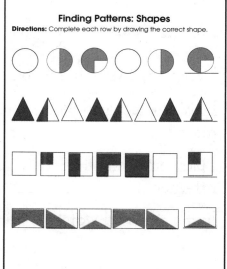

## Page 213

### Ordinal Numbers

Ordinal numbers indicate order in a series, such as **first**, **second** or **third**.

**Directions:** Follow the instructions to color the train cars. The first car is the engine.

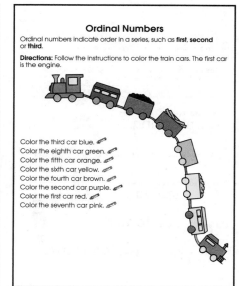

Color the third car blue.
Color the eighth car green.
Color the fifth car orange.
Color the sixth car yellow.
Color the fourth car brown.
Color the second car purple.
Color the first car red.
Color the seventh car pink.

# Answer Key

## Page 214

**Ordinal Numbers**

**Directions:** Follow the instructions.

Draw glasses on the second one.
Put a hat on the fourth one.
Color blonde hair on the third one.
Draw a tie on the first one.
Draw ears on the fifth one.
Draw black hair on the seventh one.
Put a bow on the head of the sixth one.

## Page 215

**Addition**

Addition is "putting together" or adding two or more numbers to find the sum.

**Directions:** Add.

**Example:**

$$\begin{array}{r} 2 \\ +5 \\ \hline 7 \end{array}$$

| $\begin{array}{r}3\\+4\\\hline 7\end{array}$ | $\begin{array}{r}6\\+2\\\hline 8\end{array}$ | $\begin{array}{r}7\\+1\\\hline 8\end{array}$ | $\begin{array}{r}8\\+2\\\hline 10\end{array}$ | $\begin{array}{r}5\\+4\\\hline 9\end{array}$ | $\begin{array}{r}3\\+1\\\hline 4\end{array}$ |
| $\begin{array}{r}8\\+2\\\hline 10\end{array}$ | $\begin{array}{r}9\\+5\\\hline 14\end{array}$ | $\begin{array}{r}10\\+3\\\hline 13\end{array}$ | $\begin{array}{r}6\\+6\\\hline 12\end{array}$ | $\begin{array}{r}4\\+9\\\hline 13\end{array}$ | $\begin{array}{r}7\\+7\\\hline 14\end{array}$ |
| $\begin{array}{r}9\\+3\\\hline 12\end{array}$ | $\begin{array}{r}8\\+7\\\hline 15\end{array}$ | $\begin{array}{r}6\\+5\\\hline 11\end{array}$ | $\begin{array}{r}7\\+9\\\hline 16\end{array}$ | $\begin{array}{r}7\\+6\\\hline 13\end{array}$ | $\begin{array}{r}9\\+9\\\hline 18\end{array}$ |

## Page 216

**Addition: Commutative Property**

The commutative property of addition states that even if the order of the numbers is changed in an addition sentence, the sum will stay the same.

**Example:** 2 + 3 = 5
3 + 2 = 5

**Directions:** Look at the addition sentences below. Complete the addition sentences by writing the missing numerals.

5 + 4 = 9      3 + 1 = 4      2 + 6 = 8
4 + 5 = 9      1 + 3 = 4      6 + 2 = 8

6 + 1 = 7      4 + 3 = 7      1 + 9 = 10
1 + 6 = 7      3 + 4 = 7      9 + 1 = 10

**Now try these:**

6 + 3 = 9      10 + 2 = 12      8 + 3 = 11
3 + 6 = 9      2 + 10 = 12      3 + 8 = 11

Look at these sums. Can you think of two number sentences that would show the commutative property of addition?

__ + __ = 7      __ + __ = 11      __ + __ = 9

__ + __ = 7      __ + __ = 11      __ + __ = 9

**Answers will vary.**

## Page 217

**Adding 3 or More Numbers**

**Directions:** Add all the numbers to find the sum. Draw pictures to help or break up the problem into two smaller problems.

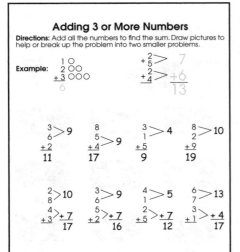

**Example:**

$$\begin{array}{r}1\\2\\+3\\\hline 6\end{array} \qquad \begin{array}{r}2\\+5\\\hline 7 \\ \begin{array}{r}+4\\\hline\end{array} \\ +6 \\ \hline 13\end{array}$$

| $\begin{array}{r}3\\6\\+2\\\hline 11\end{array}$ 9 | $\begin{array}{r}8\\5\\+4\\\hline 17\end{array}$ 9 | $\begin{array}{r}3\\1\\+5\\\hline 9\end{array}$ 4 | $\begin{array}{r}8\\2\\+9\\\hline 19\end{array}$ 10 |
| $\begin{array}{r}2\\8\\4\\+3\\\hline 17\end{array}$ 10, +7 | $\begin{array}{r}3\\6\\5\\+2\\\hline 16\end{array}$ 9, +7 | $\begin{array}{r}4\\1\\5\\+2\\\hline 12\end{array}$ 5, +7 | $\begin{array}{r}6\\7\\3\\+1\\\hline 17\end{array}$ 13, +4 |

## Page 218

**Subtraction**

Subtraction is "taking away" or subtracting one number from another to find the difference.

**Directions:** Subtract.

**Example:**

$$\begin{array}{r} 4 \\ -3 \\ \hline 1 \end{array}$$

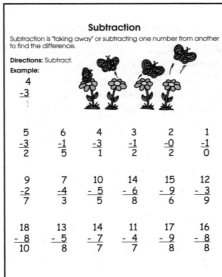

| $\begin{array}{r}5\\-3\\\hline 2\end{array}$ | $\begin{array}{r}6\\-1\\\hline 5\end{array}$ | $\begin{array}{r}4\\-3\\\hline 1\end{array}$ | $\begin{array}{r}3\\-1\\\hline 2\end{array}$ | $\begin{array}{r}2\\-0\\\hline 2\end{array}$ | $\begin{array}{r}1\\-1\\\hline 0\end{array}$ |
| $\begin{array}{r}9\\-2\\\hline 7\end{array}$ | $\begin{array}{r}7\\-4\\\hline 3\end{array}$ | $\begin{array}{r}10\\-5\\\hline 5\end{array}$ | $\begin{array}{r}14\\-6\\\hline 8\end{array}$ | $\begin{array}{r}15\\-9\\\hline 6\end{array}$ | $\begin{array}{r}12\\-3\\\hline 9\end{array}$ |
| $\begin{array}{r}18\\-8\\\hline 10\end{array}$ | $\begin{array}{r}13\\-5\\\hline 8\end{array}$ | $\begin{array}{r}14\\-7\\\hline 7\end{array}$ | $\begin{array}{r}11\\-4\\\hline 7\end{array}$ | $\begin{array}{r}17\\-9\\\hline 8\end{array}$ | $\begin{array}{r}16\\-8\\\hline 8\end{array}$ |

## Page 219

**Addition and Subtraction**

Addition is "putting together" or adding two or more numbers to find the sum. Subtraction is "taking away" or subtracting one number from another to find the difference.

**Directions:** Add or subtract. Circle the answers that are less than 10.

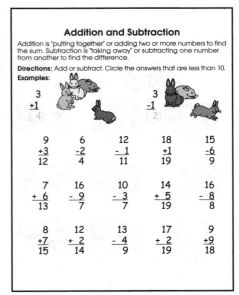

**Examples:**

$$\begin{array}{r} 3 \\ +1 \\ \hline 4 \end{array} \qquad \begin{array}{r} 3 \\ -1 \\ \hline 2 \end{array}$$

| $\begin{array}{r}9\\+3\\\hline 12\end{array}$ | $\begin{array}{r}6\\-2\\\hline 4\end{array}$ | $\begin{array}{r}12\\-1\\\hline 11\end{array}$ | $\begin{array}{r}18\\+1\\\hline 19\end{array}$ | $\begin{array}{r}15\\-6\\\hline 9\end{array}$ |
| $\begin{array}{r}7\\+6\\\hline 13\end{array}$ | $\begin{array}{r}16\\-9\\\hline 7\end{array}$ | $\begin{array}{r}10\\-3\\\hline 7\end{array}$ | $\begin{array}{r}14\\+5\\\hline 19\end{array}$ | $\begin{array}{r}16\\-8\\\hline 8\end{array}$ |
| $\begin{array}{r}8\\+7\\\hline 15\end{array}$ | $\begin{array}{r}12\\+2\\\hline 14\end{array}$ | $\begin{array}{r}13\\-4\\\hline 9\end{array}$ | $\begin{array}{r}17\\+2\\\hline 19\end{array}$ | $\begin{array}{r}9\\+9\\\hline 18\end{array}$ |

# Answer Key

## Page 220

### Place Value: Ones, Tens

The place value of a digit or numeral is shown by where it is in the number. For example, in the number **23**, **2** has the place value of **tens**, and **3** is **ones**.

**Directions:** Add the tens and ones and write your answers in the blanks.

**Example:**

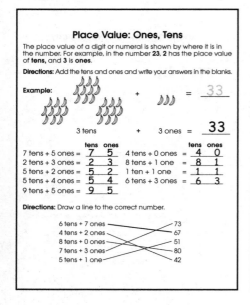

3 tens  +  3 ones  =  **33**

|  | tens | ones |  |  | tens | ones |
|---|---|---|---|---|---|---|
| 7 tens + 5 ones = | 7 | 5 | 4 tens + 0 ones = | | 4 | 0 |
| 2 tens + 3 ones = | 2 | 3 | 8 tens + 1 one = | | 8 | 1 |
| 5 tens + 2 ones = | 5 | 2 | 1 ten + 1 one = | | 1 | 1 |
| 5 tens + 4 ones = | 5 | 4 | 6 tens + 3 ones = | | 6 | 3 |
| 9 tens + 5 ones = | 9 | 5 | | | | |

**Directions:** Draw a line to the correct number.

6 tens + 7 ones — 73
4 tens + 2 ones — 67
8 tens + 0 ones — 51
7 tens + 3 ones — 80
5 tens + 1 one — 42

## Page 221

### Place Value: Ones, Tens

**Directions:** Write the numbers for the tens and ones. Then add.

**Example:**

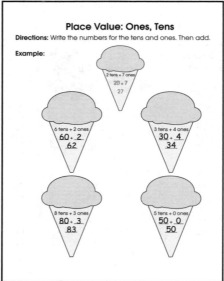

2 tens + 7 ones
20 + 7
27

6 tens + 2 ones
60 + 2
62

3 tens + 4 ones
30 + 4
34

8 tens + 3 ones
80 + 3
83

5 tens + 0 ones
50 + 0
50

## Page 222

### 2-Digit Addition

**Directions:** Study the example. Follow the steps to add.

**Example:**
```
  33
 +41
```

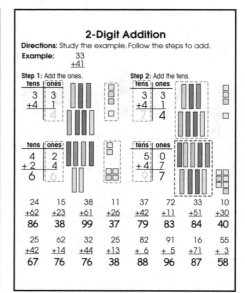

**Step 1:** Add the ones.

| tens | ones |
|---|---|
| 3 | 3 |
| +4 | 1 |
| | 4 |

**Step 2:** Add the tens.

| tens | ones |
|---|---|
| 3 | 3 |
| +4 | 1 |
| 7 | 4 |

| tens | ones |
|---|---|
| 4 | 2 |
| + 2 | |
| 6 | 6 |

| tens | ones |
|---|---|
| 5 | 0 |
| +4 | 7 |
| 9 | 7 |

| 24 | 15 | 38 | 11 | 37 | 72 | 33 | 10 |
|---|---|---|---|---|---|---|---|
| +62 | +23 | +61 | +26 | +42 | +11 | +51 | +30 |
| 86 | 38 | 99 | 37 | 79 | 83 | 84 | 40 |

| 25 | 62 | 32 | 25 | 82 | 91 | 16 | 55 |
|---|---|---|---|---|---|---|---|
| +42 | +14 | +44 | +13 | + 6 | + 5 | +71 | + 3 |
| 67 | 76 | 76 | 38 | 88 | 96 | 87 | 58 |

## Page 223

### 2-Digit Addition

**Directions:** Add the total points scored in each game. Remember to add **ones** first and **tens** second.

**Example:**

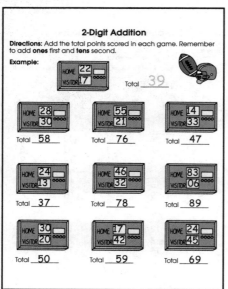

HOME 22 / VISITOR 17    Total **39**

HOME 28 / VISITOR 30    Total **58**
HOME 55 / VISITOR 21    Total **76**
HOME 14 / VISITOR 33    Total **47**

HOME 24 / VISITOR 13    Total **37**
HOME 46 / VISITOR 32    Total **78**
HOME 83 / VISITOR 06    Total **89**

HOME 30 / VISITOR 20    Total **50**
HOME 17 / VISITOR 42    Total **59**
HOME 24 / VISITOR 45    Total **69**

## Page 224

### 2-Digit Addition: Regrouping

Addition is "putting together" or adding two or more numbers to find the sum. Regrouping is using **ten ones** to form **one ten**, **ten tens** to form **one 100**, **fifteen ones** to form **one ten** and **five ones** and so on.

**Directions:** Study the examples. Follow the steps to add.

**Example:**
```
  14
 + 8
```

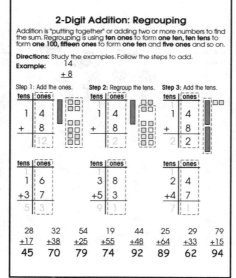

**Step 1:** Add the ones.

| tens | ones |
|---|---|
| 1 | 4 |
| + | 8 |
| | 12 |

**Step 2:** Regroup the tens.

| tens | ones |
|---|---|
| 1 | 4 |
| + | 8 |
| | 2 |

**Step 3:** Add the tens.

| tens | ones |
|---|---|
| 1 | 4 |
| + | 8 |
| 2 | 2 |

| tens | ones |
|---|---|
| 1 | 6 |
| +3 | 7 |
| 5 | 3 |

| tens | ones |
|---|---|
| 3 | 8 |
| +5 | 3 |
| 9 | 1 |

| tens | ones |
|---|---|
| 2 | 4 |
| +4 | 7 |
| 7 | 1 |

| 28 | 32 | 54 | 19 | 44 | 25 | 29 | 79 |
|---|---|---|---|---|---|---|---|
| +17 | +38 | +25 | +55 | +48 | +64 | +33 | +15 |
| 45 | 70 | 79 | 74 | 92 | 89 | 62 | 94 |

## Page 225

### 2-Digit Addition: Regrouping

**Directions:** Add the total points scored in the game. Remember to add the ones, regroup, and then add the tens.

**Example:**

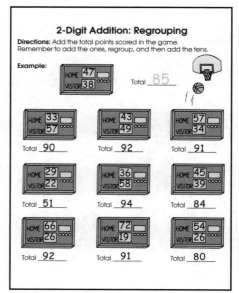

HOME 47 / VISITOR 38    Total **85**

HOME 33 / VISITOR 57    Total **90**
HOME 43 / VISITOR 49    Total **92**
HOME 57 / VISITOR 34    Total **91**

HOME 29 / VISITOR 22    Total **51**
HOME 36 / VISITOR 58    Total **94**
HOME 45 / VISITOR 39    Total **84**

HOME 66 / VISITOR 26    Total **92**
HOME 72 / VISITOR 19    Total **91**
HOME 54 / VISITOR 26    Total **80**

# Answer Key

## Page 226

### 2-Digit Subtraction

**Directions:** Study the example. Follow the steps to subtract.

**Example:**
```
  28
 -14
```

**Step 1: Subtract the ones.**

| tens | ones |
|------|------|
| 2 | 8 |
| -1 | 4 |
| | 4 |

| tens | ones |
|------|------|
| 2 | 4 |
| -1 | 2 |
| 1 | |

**Step 2: Subtract the tens.**

| tens | ones |
|------|------|
| 2 | 8 |
| -1 | 4 |
| | 4 |

| tens | ones |
|------|------|
| 3 | 8 |
| -1 | 5 |
| 2 | 3 |

| | | | | | | | |
|--|--|--|--|--|--|--|--|
| 24 | 61 | 77 | 85 | 57 | 87 | 59 | 96 |
| −12 | −30 | −44 | −24 | −23 | −33 | −34 | −16 |
| 12 | 31 | 33 | 61 | 34 | 54 | 25 | 80 |

| | | | | | | | |
|--|--|--|--|--|--|--|--|
| 29 | 74 | 46 | 69 | 95 | 33 | 78 | 22 |
| −15 | −51 | −32 | −35 | −32 | −33 | −26 | −11 |
| 14 | 23 | 14 | 34 | 63 | 0 | 52 | 11 |

## Page 227

### 2-Digit Subtraction: Regrouping

Subtraction is "taking away" or subtracting one number from another to find the difference. Regrouping is using **one ten to form ten ones, one 100 to form ten tens** and so on.

**Directions:** Study the examples. Follow the steps to subtract.

**Example:**
```
  37
 -19
```

**Step 1: Regroup.**

| tens | ones |
|------|------|
| 2 | 17 |
| 3 | 7 |
| -1 | 9 |

**Step 2: Subtract the ones.**

| tens | ones |
|------|------|
| 2 | 17 |
| 3 | 7 |
| -1 | 9 |
| | 8 |

**Step 3: Subtract the tens.**

| tens | ones |
|------|------|
| 2 | 17 |
| 3 | 7 |
| -1 | 9 |
| 1 | 8 |

| tens | ones |
|------|------|
| 1 | 12 |
| 2 | 2 |
| | 9 |
| | 3 |

| tens | ones |
|------|------|
| 2 | 14 |
| 3 | 4 |
| -1 | 6 |
| 1 | 8 |

| tens | ones |
|------|------|
| 3 | 15 |
| 4 | 5 |
| -2 | 9 |
| 1 | 6 |

| | | | | | | | |
|--|--|--|--|--|--|--|--|
| 28 | 46 | 12 | 30 | 52 | 47 | 21 | 45 |
| −19 | −18 | − 8 | −12 | −25 | −35 | −13 | −25 |
| 9 | 28 | 4 | 18 | 27 | 12 | 8 | 20 |

## Page 228

### 2-Digit Subtraction: Regrouping

**Directions:** Study the steps for subtracting. Solve the problems using the steps.

**STEPS FOR SUBTRACTING**

DO YOU REGROUP? YES, WHEN BOTTOM NUMBER IS BIGGER THAN THE TOP.
2. SUBTRACT THE ONES.
3. SUBTRACT THE TENS.

| tens | ones |
|------|------|
| 4 | 7 |
| - 2 | 8 |
| 1 | 9 |

| tens | ones |
|------|------|
| 6 | 4 |
| - 3 | 4 |
| 3 | 0 |

| tens | ones |
|------|------|
| 5 | 3 |
| - 3 | 9 |
| 1 | 4 |

| | | | | |
|--|--|--|--|--|
| 56 | 83 | 43 | 75 | 91 |
| − 27 | − 47 | − 39 | − 53 | − 18 |
| 29 | 36 | 4 | 22 | 73 |

| | | | | |
|--|--|--|--|--|
| 73 | 35 | 67 | 26 | 68 |
| − 66 | − 14 | − 58 | − 7 | − 45 |
| 7 | 21 | 9 | 19 | 23 |

## Page 229

### 2-Digit Addition and Subtraction

Addition is "putting together" or adding two or more numbers to find the sum. Subtraction is "taking away" or subtracting one number from another to find the difference. Regrouping is using **one ten** to form **ten ones, one 100** to form **ten tens**, and so on.

**Directions:** Add or subtract using regrouping.

**Example:**

| tens | ones |
|------|------|
| 2 | 15 |
| 3 | 5 |
| -2 | 7 |
| | 8 |

| | | | | | | | |
|--|--|--|--|--|--|--|--|
| 56 | 40 | 35 | 42 | 53 | 97 | 44 | 93 |
| − 27 | − 16 | + 27 | − 14 | +38 | − 48 | + 27 | − 39 |
| 29 | 24 | 62 | 28 | 91 | 49 | 71 | 54 |

| | | | | | | | |
|--|--|--|--|--|--|--|--|
| 56 | 44 | 68 | 73 | 33 | 49 | 77 | 27 |
| − 17 | + 28 | − 49 | − 24 | + 18 | + 32 | − 68 | + 19 |
| 39 | 72 | 19 | 49 | 51 | 81 | 9 | 46 |

## Page 230

### 2-Digit Addition and Subtraction

**Directions:** Add or subtract using regrouping.

| | | | |
|--|--|--|--|
| 23 | 84 | 69 | 41 |
| +48 | -56 | +29 | -17 |
| 71 | 28 | 98 | 24 |

| | | | |
|--|--|--|--|
| 52 | 73 | 84 | 57 |
| -28 | +18 | -27 | -39 |
| 24 | 91 | 57 | 18 |

| | | | |
|--|--|--|--|
| 33 | 64 | 37 | 36 |
| -15 | +17 | +58 | -19 |
| 18 | 81 | 95 | 17 |

| | | | |
|--|--|--|--|
| 65 | 48 | 33 | 25 |
| -28 | -30 | +18 | +35 |
| 37 | 18 | 51 | 60 |

## Page 231

### Place Value: Hundreds

The place value of a digit or numeral is shown by where it is in the number. For example, in the number **123**, 1 has the place value of **hundreds**, 2 is **tens** and 3 is **ones**.

**Directions:** Study the examples. Then write the missing numbers in the blanks.

**Examples:**

2 hundreds + 3 tens + 6 ones =

| hundreds | tens | ones |
|----------|------|------|
| 2 | 3 | 6 | = 236 |

1 hundred + 4 tens + 9 ones =

| hundreds | tens | ones |
|----------|------|------|
| 1 | 4 | 9 | = 149 |

| | hundreds | tens | ones | total |
|--|----------|------|------|-------|
| 3 hundreds + 4 tens + 8 ones = | 3 | 4 | 8 | = 348 |
| 2 hundreds + 1 tens + 7 ones = | 2 | 1 | 7 | = 217 |
| 6 hundreds + 3 tens + 5 ones = | 6 | 3 | 5 | = 635 |
| 4 hundreds + 7 tens + 9 ones = | 4 | 7 | 9 | = 479 |
| 2 hundreds + 9 tens + 4 ones = | 2 | 9 | 4 | = 294 |
| 4 hundreds + 5 tens + 6 ones = | 4 | 5 | 6 | = 456 |
| 3 hundreds + 1 tens + 3 ones = | 3 | 1 | 3 | = 313 |
| 3 hundreds + 5 tens + 7 ones = | 3 | 5 | 7 | = 357 |
| 6 hundreds + 2 tens + 8 ones = | 6 | 2 | 8 | = 628 |

# Answer Key

## Page 232

### Place Value: Hundreds

**Directions:** Write the numbers for hundreds, tens and ones. Then add.

**Example:**

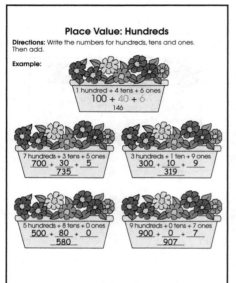

1 hundred + 4 tens + 6 ones
100 + 40 + 6
146

7 hundreds + 3 tens + 5 ones
700 + 30 + 5
735

3 hundreds + 1 ten + 9 ones
300 + 10 + 9
319

5 hundreds + 8 tens + 0 ones
500 + 80 + 0
580

9 hundreds + 0 tens + 7 ones
900 + 0 + 7
907

## Page 233

### 3-Digit Addition: Regrouping

**Directions:** Study the examples. Follow the steps to add.

**Example:**

**Step 1:** Add the ones.
**Step 2:** Add the tens.
**Step 3:** Add the hundreds.

Do you regroup?     Do you regroup?

| hundreds | tens | ones | | hundreds | tens | ones | | hundreds | tens | ones |
|---|---|---|---|---|---|---|---|---|---|---|
| 3 | 4 | 8 | | 3 | 4 | 8 | | 3 | 4 | 8 |
| +4 | 4 | 4 | | +4 | 4 | 4 | | +4 | 4 | 4 |
| | | 2 | | | 9 | 2 | | 7 | 9 | 2 |

| hundreds | tens | ones | | hundreds | tens | ones | | hundreds | tens | ones |
|---|---|---|---|---|---|---|---|---|---|---|
| 2 | 1 | 4 | | 3 | 6 | 8 | | 1 | 1 | 9 |
| +2 | 3 | 8 | | +2 | 1 | 3 | | +5 | 6 | 5 |
| 4 | 5 | 2 | | 5 | 8 | 1 | | 6 | 8 | 4 |

| 418 | 471 | 334 | 659 | 736 | 426 | 567 | 327 |
|---|---|---|---|---|---|---|---|
| +323 | +319 | +528 | +127 | +145 | +165 | +228 | +354 |
| 741 | 790 | 862 | 786 | 881 | 591 | 795 | 681 |

## Page 234

### 3-Digit Addition: Regrouping

**Directions:** Study the example. Follow the steps to add. Regroup when needed.

**Step 1:** Add the ones.
**Step 2:** Add the tens.
**Step 3:** Add the hundreds.

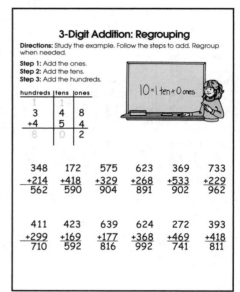

10 = 1 ten + 0 ones

| hundreds | tens | ones |
|---|---|---|
| 3 | 4 | 8 |
| +4 | 5 | 4 |
| 8 | 0 | 2 |

| 348 | 172 | 575 | 623 | 369 | 733 |
|---|---|---|---|---|---|
| +214 | +418 | +329 | +268 | +533 | +229 |
| 562 | 590 | 904 | 891 | 902 | 962 |

| 411 | 423 | 639 | 624 | 272 | 393 |
|---|---|---|---|---|---|
| +299 | +169 | +177 | +368 | +469 | +418 |
| 710 | 592 | 816 | 992 | 741 | 811 |

## Page 235

### 3-Digit Subtraction: Regrouping

**Directions:** Study the example. Follow the steps to subtract.

**Step 1:** Regroup ones.
**Step 2:** Subtract ones.
**Step 3:** Subtract tens.
**Step 4:** Subtract hundreds.

**Example:**

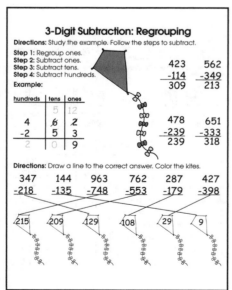

| hundreds | tens | ones |
|---|---|---|
| 4 | 6 | 2 |
| -2 | 5 | 3 |
| 2 | 0 | 9 |

| 423 | 562 |
|---|---|
| -114 | -349 |
| 309 | 213 |

| 478 | 651 |
|---|---|
| -239 | -333 |
| 239 | 318 |

**Directions:** Draw a line to the correct answer. Color the kites.

| 347 | 144 | 963 | 762 | 287 | 427 |
|---|---|---|---|---|---|
| -218 | -135 | -748 | -553 | -179 | -398 |

215   209   129   108   29   9

## Page 236

### 3-Digit Subtraction: Regrouping

**Directions:** Subtract. Circle the 7's that appear in the **tens place**.

score
257

| 492 | 184 |
|---|---|
| -221 | -129 |
| 271 | 55 |

| 358 | 765 | 584 | 693 | 921 |
|---|---|---|---|---|
| -238 | -326 | -435 | -314 | -362 |
| 120 | 439 | 149 | 379 | 559 |

| 128 | 744 | 835 | 248 | 635 |
|---|---|---|---|---|
| -109 | -674 | -217 | -199 | -428 |
| 19 | 70 | 618 | 49 | 207 |

## Page 237

### Graphs

A graph is a drawing that shows information about numbers.

**Directions:** Count the apples in each row. Color the boxes to show how many apples have bites taken out of them.

**Example:**

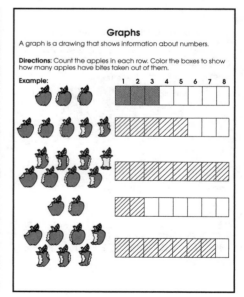

# Answer Key

## Page 238

### Graphs

**Directions:** Count the bananas in each row. Color the boxes to show how many have been eaten by the monkeys.

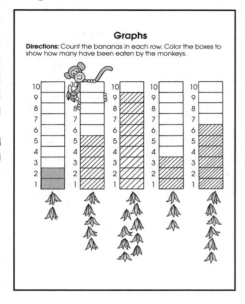

## Page 239

### Graphs

**Directions:** Count the fish. Color the bowls to make a graph that shows the number of fish.

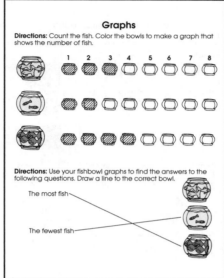

**Directions:** Use your fishbowl graphs to find the answers to the following questions. Draw a line to the correct bowl.

The most fish

The fewest fish

## Page 240

### Multiplication

Multiplication is a short way to find the sum of adding the same number a certain amount of times. For example, **7 x 4 = 28** instead of **7 + 7 + 7 + 7 = 28**.

**Directions:** Study the example. Solve the problems.

**Example:**

3 + 3 + 3 = 9
3 threes = 9
3 x 3 = 9

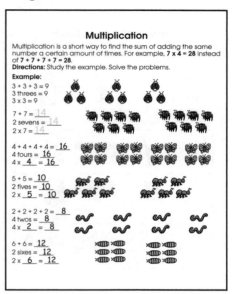

7 + 7 = 14
2 sevens = 14
2 x 7 = 14

4 + 4 + 4 + 4 = 16
4 fours = 16
4 x 4 = 16

5 + 5 = 10
2 fives = 10
2 x 5 = 10

2 + 2 + 2 + 2 = 8
4 twos = 8
4 x 2 = 8

6 + 6 = 12
2 sixes = 12
2 x 6 = 12

## Page 241

### Multiplication

Multiplication is repeated addition.

**Directions:** Draw a picture for each problem. Then write the missing numbers.

**Example:**

Draw 2 groups of three apples.

3 + 3 = 6
or   2 x 3 = 6

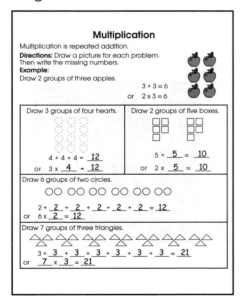

Draw 3 groups of four hearts.

4 + 4 + 4 = 12
or  3 x 4 = 12

Draw 2 groups of five boxes.

5 + 5 = 10
or  2 x 5 = 10

Draw 6 groups of two circles.

○○ ○○ ○○ ○○ ○○ ○○

2 + 2 + 2 + 2 + 2 + 2 = 12
or  6 x 2 = 12

Draw 7 groups of three triangles.

3 + 3 + 3 + 3 + 3 + 3 + 3 = 21
or  7 x 3 = 21

## Page 242

### Multiplication

**Directions:** Study the example. Draw the groups and write the total.

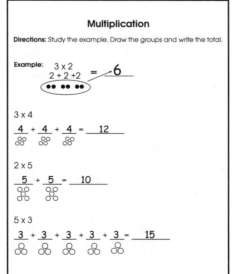

**Example:**   3 x 2
2 + 2 + 2  = 6

3 x 4

4 + 4 + 4 = 12

2 x 5

5 + 5 = 10

5 x 3

3 + 3 + 3 + 3 + 3 = 15

## Page 243

### Multiplication

**Directions:** Solve the problems.

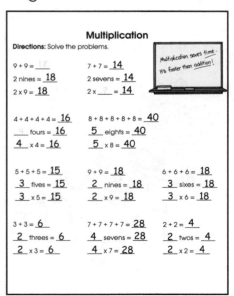

9 + 9 = 18
2 nines = 18
2 x 9 = 18

7 + 7 = 14
2 sevens = 14
2 x 7 = 14

4 + 4 + 4 + 4 = 16
4 fours = 16
4 x 4 = 16

8 + 8 + 8 + 8 + 8 = 40
5 eights = 40
5 x 8 = 40

5 + 5 + 5 = 15
3 fives = 15
3 x 5 = 15

9 + 9 = 18
2 nines = 18
2 x 9 = 18

6 + 6 + 6 = 18
3 sixes = 18
3 x 6 = 18

3 + 3 = 6
2 threes = 6
2 x 3 = 6

7 + 7 + 7 + 7 = 28
4 sevens = 28
4 x 7 = 28

2 + 2 = 4
2 twos = 4
2 x 2 = 4

# Answer Key

## Page 244

### Fractions: Half, Third, Fourth

A fraction is a number that names part of a whole, such as $\frac{1}{2}$ or $\frac{1}{3}$.

**Directions:** Study the examples. Color the correct fraction of each shape.

**Examples:**

shaded part 1
equal parts 2
$\frac{1}{2}$ (one-half) shaded

shaded part 1
equal parts 3
$\frac{1}{3}$ (one-third) shaded

shaded part 1
equal parts 4
$\frac{1}{4}$ (one-fourth) shaded

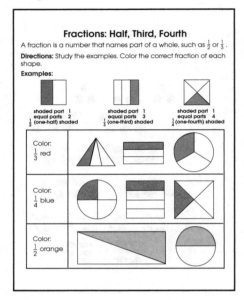

Color: $\frac{1}{3}$ red

Color: $\frac{1}{4}$ blue

Color: $\frac{1}{2}$ orange

## Page 245

### Fractions: Half, Third, Fourth

**Directions:** Study the examples. Circle the fraction that shows the shaded part. Then circle the fraction that shows the white part.

**Examples:**

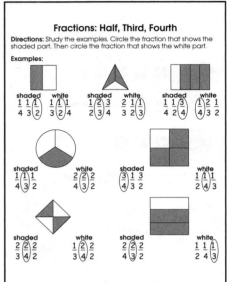

## Page 246

### Fractions: Half, Third, Fourth

**Directions:** Draw a line from the fraction to the correct shape.

$\frac{1}{4}$ shaded

$\frac{2}{4}$ shaded

$\frac{1}{2}$ shaded

$\frac{1}{3}$ shaded

$\frac{2}{3}$ shaded

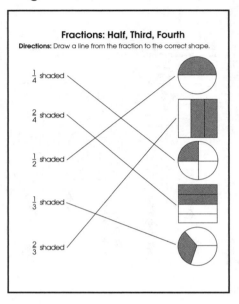

## Page 247

### Geometry

Geometry is mathematics that has to do with lines and shapes.

**Directions:** Color the shapes.

Color the triangles blue.
Color the circles red.
Color the squares green.
Color the rectangles pink.

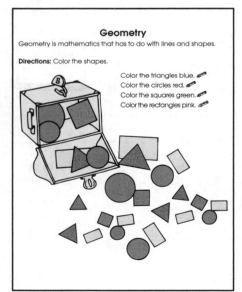

## Page 248

### Geometry

**Directions:** Draw a line from the word to the shape.

Use a red line for circles.    Use a yellow line for rectangles.
Use a blue line for squares.    Use a green line for triangles.

Circle    Square    Triangle    Rectangle

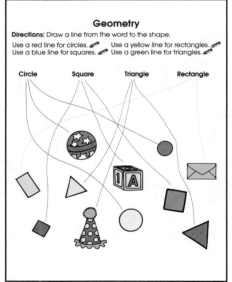

## Page 249

### Geometry

**Directions:** Cut out the tangram below. Mix up the pieces. Try to put it back together into a square.

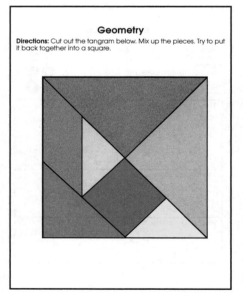

# Answer Key

## Page 251

### Measurement: Inches

**Directions:** Cut out the ruler. Measure each object to the nearest inch.

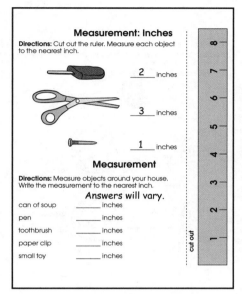

___2___ inches

___3___ inches

___1___ inches

### Measurement

**Directions:** Measure objects around your house. Write the measurement to the nearest inch.

**Answers will vary.**

can of soup _____ inches

pen _____ inches

toothbrush _____ inches

paper clip _____ inches

small toy _____ inches

## Page 253

### Measurement: Inches

An inch is a unit of length in the standard measurement system.

**Directions:** Use a ruler to measure each object to the nearest inch.

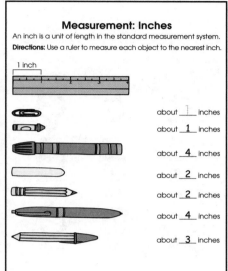

1 inch

about __1__ inches

about __1__ inches

about __4__ inches

about __2__ inches

about __2__ inches

about __4__ inches

about __3__ inches

## Page 254

### Measurement: Inches

**Directions:** Use the ruler to measure the fish to the nearest inch.

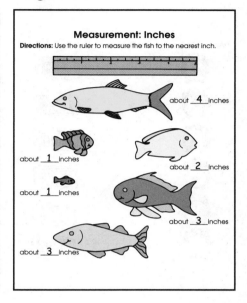

about __4__ inches

about __1__ inches

about __2__ inches

about __1__ inches

about __3__ inches

about __3__ inches

## Page 255

### Measurement: Centimeters

A centimeter is a unit of length in the metric system. There are 2.54 centimeters in an inch.

**Directions:** Use a centimeter ruler to measure the crayons to the nearest centimeter.

**Example:** The first crayon is about 7 centimeters long.

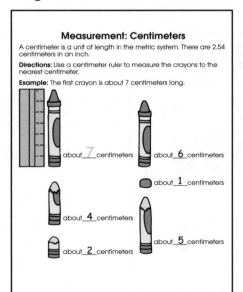

about __7__ centimeters

about __6__ centimeters

about __1__ centimeters

about __4__ centimeters

about __5__ centimeters

about __2__ centimeters

## Page 256

### Measurement: Centimeters

**Directions:** The giraffe is about 8 centimeters high. How many centimeters (cm) high are the trees? Write your answers in the blanks.

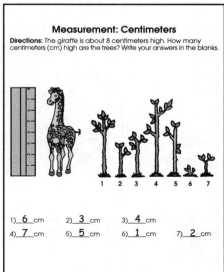

1) __6__ cm

2) __3__ cm

3) __4__ cm

4) __7__ cm

5) __5__ cm

6) __1__ cm

7) __2__ cm

## Page 257

### Time: Hour, Half-Hour

An hour is sixty minutes. The short hand of a clock tells the hour. It is written **0:00**, such as **5:00**. A half-hour is thirty minutes. When the long hand of the clock is pointing to the six, the time is on the half-hour. It is written **:30**, such as **5:30**.

**Directions:** Study the examples. Tell what time it is on each clock.

**Examples:**

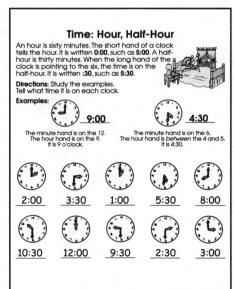

9:00

The minute hand is on the 12.
The hour hand is on the 9.
It is 9 o'clock.

4:30

The minute hand is on the 6.
The hour hand is *between* the 4 and 5.
It is 4:30.

2:00    3:30    1:00    5:30    8:00

10:30    12:00    9:30    2:30    3:00

# Answer Key

## Page 258

### Time: Hour, Half-Hour

**Directions:** Draw lines between the clocks that show the same time.

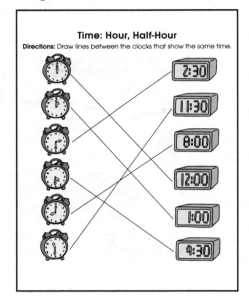

2:30
11:30
8:00
12:00
1:00
9:30

## Page 259

### Time: Counting by 5's

The minute hand of a clock takes 5 minutes to move from one number to the next. Start at the 12 and count by fives to tell how many minutes it is past the hour.

**Directions:** Study the examples. Tell what time is on each clock.

**Examples:**

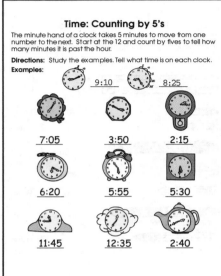

9:10     8:25

7:05     3:50     2:15

6:20     5:55     5:30

11:45    12:35    2:40

## Page 260

### Time: Quarter-Hours

Time can also be shown as fractions. 30 minutes = $\frac{1}{2}$ hour.

**Directions:** Shade the fraction of each clock and tell how many minutes you have shaded.

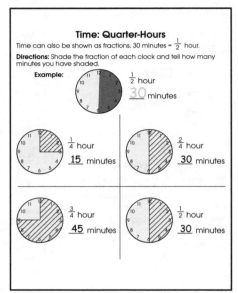

**Example:**   $\frac{1}{2}$ hour   30 minutes

$\frac{1}{4}$ hour   15 minutes

$\frac{2}{4}$ hour   30 minutes

$\frac{3}{4}$ hour   45 minutes

$\frac{1}{2}$ hour   30 minutes

## Page 261

### Money: Penny, Nickel

Penny 1¢     Nickel 5¢

**Directions:** Count the coins and write the amount.

**Example:**

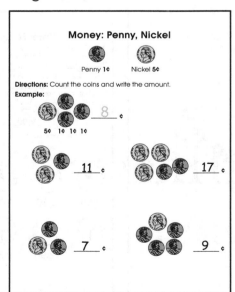

8 ¢
5¢ 1¢ 1¢ 1¢

11 ¢     17 ¢

7 ¢     9 ¢

## Page 262

### Money: Penny, Nickel, Dime

Penny 1¢     Nickel 5¢     Dime 10¢

**Directions:** Count the coins and write the amount.

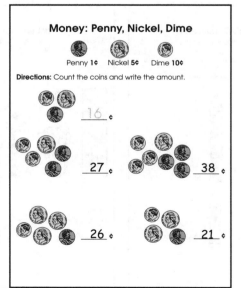

16 ¢

27 ¢     38 ¢

26 ¢     21 ¢

# Answer Key

## Page 263

### Money: Penny, Nickel, Dime
**Directions:** Draw a line from the toy to the amount of money it costs.

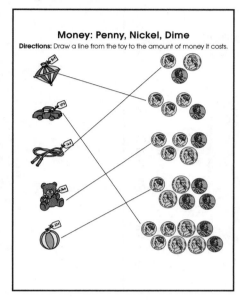

## Page 264

### Money: Penny, Nickel, Dime
**Directions:** Draw a line to match the amounts of money.

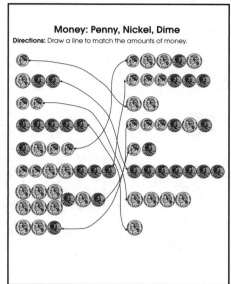

## Page 265

### Money: Quarter
A quarter is worth 25¢.
**Directions:** Count the coins and write the amounts.

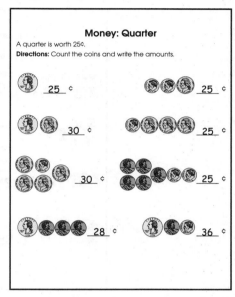

_25_ ¢        _25_ ¢

_30_ ¢        _25_ ¢

_30_ ¢        _25_ ¢

_28_ ¢        _36_ ¢

## Page 266

### Money: Decimal
A decimal is a number with one or more places to the right of a decimal point, such as 6.5 or 2.25. Money amounts are written with two places to the right of the decimal point.

25¢    10¢    5¢    1¢
$.25   $.10   $.05  $.01

**Directions:** Count the coins and circle the amount shown.

**Example:**

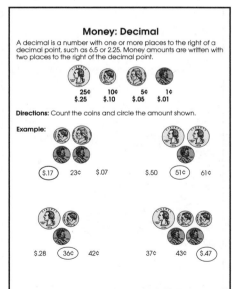

($.17)   23¢   $.07        $.50  (51¢)  61¢

$.28  (36¢)  42¢        37¢   43¢  ($.47)

## Page 267

### Money: Decimal
**Directions:** Draw a line from the coins to the correct amount in each column.

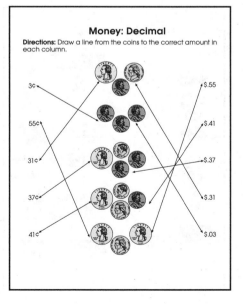

3¢                          $.55

55¢                         $.41

31¢                         $.37

37¢                         $.31

41¢                         $.03

# Answer Key

## Page 268

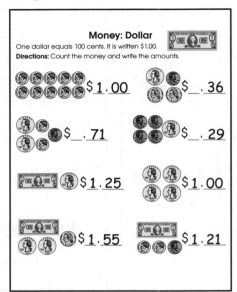

**Money: Dollar**

One dollar equals 100 cents. It is written $1.00.

**Directions:** Count the money and write the amounts.

$1.00        $ .36

$ .71        $ .29

$1.25        $1.00

$1.55        $1.21

## Page 269

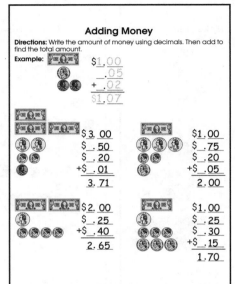

**Adding Money**

**Directions:** Write the amount of money using decimals. Then add to find the total amount.

**Example:**
$1.00
.05
+ .02
$1.07

$3.00
$ .50
$ .20
+$ .01
3.71

$1.00
$ .75
$ .20
+$ .05
2.00

$2.00
$ .25
+$ .40
2.65

$1.00
$ .25
$ .30
+$ .15
1.70

## Page 270

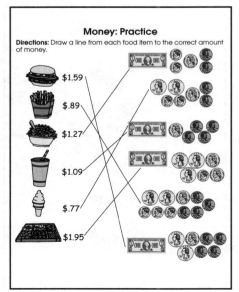

**Money: Practice**

**Directions:** Draw a line from each food item to the correct amount of money.

$1.59

$.89

$1.27

$1.09

$.77

$1.95

## Page 271

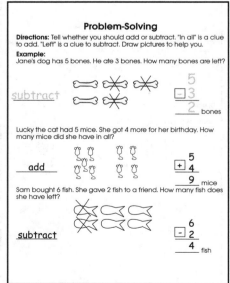

**Problem-Solving**

**Directions:** Tell whether you should add or subtract. "In all" is a clue to add. "Left" is a clue to subtract. Draw pictures to help you.

**Example:**
Jane's dog has 5 bones. He ate 3 bones. How many bones are left?

subtract

5
- 3
2 bones

Lucky the cat had 5 mice. She got 4 more for her birthday. How many mice did she have in all?

add

5
+ 4
9 mice

Sam bought 6 fish. She gave 2 fish to a friend. How many fish does she have left?

subtract

6
- 2
4 fish